ADVANCED METHODS IN NEURAL COMPUTING

Philip D. Wasserman

VNR VAN NOSTRAND REINHOLD
New York

Van Nostrand Reinhold is a division of
International Thomson Publishing, ITP logo is a
trademark under license.

Printed in the United States of America

Van Nostrand Reinhold
115 Fifth Avenue
New York, NY 10003

International Thomson Publishing
Berkshire House
168–173 High Holborn
London WC1V7AA, England

Thomas Nelson Australia
102 Dodds Street
South Melbourne 3205
Victoria, Australia

Nelson Canada
1120 Birchmount Road
Scarborough, Ontario
M1K 5G4, Canada

16 15 14 13 12 11 10 9 8 7 6 5 4 3 2 1

Library of Congress Cataloging in Publication Data

Wasserman, Philip D., 1937–
　　Advanced methods in neural computing/Philip D. Wasserman.
　　　p.　cm.
　　Includes bibliographical references and index.
　　ISBN 0-442-00461-3
　　1. Neural networks (Computer science) I. Title.
　QA78.87.W37　1993
　006.3—dc20
　　　　　　　　　　　　　　　　　　　93-12320
　　　　　　　　　　　　　　　　　　　CIP

Preface

Neural computing techniques are expanding rapidly, both in number and power. Research and application activity have produced important new paradigms, revived interest in some that have seen long use, and resurrected a few that were all but moribund. As a result, tools available to the artificial neural network practitioner have been substantially increased. Finding and evaluating these methods can be a serious problem. With more than 1000 papers published in 1992 alone, it is difficult to sort the important from the trivial, the innovative from the derivative, and the proven from the speculative. This book attempts this separation, providing the reader with a set of useful methods, along with enough theory and applications information to apply them.

Choosing the topics for this volume was difficult; dozens of paradigms with hundreds of variations were considered for inclusion. To select among what seemed at times an excess of riches, the following five major criteria were used:

1. **Modernity:** The approach must be new, but only in the sense that it has only recently received interest and application. This liberal definition of "new" resulted in the inclusion of recent work as well as some produced in the 1960's that is only now receiving proper appreciation.

2. **Utility:** Only paradigms proven, or showing exceptional promise to be useful, advantageous, and important were considered. This necessarily excluded many minor improvements and purely theoretical results that may lead to future breakthroughs.

3. Trainability: The method must be capable of some form of learning, either supervised or unsupervised. A set of operations involving a training set must change the function of the network in some desirable way.
4. Generalization: Similar inputs must produce similar responses. This is consistent with human abilities. For example, a young child learns to recognize his/her mother despite variations in lighting, distance, angle, and clothing. While no artificial neural network has duplicated the recognition ability of a human toddler, significant ability to generalize has been demonstrated.
5. Concurrent Operation: It must be possible to make efficient use of a large number of processors; ideally, computational rate would increase linearly with the number of processors employed.

Of these criteria, the last may prove the most significant in the long run. The computational load implied by important, real-time neural network applications exceeds the capacity of today's fastest super computers. Throughput must be increased by orders of magnitude if neural networks are to be applied to important applications such as real-time image processing.

Since the early 1960's, hardware improvements have doubled computation rates every two or three years (at constant cost). We cannot rely on this to continue much longer as fundamental limits are being approached. Throughput of single processors will soon be limited by the speed of light. Thus, in the near future, speed increases must come from efficient use of multiprocessor systems rather than brute force acceleration of single processor hardware.

While multiprocessor hardware is readily available, there are few algorithms that can efficiently employ a large number of concurrent processors. Unfortunately, most algorithms devised over the past several thousand years are inherently serial, perhaps mirroring the sequential nature of human problem solving.

Artificial neural networks promise a solution. Their computation is inherently parallel, modeled after the human brain that performs its functions through the use of about 10^{11} simple, slow processors (neurons) operating concurrently.

It is this parallel computing ability that most clearly distinguishes artificial neural network paradigms from more conventional computational approaches. Indeed, some neural networks are well-known mathematical methods, recast for efficient concurrent computation. Some researchers object to calling these neural networks, citing their lack of biological plausibility; there are no known structures in the brain that perform similar operations. This argument points out a fundamental split between those who are using artificial neural networks to study brain function, versus those who view them as a solution to practical engineering problems. This book will take the latter position (without denigrating the former), due to the inclination of the author and the perceived preponderance of interest.

Inevitably, much important work had to be excluded even though it satisfied all of the criteria for inclusion. For example, some was reluctantly omitted that is promising but not fully developed; perhaps it can be included in future volumes as it matures.

As artificial neural networks emerge from the research labs into real-world applications, a broad range of scientifically trained practitioners need to understand how they can use the new techniques. Many have found this to be difficult, as the literature on artificial neural networks is often rendered opaque by the diversity of terminology, the lack of standard notation, and the use of sophisticated mathematics. While professional mathematicians have learned to deal with this problem, many competent researchers in other fields have found important works to be inaccessible. This situation has slowed the dissemination of knowledge and impeded the application of neural network technology.

This book attempts to bridge the gap. Bringing together a diverse set of important paradigms, its explanations are intended to make them understandable to a broad range of scientific professionals. Notation is standardized; qualitative explanations precede the quantitative, and illustrations are used freely to clarify obscure concepts. Nowhere does the mathematics exceed that provided by an undergraduate degree in the sciences, not out of condescension, but because it is simply unnecessary to support applications-oriented explanations. Throughout, the emphasis is on clarity rather than elegance, explanation rather than proof, and exposition rather than mathematical rigor. Still, there has been no deliberate compromise with accuracy; the reader should have nothing to unlearn when going on to the more specialized and theoretical works listed in the references.

In no way does this emphasis imply that the mathematical rigor and deep theoretical study are unimportant. In fact, the field suffers from the general poverty of rigorous theory, and its progress depends heavily on the success of the theoreticians. For those so inclined, a substantial reference section at the end of each chapter leads to the wealth of research papers that provide the theoretical and mathematical support for the paradigms in the book.

These references were selected for clarity of presentation; there was no attempt to be complete or to determine priority. I apologize in advance to authors who find that their earlier work has been excluded.

The explanations in this book are in algorithmic form. This is consistent with the way that most neural computing is now being done—on general-purpose digital computers. For this reason, difference equations are used instead of differential equations, and explanations tend to be program oriented. It is assumed that the reader wishes to apply artificial neural networks, not just to study them; this book is written to facilitate that objective.

The chapters have been written to be largely self-contained. This makes information on a topic accessible without reading the entire book, or paging back to references in previous chapters. This policy implies repetition; in some cases the same concepts are presented in two or more chapters. It is hoped that the utility of this organization will make the redundancy worthwhile.

Some authors avoid the use of the term "neuron," preferring names such as "unit" for this building block. While this respects the profound simplicity of artificial neurons relative to their biological counterparts, it sacrifices comprehensibility, a major objective of this book. For this reason I shall, without further apology, refer to the computational elements of artificial neural networks as neurons.

While this is not a book for beginners, neither does it assume great expertise in the field of artificial neural networks. If you need a review of fundamentals, I recommend the book *Neutral Computing Theory and Practice*, Van Nostrand Reinhold, 1989; it explains the theory that underlies most of the modern paradigms. Equipped with this background and an eagerness to learn more about neural computing, this book provides the logical next step.

Philip D. Wasserman
Cupertino, CA

Contents

Acknowledgments

I would like to express my gratitude to those who have reviewed parts of this book: Dr. Walter J. Freeman, Dr. Donald F. Specht, Dr. Douglas L. Reilly, Dr. Pentti Kanerva, Mr. Mark Jurik, and Mr. Charles Rockwell. Their suggestions have substantially improved the clarity of the book, as did their correction of errors, removal of superfluous material, and expansion of important topics. For any residual errors, I must, of course, take full responsibility.

For the illustrations, proofreading, and general assistance, I would like to thank Mr. Robert Gmelin who took time out from his teaching career to help me with this project. For unparalleled patience, perseverance, and tolerance of my procrastination, I would like to thank my editor, Ms. Dianne Littwin. Without her unflagging support and gentle nudging this book would never have been finished. Finally, I would like to thank my wife, Sarah, who has provided the encouragement and supportive environment that has made this effort possible and worthwhile.

1

Fundamentals

The current interest in artificial neural networks is largely a result of their ability to mimic natural intelligence. Although limited and imperfect, artificial neural networks have, in some applications, performed impressively, in other cases, disappointingly. This mix of failure and success offers the tantalizing suggestion that research will eventually produce artificial systems capable of performing a large percentage of the tasks that now require human intelligence, hence the exponentially increasing growth of neural network research.

As a result of this research, artificial neural networks have been used in a broad range of applications. These include pattern classification, pattern completion, function approximation, optimization, prediction, and automatic control. Furthermore, research has produced a large number of network paradigms, each with its own distinctive name.

Faced with this diversity one might conclude that the field is highly fragmented, consisting of a set of unrelated methods and objectives. Despite appearances, all artificial neural networks perform essentially the same function: They accept a set of inputs (an input vector) and produce a corresponding set of outputs (an output vector), an operation called vector mapping. Likewise, all neural network applications are special cases of vector mapping.

As shown in Figure 1-1, a vector mapper accepts a set of inputs and produces a set of outputs according to some mapping relationship encoded in its

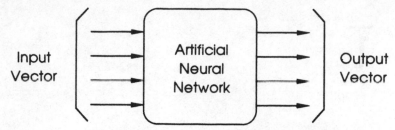

Figure 1-1. A general view of a neural network as a vector mapper.

structure. For example, Figure 1-2 shows a system that maps an input vector with three components—height, weight, and age, into an output vector with two components—life expectancy and insurance premium. Seen from this unifying viewpoint, the various paradigms may be viewed as related approaches, all attempting to solve the same problem.

The nature of the mapping relationship between input and output vectors is defined by the values of free variables (often called weights) within the network. Figure 1-3 shows a configuration where weights (the numbers on

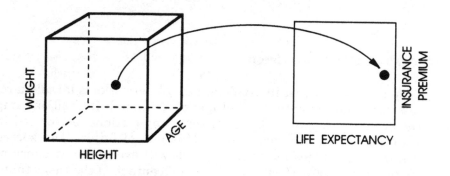

(height, weight, age) ⟶ (life expectancy, insurance premium)

Figure 1-2. Vector mapping accepts one vector (or point) and converts it into another vector (or point).

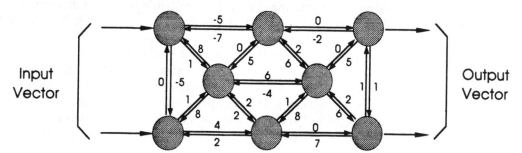

Figure 1-3. Weights in a neural network scale the output value from one processing cell to another.

the arcs) scale the inputs to processing units (circles). Figure 1-4 shows a special case, the feed-forward network, in which the signals flow only from input to output. The mapping relationship between input and output vectors may be *static*, where each application of a given input vector always produces the same output vector, or it may be a *dynamic*, where the output produced depends upon previous, as well as current, inputs and/or outputs. Since feed-forward networks have no memory, they are only capable of implementing static mappings. Adding feedback allows the network to produce dynamic mappings.

Different network paradigms vary greatly in the range of mappings that they can represent. Determining the representational limits for each network type is currently an active area of research. However, recent work on feed-forward networks with one hidden layer (Hornik, Stinchcombe, and White, 1989) has produced a rigorous proof that this functional relationship may be, for all practical purposes, arbitrarily complicated (see Chapter 11). Thus, at least some artificial neural networks are quite general in their vector mapping capability. Without changing internal topology, the same network is capable of producing any functional relationship likely to be encountered by changing its weights.

Vector mapping may be heteroassociative or autoassociative. Heteroassociative mappers are the general case. They produce an output vector that can be different from the input vector. Autoassociative mappers are a subset that yields an output vector that is identical to the input vector on which it was trained. This seems unpromising. However, certain autoassociative paradigms have the ability to produce the desired output vector with a partially incomplete or incorrect input vector. This characteristic has made them useful in pattern completion and noise rejection applications.

Subsequent chapters will present specific artificial neural network paradigms, distinguishing each by its topology, algorithms, benefits, and disadvantages. In the remainder of this chapter the emphasis will be on the underlying principles, thereby providing a unifying framework and a set of terminology that will make it easier to understand the paradigms in this book, as well as other methods encountered elsewhere.

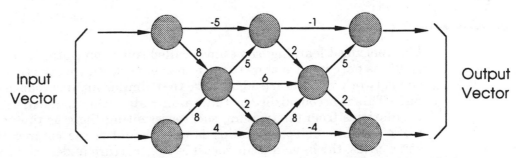

Figure 1-4. In a feed-forward network, weights may be nonzero only in the feed-forward direction.

LEARNING

Artificial neural networks learn from experience. This characteristic, perhaps more than any other, has created the current interest in these methods. In addition to the anthropomorphic implications (that are usually inappropriate), learning offers a powerful alternative to programming.

Learning methods may be broadly grouped as supervised and unsupervised, with a great many paradigms implementing each method.

Supervised Learning

The original Perceptron and, more recently, backpropagation are examples of supervised learning paradigms. In supervised learning, the network is trained on a *training set* consisting of vector pairs. One vector is applied to the input of the network; the other is used as a "target" representing the desired output.

Training is accomplished by adjusting the network weights so as to minimize the difference between the desired and actual network outputs. This process may be an iterative procedure, or weights may be calculated by closed-form equations. Paradigms using the latter form of training may seem to be so far from the biological method that they fail to qualify as an artificial neural network. Nevertheless, such methods are useful, and satisfy a broad definition of artificial neural networks.

In iterative training, application of an input vector causes the network to produce an output vector. This is compared to the target vector, thereby producing an error signal which is then used to modify the network weights. This weight correction may be general, equally applied as a reinforcement to all parts of the network, or it may be specific, with each weight receiving an appropriate adjustment. In either case the weight adjustment is intended to be in a direction that reduces the difference between the output and target vectors. Vectors from the training set are applied to the network repeatedly until the error is at an acceptably low value. If the training process is successful, the network is capable of performing the desired mapping.

Unsupervised Learning

Unsupervised learning, sometimes called self-organization (Kohonen 1988), requires only input vectors to train the network. During the training process the network weights are adjusted so that similar inputs produce similar outputs. This is accomplished by the training algorithm that extracts statistical regularities from the training set, representing them as the values of network weights. Self-organization is reminiscent of the manner in which, in some cases, the human brain modifies its structure under the influence of its experiences without a "teacher."

Applications of unsupervised learning have been limited, however, used in combination with other paradigms they have produced useful results, such as the counterpropagation method (Hecht-Nielsen 1987).

Learning Issues

No network learning paradigm is ideal; all suffer from various limitations and pathologies. For this reason, network training algorithms occupy more research hours than any other aspect of artificial neural networks. Speed, reliability, and generality are important factors in evaluating a training algorithm; improvements are being made in all of these areas.

There are many questions surrounding the learning process. For example:

1. Is the network capable of the desired representation? Does a set of weights exist that will yield the desired mapping?
2. Is the training algorithm capable of adjusting the weights to these values?
3. Will the network train to the best set of weights?
4. Will the network respond correctly to input vectors that are similar, but not identical, to the training vectors? In other words, does the network generalize well enough?
5. Does the training process require a reasonable amount of computation?
6. Is the training set adequate? Does it fully represent the set of input vectors to be encountered in the actual application?

Unfortunately, these questions do not, in general, yet have satisfactory answers. They will be discussed in more detail in Chapter 11, but applying an artificial neural network today requires experience, judgment, and patience. One is often uncertain if a given network, training algorithm, and training set will produce the desired results. Indeed, a certain amount of trial and error seems inevitable with our current state of knowledge. It is fortunate the networks are so robust and the results so striking, otherwise researchers would have long ago directed their efforts toward less ambiguous methods.

GENERALIZATION

The real world suffers from a lack of consistency; two experiences are seldom identical in every detail. Humans accommodate this variability with little effort. For example, we can recognize a friend's voice on the telephone despite a great deal of noise, limited frequency response, and variations in amplitude and pitch.

For a neural network to be useful it must accommodate this variability, producing the correct output vector despite insignificant deviations between the input and test vectors. This ability is called generalization.

Generalization may be quantitatively defined for supervised training if the training set is considered to be randomly selected examples from a specific (but unknown) probability distribution. First, a network is trained on such a set, and the resulting error rate e_1 is measured. Next, a new set of input/output vector pairs is selected from the same distribution, each input vector is applied to the network, the network's response is compared to the desired response (the output vector), and another error rate e_2 is calculated. The $|e_1 - e_2|$ is then a measure of the generalizing ability of the network. More sophisticated methods of measuring generalization are in common use; these will be discussed in Chapter 11.

Generalization as Interpolation

Generalization in neural networks may be viewed as multidimensional interpolation. Poggio and Girosi (1990) use this idea to provide an insightful treatment of artificial neural networks. To see how this idea relates to neural networks, suppose that we have a one-dimensional problem; the input vectors have one component. Suppose also that we are given as a training set the five points plotted in Figure 1-5. We generally assume that these points are samples of some underlying curve. We interpolate between these points so that given intermediate values for x we can determine values for $y = F(x)$ that lie on the underlying (and unknown) curve.

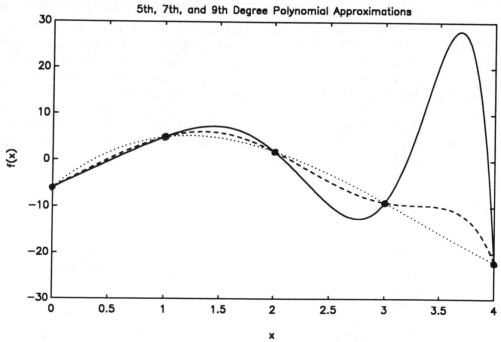

Figure 1-5. An example of smooth continuous interpolation between known points on the X–Y graph.

Three smooth curves have been drawn through the five points, generated by 5th-, 7th-, and 9th-degree polynomial curve fits. Each line constitutes an interpolation, defining a continuum of interpolated points between each of the known points. Since there are three such curves, all of which fit the available information (the training set) perfectly, how can one decide which curve provides "correct" values for intermediate points? In fact, without further information, all three curves are equally valid. We may prefer the smoothest curve based on the lowest degree approximation, however, this is based upon a premise that may be false; we have no certain knowledge of any points other than the five that have been given.

This example demonstrates a fundamental aspect of generalization; that is, with only the data points in a training set, determining other points is an ill-posed problem: There is no unique solution. Therefore, we must supply additional constraints based upon our knowledge of the application. For example, we may choose the 5th-degree fit because we know that the system that generated the points produces smooth curves, or, lacking any other information, we may choose the smoothest curve because we feel that nature favors simple solutions. Such decisions constitute a bias; they restrict the permissible approximations to those involving polynomials with few coefficients. Similarly, we may decide to restrict our neural network topology to the smallest number of weights that produce accurate performance on the training set. While such decisions are often made, we must recognize them as arbitrary and subject to error. In Chapter 11 we develop objective methods for sizing a network to produce good generalization.

Interpolation (generalization) requires an adequate number of points (training set size). Obviously, if there are only a few points (a sparse training set) there is much uncertainty regarding the shape of the curve between points. Much has been written about this problem, and Chapter 11 treats it in detail. It is appropriate here to state merely that there is a close relationship between the number of elements in the input vector (which determines the number of weights in the input layer of the network), the total number of nodes and weights in the network, and the number of vectors required in the training set to generalize with acceptable accuracy.

CLASSIFICATION

Classification, a special case of vector mapping, has an extremely broad range of applications. Here, the network operates to assign each input vector to a category. For example, an input vector might represent the values of the leading economic indicators on a specific date; the two classes might be "Dow Jones Up" and "Dow Jones Down" on the following day.

A classifier may be implemented by modifying a general vector mapping network to produce mutually exclusive binary outputs, namely, an output vector whose components are either 1 or 0. Only a single output (representing category membership) is 1 for a given input vector; all other outputs are 0.

Classification is a central concern in the study of artificial intelligence. An efficient and effective replication of the human's ability to classify patterns would open the door to a host of important applications. These include interpretation of handwriting, connected speech, and visual images. Unfortunately, this goal has been elusive. In most cases humans still perform these tasks far better than any machine devised to date.

The traditional classifiers are either *ad hoc* computer programs or statistical algorithms. Nonstatistical computer programs written for pattern recognition are often "brittle," and easily broken by new data. Such a program will often successfully recognize all examples seen so far, but a new pattern will cause it to fail. This is a consequence of the nature of computer programs; small variations in the input data can produce disproportionately large effects. Thus, it has proven difficult to devise programs that generalize; that produce correct responses to inputs that are similar but not identical to those seen previously. Programmers often find themselves in a frustrating situation: They can correctly classify patterns themselves, but are unable to program a machine to do the task with similar accuracy.

Statistical classifiers have been more successful. Bayesian classifiers and their artificial neural network counterparts are presented in Chapter 3.

A number of artificial neural network paradigms show promise as vector classifiers. Learning from experience rather than being programmed for each problem, they generalize naturally, producing correct answers despite the highly variable, noisy, inconsistent data that is characteristic of real-world problems.

Because of the importance of the classification problem and the power of the neural network approach, a substantial portion of this book will be devoted to the study of this application.

The classification decision is based both upon measurements of the object's characteristics and upon a data base containing information about the characteristics and classifications of similar objects. Therefore, implicit in this process is the collection of data that characterize the statistical properties of the objects being classified.

For example, a lumber mill might wish to automatically separate pieces of pine, spruce, oak, and redwood, putting them into separate bins. This classification could be accomplished by making a set of measurements on the piece, such as color, density, hardness, etc. This set of measurements, expressed numerically, forms a feature vector for that piece, where each measurement is a vector component. The feature vector is compared with a set of recorded feature vectors and their known classifications, those comprising a training set. By some method, a decision is made regarding the correct classification.

Often the classification problem is complicated by the poor quality of the data. Measurements of the sample as well as those in the training set may be noisy and inaccurate. In addition, the training set may be too small to fully characterize the statistics of the data, and overlapping classes can create ambiguities that no classifier can resolve. For these reasons, perfect classification is often a theoretical impossibility. The task then becomes one of producing the best possible classification, given the information which is available.

Decision Regions and Boundaries

The classification problem is perhaps most easily understood in geometric terms. As an example, suppose that a bank wants to classify loan applications into "Accept" and "Reject" categories. They have accumulated a large data base containing a record for each loan made in the past, having entries for income and credit rating of a customer along with the outcome of the loan; either paid or defaulted. Consider income and credit rating to be numbers organized as components of a vector associated with each customer. In Figure 1-6, each person (vector) is represented as a point in a two-dimensional space (a plane), with the position determined by income and credit rating.

After plotting a large number of points, it is observed that most defaulted loans have occurred when the borrower was in the region marked "Region where loans have always defaulted." If a new loan application is received, the loan officer could determine where the applicant falls on the plane, and thereby classify the application appropriately according to risk.

In this book, each pair of numbers will be called a *feature vector*; the data base information used to construct the drawing is named a *training set*; each two component record will be referred to as a *training vector*. The new loan application provides two numbers that comprise a *test vector*. The default region is called a *decision region*, and its boundary is a *decision boundary*.

Sometimes, the points divide nicely into two groups, allowing the decision regions to be separated by a straight line in two dimensions. Vectors with three components require a separating plane in three dimensions; those with

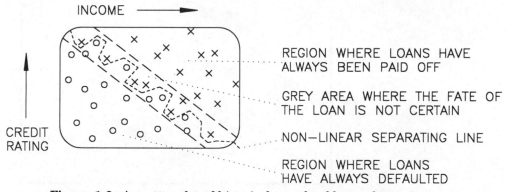

Figure 1-6. A scatter-plot of historical records of loans that were eventually either paid up or defaulted.

four or more components may be separated by a hyperplane. All of these are examples of *linearly separable* decision regions (Figure 1-7). While such regions lead to simple classifiers (a single layer Perceptron will do) they are very unlikely to occur in applications with large feature vectors.

A more common decision region configuration is shown in the central region of Figure 1-8. Here, decision regions are intertwined in a way that makes it impossible to separate them with a straight line. This results in a *nonlinearly separable* problem. Figure 1-9 shows the same situation in three dimensions. A multilayer network is required for classifiers of this type, as it is capable of generating the needed piecewise linear separator.

Overlapping decision regions can require a very complex classifier. For

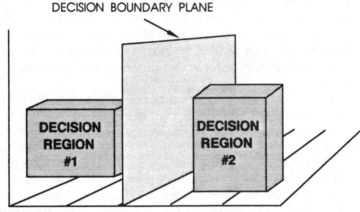

Figure 1-7. A two-dimensional decision boundary is needed to separate three-dimensional decision regions, provided the regions are linearly separable.

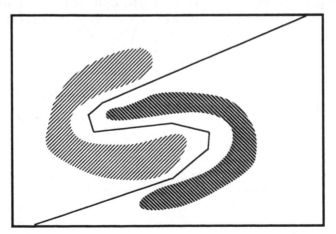

Figure 1-8. These two regions can be nonlinearly separated by piecing together small-sized linear segments.

example, the cases in the central region of Figure 1-6 require a jagged separating line that is difficult to implement. This situation can arise from incorrect data, however, it may also be the result of inadequate dimensionality of the input vector. Suppose, for example, that the two training sets of Figure 1-6 were plotted on two parallel panes of glass. The problem with the overlap in the central region would be easily solved if it were realized that there was a third dimension in which the planes are separated. Adding this information (that the problem is three dimensional rather than two) would produce the situation shown in Figure 1-10 where the two classes can be separated with a simple plane between them. Thus, a complex neural network could be replaced by a simple one.

Sometimes a transformation, such as a Fourier transform, will dramatically simplify a problem. Since the number of possible transformations is infinite, each allowing the problem to be viewed in a different way, selecting

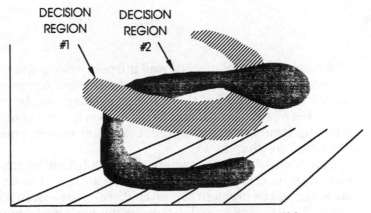

Figure 1-9. These two regions are nonlinearly separable.

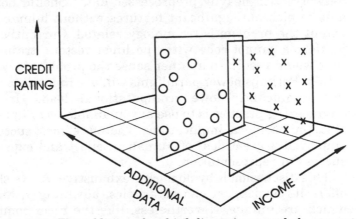

Figure 1-10. The addition of a third dimension may help separate two classes of input data.

the appropriate transformation is a difficult problem. Some transformations may make the problem easier; others may make it nearly impossible. The selection of an appropriate transformation will be discussed in Chapter 11.

Training and test vectors often have a large number of components. For example, a classification based on ten characteristics would input a training vector with ten components. Each such vector would represent a point in ten-dimensional space, well beyond human capability to draw or visualize.

Decision boundaries enclosing these points may define highly complicated regions in high-dimensional space, with no visual representation possible. Nevertheless, the concepts shown in two dimensions are applicable by analogy, with faith in mathematics allowing extension beyond graphical representation.

DISCUSSION

The commonality of method and purpose among the various artificial neural network paradigms is significant. Still more important are the unresolved issues that affect all of them to various degrees. In particular, the relationships between input vector size, network size, generalization ability, and training time are complex and, to a great extent, open issues. These will be discussed in Chapter 11.

Selection of an appropriate representation of the input data has been shown to be crucial, and still largely an art. Human creativity and understanding of the problem can often discern the essential features, ignore irrelevant details, and greatly improve network performance.

This approach may seem wrongheaded. Why should we "spoon feed" the network with heavily preprocessed data? Should not the network itself be able to pick out significant features without human intervention? To some extent the problem is technology related. Currently available computation platforms cannot cope with the huge vectors, training sets, and networks that would result. In another sense the problem is with the networks themselves. Perhaps newer paradigms will use input data more efficiently, requiring significantly lower computational loads. In any case, pragmatic engineering practice is to use any available technique that works, regardless of its philosophical implications. Therefore, most successful applications have employed a great deal of human intellect and experience in discovering a successful representation.

This discussion is by no means exhaustive. As we shall see, each paradigm offers its own set of characteristics, advantages, and limitations, some of which are unique. Nevertheless, like the races comprising mankind, their similarities far outweigh their differences when fundamental characteristics are considered rather than superficial variations.

REFERENCES

Hecht-Nielsen, R. 1987. Counterpropagation Networks. In *Proceedings of the IEEE First International Conference on Neural Networks*, eds. M. Caudill and C. Butler, vol. 2, pp. 19–32. San Diego, CA: SOS Printing.

Hornik, K. M., M. Stinchcombe, and H. White. 1989. Multilayer Feedforward Networks are Universal Approximators. *Neural Networks*, 2:359–366.

Kohonen, T. 1988. *Self-Organization and Associative Memory*. New York: Springer-Verlag.

Oppenheim, A. V. and R. W. Schafer. 1975. *Digital Signal Processing*. New Jersey: Prentice-Hall.

Papoulis, A. 1965. *Probability, Random Variables and Stochastic Processes*. New York: McGraw-Hill.

Poggio, T. and F. Girosi. 1990. Regularization algorithms for learning that are equivalent to multilayer networks. *Science* 247:978–81.

2

Field Theory Methods

A number of paradigms have been developed that treat a network as a dynamic system. Given an initial state, the system relaxes to a minimum energy condition that constitutes a solution to some vector mapping problem. Metropolis *et al.* (1953) introduced a system based upon thermodynamic principles. Here the minimum energy configuration was reached through random adjustments of system states, retaining those that reduce overall system energy. The final state may be interpreted as the minimum error solution if the network represents an optimization problem such as the well-known "traveling salesman" application. Here, the final state of the network would represent the minimum distance multi-city route that a salesman could take, returning to the starting city.

More recently Hopfield (1982) developed a fully connected, symmetrical feedback network of binary valued neurons whose weights represent stored memories. Given a set of inputs, the network weights are repeatedly updated by a simple local algorithm. As a result, the network relaxes to a state representing a stored memory. This state exists at a local minimum of an energy function (a Lyapunov function) so defined as to be nonincreasing with network state updates. The energy value calculated by this function represents the degree of nonoptimality of the current network state.

The Hopfield network, while interesting and sometimes usful, has serious memory capacity limitations. In its original form, its typical maximum memory capacity is $0.1N$ (where N is the number of neurons). Exceeding this bound produces spurious states with incorrect outputs. This is called the "déjà vu" phenomenon; the network recalls states which it was never taught.

Subsequent work has improved this problem but memory capacity is still severely limited.

COULOMB POTENTIAL MODEL (CPM)

Bachmann *et al.* (1987) proposed a system that overcomes the memory capacity limitations of the Hopfield model; no spurious responses are produced regardless of the number of memories stored in the network. It is a relaxation model, i.e., its algorithm minimizes an energy function. In one of its many forms it is analogous to placing a positively charged particle or test charge among a fixed set of negative charges and allowing it to move freely to a minimum energy location.

The system may be viewed as a classifier using supervised training; its function is to categorize an object represented by a set of characteristics. Each characteristic is expressed as a number. The set of numbers associated with each object is called a *test vector*. Since most applications require the classification of many test vectors, these are referred to collectively as a *test set*.

Classification is performed by determining the similarity between a test vector and each of a group of *training vectors*. A training vector is also a set of numbers representing the characteristics of a prototype object. Associated with every training vector is an additional number indicating its *class*. A *training set* consists of a set of training vectors, each with its associated class. The classifier functions by assigning each test vector to the same class as the training vector that it most nearly resembles.

In the coulomb potential method, each training vector is represented as a negative charge <u>fixed</u> in a specific location. Borrowing from electrostatic theory, each such training vector will be referred to as a *training charge*. Every training charge is located initially in space at its vector coordinates. For example, if the vectors have three components, each defines a point in three dimensional space. The act of locating these training charges may be viewed as a form of deterministic supervised training.

The test vector is represented as a <u>freely</u> <u>moving</u> positive charge, analogous to a *test charge* in electrostatic theory. The test charge is allowed to move under the influence of the net electrostatic field created by the training charges, attracted in varying degrees toward their locations. Eventually it is captured by the attraction of one of the training charges, pulled into its position, and assigned its classification.

Equations of Motion

The test charge is accelerated by the vector sum of the fields of the training charges. Assuming that training and test charges have a magnitude of 1.0, that field may be calculated as follows (ignoring a multiplicative constant)

$$\mathbf{E_u} = -\sum_{i=1}^{m} \|\mathbf{u} - \mathbf{x_i}\|^{-L} \frac{(\mathbf{u} - \mathbf{x_i})}{\|\mathbf{u} - \mathbf{x_i}\|} \tag{2-1}$$

where

$\mathbf{E_u}$ = the field vector at the point $\mathbf{u}$
$\mathbf{u}$ = the vector representing the position of the test charge
$\mathbf{x_i}$ = the ith training vector
$\|\ldots\|$ = Euclidian distance
L = a constant ($L = 2$ for ordinary electrostatic fields)

For electrostatic fields it is intuitively obvious that this system cannot produce a false stabilization. Electrons do not become "stuck" between positive charges even if the field is zero at that point. This would be a condition of unstable equilibrium, quickly broken by the random motions inherent in any physical system.

It is easy to prove by contradiction that a test charge cannot be in a state of stable equilibrium where there is no training charge. To do so assumes that the test charge is stopped in a state of stable equilibrium at some point $\mathbf{x}$ other than a training charge location. Since stable equilibrium was assumed, minor motions of the test charge away from $\mathbf{x}$ must always result in its return to $\mathbf{x}$. This means there is some small volume around $\mathbf{x}$ (which by definition contains no training charge), where the inward component of the field (and hence the acceleration) is positive at all points on its surface. Thus, with the test charge removed, the integral of the field over that surface is positive. By Gauss's law, this integral is equal to the charge enclosed in the region. Since the enclosed charge (with the test charge removed) was assumed to be zero, a contradiction results. In other words, the only way that all points on the surface of the sphere can be forcing the test charge inward is if there is a positive charge in the sphere. Since by definition there is no such positive charge, the assumption must be wrong. Therefore, it is impossible for the test charge to become "stuck" at any point where there is no training charge.

Digital Computer Implementation

Implementing Equation (2-1) on a digital computer presents the following practical problems:

1. The system can overshoot or be unstable. Calculating the position of the test charge from the acceleration equation requires a double integration at discrete steps in time. As the test charge approaches a training charge the magnitude of the field (and hence the acceleration) approaches infinity. Thus, any fixed time step can produce an arbitrarily large step in distance, leading to a large overshoot and possible instability.
2. When the test charge is far from any training charge the field is small and convergence is slow.

3. False stabilization can occur. The determinism and discrete nature of numbers on a digital computer allows the test charge to stop at a point where the field is exactly zero; there is no inherent randomness to break the unstable equilibrium.

Problems 1 and 2 can be solved by normalizing the acceleration vector to unit length. This preserves the convergence properties while solving the problem of unbounded acceleration. Also, step size can be made proportional to the distance between the test charge and the nearest training charge.

Problem 3 can be solved by adding a small random vector to the position of the test vector, thereby moving it off of "dead center" if a state of unstable equilibrium should occur. Scaling this by the distance to the nearest training charge ensures accurate convergence.

The resulting equations can be used to calculate position of the test charge

$$\mathbf{vel}(n) = \mathbf{vel}(n - 1) + \lambda \text{ mindist } \mathbf{E_u}/\|\mathbf{E_u}\|.$$

$$\mathbf{u}(n + 1) = \mathbf{u}(n) + \mathbf{vel}(n) + (\mathbf{e} \text{ mindist}) \tag{2-2}$$

where

$$\mathbf{vel}(n) = \text{is the velocity vector at step } n.$$
$$\lambda = \text{a constant determining the step size}$$
$$\mathbf{u}(n) = \text{the position of the test charge at step } n$$
$$\text{mindist} = \text{the distance to the nearest training charge}$$
$$\mathbf{e} = \text{a small random number, perhaps averaging } 1.0 \times 10^{-12}$$

In this formulation, $\mathbf{E_u}$ is a unit vector pointing in the direction of the mean field. Note that the calculation of mindist does not add appreciably to the computational load; distance to each training vector must be calculated to determine $\mathbf{E_u}$.

Basins of Attraction

A rubber sheet can provide a useful analogy for the system in two dimensions. Suppose that such a sheet is stretched on a horizontal frame. Each training vector is represented by a point at which the sheet is pressed downward. A test vector can be thought of as a ball bearing, initially placed on the sheet at the coordinates of its vector components. The slope of the sheet represents the field at each point. The bearing rolls freely across the sheet, eventually falling into one of the training vector depressions. Thus, each training vector has a corresponding region from which a test vector cannot escape; this is called its *basin of attraction* (Figure 2-1). Once the test vector enters this region, it is drawn invariably to the associated training vector.

Although the rubber sheet analogy is limited to two-dimensional space and electrostatic fields exist in three dimensions, nothing in the equations prevents their application to four or more dimensions. The dimensionality

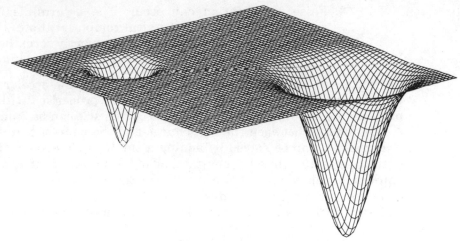

Figure 2-1. Basins of attraction.

of the space is simply the number of components in each of the test and training vectors and is limited only by the available computational power.

Nearest Neighbor Training

The test charge may not converge to the nearest training charge; the field from a single nearby training charge can be overcome by a group of training charges that are further away. Thus, this is not a simple nearest neighbor classifier. Its operation is reminiscent of a Bayesian classifier that weights its classifications in favor of classes that are more probable, as evidenced by a larger number of training vectors for that class.

In some cases this is undesirable; nearness may be closely related to similarity. Here the assignment of a test vector should be weighted more heavily toward the training vector it most resembles. The problem is solved by increasing L, thereby steepening the energy gradient associated with each basin of attraction. In the rubber sheet analogy described above, this would be equivalent to increasing the slope of the sheet in the vicinity of the training charge. As L is made very large the system approaches a nearest neighbor classifier. If this is the desired result it may be achieved with much less computation; however, this limiting case demonstrates a relationship between the two types of classification.

Alternative Distance Metrics

In Equation (2-1) $\|\mathbf{u} - \mathbf{x}_i\|$ is used to indicate distance between the two vectors. It is important to recognize that this distance definition (metric) is not restricted to the common Euclidian metric used in electrostatics. This freedom allows the selection of a metric that is most appropriate for the problem under consideration. A more general definition of distance may be expressed as follows:

$$d = \left(\sum_{j} |\mathbf{u}_j - \mathbf{x}_j|^l \right)^{1/l}$$

where j indicates a vector component. If $l = 2$, the familiar Euclidian distance metric results.

If $l = 1$ and all components of vectors **u** and **x** are restricted to the values 0 or 1, the Hamming metric results. Each vector then occupies a vertex of a unit hypercube (a square in two dimensions, a cube in three, etc.) (Figure 2-2), and the distance between vectors is simply the number of bit positions in which they differ.

As in the Euclidian metric case, a system using the Hamming metric on N dimensional Hamming space ensures that a test vector will converge to the nearest fixed vector provided that large enough values for L [the exponent in Equation 2-1)] and N are selected. In fact, Bachmann *et al.* (1987) have shown that if the distance between the closest pair of training vectors is greater than K bits, then the input vector may differ from its nearest training vector by up to $K/2$ bits, and still be correctly classified. Thus, a test vector can have a large percentage of its bits corrupted and still receive a correct classification.

If all vectors are normalized to unit length, distance may be calculated by the computationally efficient inner product operation. Unit vectors may be visualized as points on the surface of a unit hypersphere (a circle with radius

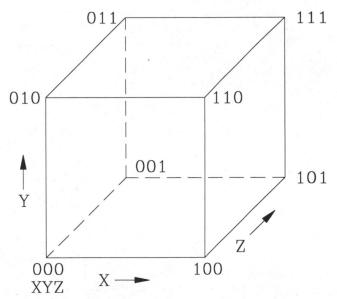

Figure 2-2. Three-dimensional hypercube.

1.0 in two dimensions, a sphere in three, etc.) (Figure 2-3). By definition, the inner product of vectors **u** and **v** is:

$$\langle \mathbf{u}, \mathbf{v} \rangle = \| \mathbf{u_i} \| \, \| \mathbf{x_i} \| \, \cos(\Theta)$$

where $\langle . \rangle$ indicates the inner product operation:

$$\langle \mathbf{u}, \mathbf{v} \rangle = \sum_i (u_i \, v_i)$$

Since both vectors are normalized to length 1.0, their inner product equals the cosine Θ, the angle between the two vectors. This cosine may be used as a measure of the distance between the two vectors. Calculating distance using the inner product greatly reduces the computational load and is a useful method where normalization does not adversely affect the classification. Note, however, that all colinear vectors (those pointing in the same direction) will become identical after normalization and cannot be distinguished by the classifier. Thus, this simplification is only feasible where the normalization operation does not create ambiguity.

RESTRICTED COULOMB ENERGY SYSTEM (RCE)

A classifier designed around the coulomb model described above has certain disadvantages. First, classification is an iterative process; convergence to the correct training vector can be lengthy. It has been proven that the test charge

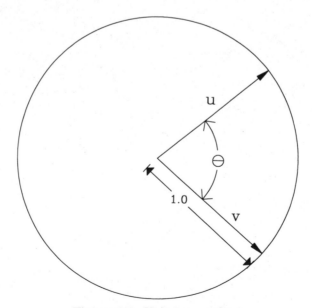

Figure 2-3. Unit hypersphere.

will eventually end up at a training charge, but the path may be circuitous, requiring a prohibitive time with large training sets. If simulated on a digital computer, each step requires the calculation of the field from every training charge, a task which can become impractical with large training sets. Also, the entire training set must be available during classification. In some cases this may require excessive computer memory.

RCE[1] (Cooper, Elbaum, and Reilly 1983), is a linear descendant of the Coulomb Potential Method (CPM) and overcomes many of its problems. It lowers the computational load and memory requirements while maintaining the ability to perform arbitrarily complex classifications with high accuracy.

Rather than the electrostatic energy formula of Equation (2-1), an energy function of the following form is used:

$$E_j = -Q_j/R_o \quad \text{for } \| u - x_j \| \le \lambda_j$$

$$E_j = 0 \quad\quad\quad \text{for } \| u - x_j \| > \lambda_j \quad\quad (2\text{-}4)$$

where

E_j = the energy contribution of the jth training vector
Q_j = the charge associated with the jth training vector
$\mathbf{u}$ = the current location of the test vector
$\mathbf{x_j}$ = the jth training vector location (fixed)
λ_j = radius of the jth basin of attraction
R_o = a constant

This produces an energy surface where each basin of attraction consists of a radially symmetrical, flat-bottomed region centered at the training vector. Within a basin the energy is constant; no field exists. Each basin is surrounded by a zero energy plateau. Thus, here again, the field is zero. A test charge in either region has no field acting upon it; it does not move.

From this it may be seen that RCE is not a relaxation system, a fact that accounts for the small amount of computation needed to perform a classification. A test vector stays where it is initially placed; if it is within a basin of attraction formed by a training vector, it is assigned to that class. If a test vector falls outside of any basin it is motionless and will never be classified. Thus, to make this scheme work, some method is required to fill the space with basins of attraction.

As we shall see, RCE differs from CPM in that it does not store all training vectors. It uses only those needed to accomplish correct classifications, thereby economizing on memory and computation.

Figure 2-4 shows two decision regions A and B in two-dimensional space. Clearly, these regions are not linearly separable as no straight line can be drawn that divides them. The decision regions are implied by the training set; they are not known *a priori*. This simple training set consists of vectors with two components and a predetermined classification for each. Each vec-

---

[1]Restricted Coulomb Energy is a trademark of Nestor Inc.

tor may be interpreted as defining a point in two-dimensional space, and are so drawn as points x_1 and x_2 in Figure 2-4.

RCE Training

The RCE training algorithm attempts to create basins of attraction which cover each nonoverlapping decision region (Figure 2-5). Since each basin is

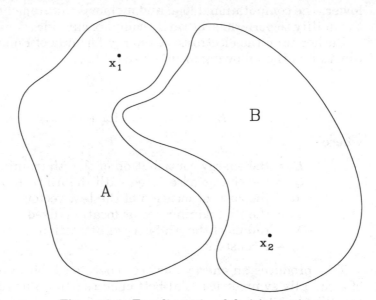

Figure 2-4. Two-dimensional decision regions.

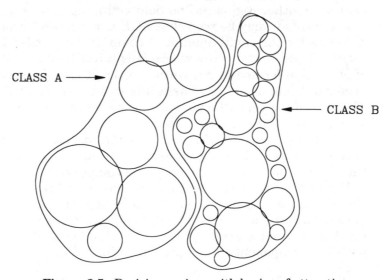

Figure 2-5. Decision regions with basins of attraction.

associated with a training vector, the basin inherits the vector's class. No basin of attraction should intrude into an incorrect decision region, however, basins of attraction of the same class may overlap. Once the network is trained, an input vector is categorized by assigning it to the class of the basin of attraction in which it lies.

The training process starts with no basins of attraction; the system creates them as a result of actions taken when training vectors are presented sequentially. The following two rules, applied to each training vector in turn, suffice to produce these basins:

1. If a training vector is applied that does not lie within a basin of attraction of the same class as that of the training vector, a basin of radius λ_0 is created, centered at that training vector. The maximum size of λ_0 is a system constant, but it is chosen to be less than the distance to the center of the nearest basin of any other class.

2. If the applied training vector falls in the basin of attraction of a different class, the diameter of that basin is reduced until the training vector lies just outside of the basin.

Training proceeds by attempting to classify each training vector. Appropriate action is taken depending upon the result, applying the two rules above to the following four cases:

Unidentified

A training vector x_{ia}, of class A, is presented to the system. If it falls within no basin of attraction, it is considered "unidentified," rule 1 applies, and the training algorithm creates a basin of attraction of radius λ_0 centered at its coordinates.

Figure 2-6 shows the result of applying three such training vectors, x_{1a}, x_{2a}, and x_{3b}. Note that many basins of attraction can be created for each class.

Correct

If a training vector falls within the basin of attraction of its own class, and no other, then the classification is correct, neither rule 1 nor rule 2 applies, and the basins of attraction are unchanged.

Figure 2-7 shows a case where a training vector x_{4a} falls with the basin of attraction of vector x_{1a} of the same class. In this case the vector is correctly classified, and no new basin of attraction is created.

Incorrect

If the training vector falls within the basin of attraction of a different class, but not within a basin of its own class, the classification is incorrect and rule 2 applies, shrinking the basin of attraction of the incorrect class.

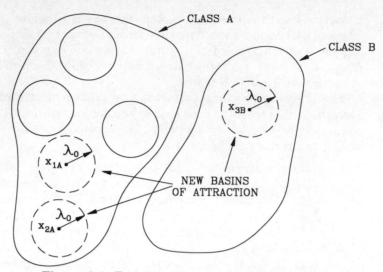

Figure 2-6. Training vectors and basins of attraction.

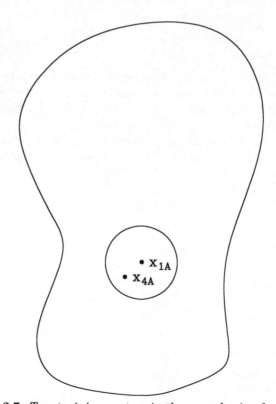

Figure 2-7. Two training vectors in the same basin of attraction.

In Figure 2-8, the class of x_{5b} is not the same as the class of x_{1a}; the vector is misclassified. The system responds by shrinking the basin of attraction of x_{1a} until x_{5b} lies just outside.

Rule 1 is now applied, creating a new basin of attraction for this point.

Confused

If the training vector lies within basins of attraction of two or more classes, then the classification is confused. If one of these basins is of its own class, then that basin is unchanged; if not, rule 1 causes a new basin to be created. All basins of different classes into which the training vector falls are shrunk according to rule 2.

The classifier is trained by repeated, sequential applications of training vectors. Rule 1 or rule 2 is applied as appropriate to create new basins of attraction and/or adjust existing basins. Note that rule 2 may cause a vector that was previously classified to fall outside of all basins of attraction. Therefore, repeated applications of the training procedure are necessary to ensure that each training vector is enclosed by its corresponding basin of attraction and no other.

Characteristics of RCE

RCE is completely general. The trained network can approximate arbitrarily complicated decision regions, including those which are concave, convex, and even disjoint. Since the approximation is done with scaled hyperspheres,

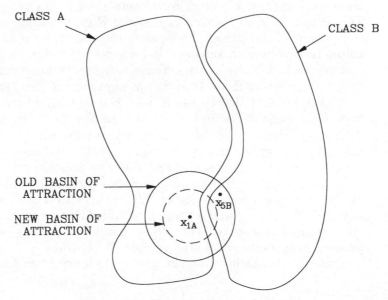

Figure 2-8. Shrinking basin of attraction.

it may require a substantial number of training vectors to adequately fit a highly convoluted decision region.

When training is complete, RCE classification is done in one computational sequence, whereas the training process is iterative, requiring many applications of the training vectors to form the decision regions. CPM is the exact opposite; training is virtually instantaneous (just load the vectors) but classification is iterative. Fast classification is generally preferable to fast training; a network is usually trained once off-line but used to classify many vectors thereafter.

Digital computer implementations of CPM require the full training set to be available in memory if the classification is to be performed rapidly. RCE relaxes this requirement; only those training vectors which are needed to define the decision regions must be in memory. This reduces memory requirements, but more importantly, reduces the computation required to perform a classification.

Unlike backpropagation and similar algorithms, RCE allows new training vectors to be included with only moderate additional training time. This allows a network to learn "on the job," incorporating new information as it becomes available.

NESTOR LEARNING SYSTEM (NLS)

Object classification can require the consideration of many characteristics. For example, a human identifies objects using data from the senses of sight, sound, touch, smell, and taste. For a given object, each sense supplies multiple data values. A sound, for example, excites a set of sensors in the ear. The output of each sensor represents the amplitude of a given frequency component of the sound. Thus, each may be thought of as a component of a sound feature vector. In ways that are poorly understood, a human combines feature vectors from the various sensory inputs when making a classification decision, ignoring those that do not apply to the problem at hand.

It is difficult to determine in advance which features are significant and how they should be incorporated into the final decision. This creates a dilemma: failure to include an important feature can adversely affect the classifier. However, incorporating irrelevant features will reduce accuracy, raise memory requirements, and slow the decision process.

It may seem that one could simply concatenate all feature vectors and apply them to a single classifier. While this will sometimes work, it is seldom optimal. For example, if a human included taste, touch, and smell data when classifying a remote aircraft, these irrelevant inputs would slow the classification process and probably reduce its accuracy.

The NLS[2] classifier has the ability to learn from the training set which

---

[2]Nestor Learning System is a trademark of Nestor Inc.

types of input are important to the classification task, automatically deemphasizing those which do not contribute to classification accuracy. This is done by defining a feature type for each type of input. For example, sight, smell, and sound might each be a feature type. NLS assigns a separate classifier to each type of input. Each input vector is applied to only the classifier of its type. A system level controller then directs the training of the classifiers, determines how they participate in the decision process, and interprets their outputs.

A Multiple Classifier Architecture

In the NLS system, a classification decision is determined by the combined responses from a set of trained RCE classifiers, one for each type of data. Each such classifier receives only feature vectors of its type. Of course, a human must determine which types of data to include, a crucial decision based on knowledge of the problem as well as intuition. However they are selected, these data types are initially thought to be useful in making a correct classification. Thus, each RCE classifier is trained to specialize on one type of data, making decisions as well as it can.

A class selection device (CSD), a component of the NLS, operates at a higher level. It supervises the group of classifiers, learning to select and combine information from all of them in a way that produces better performance than could be provided by any single classifier.

As an example of its operation, suppose that two types of measurements—temperature and pressure—are made on a chemical process. The object is to determine if the plant operation is normal (operating region A) or abnormal (operating region B). Simultaneous measurements are made of temperature at locations X and Y, and pressure at points P and Q. Thus, both a temperature and a pressure vector, each having two components, is formed for each measurement.

As a result of a series of measurements covering normal and abnormal conditions of the process, a training set of temperature-pressure vector pairs is produced, one pair for each measurement. Two RCE classifiers are assigned, one for temperature, the other for pressure. Figure 2-9 shows how each classifier forms decision regions. The temperature RCE unit creates separated regions, whereas, the pressure RCE unit produces overlapping regions. A classifier can only make unambiguous decisions on nonoverlapping regions; test vectors falling into the overlap region will produce a "confused" response. Thus, the temperature classifier will, on average, produce more accurate results than the pressure classifier.

During training the CSD must learn to give precedence to the temperature classifier in those cases where it makes better decisions than the pressure unit. The CSD algorithm accomplishes this by assigning arbitrary priorities to the classifiers prior to training. More than one classifier can have the same priority; hence, all classifiers with the same priority are said to be at the same level. During training each classifier is polled in priority

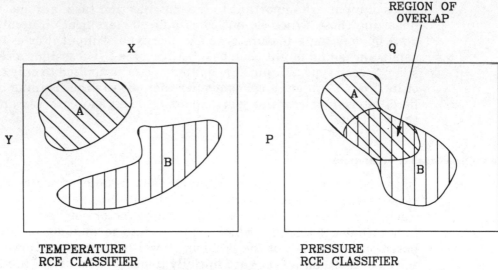

Figure 2-9. Class regions for two feature sets.

order and the RCE training algorithm is applied using the current feature vector.

If the temperature is assigned the highest priority it is polled first. If it produces an ambiguous response (either Unidentified or Confused), the pressure classifier is polled. If it produces an unambiguous response, it is trained according to the RCE rules, otherwise the temperature classifier is trained.

This procedure is generalized by the following rules:

1. Given a training vector, train the highest priority classifier that produces an unambiguous response
2. If no classifier produces an unambiguous response, train the highest priority classifier

If there are multiple classifiers with the same priority, a second ordering relationship is required. A system of ordering by resolution will be discussed later in this chapter.

Figure 2-10 shows how such a classifier might be trained in the case where regions A and B are disjoint for classifier C1 and with a significant overlap for C2. Assuming that the highest initial priority was assigned to C1, Most of the training vectors would be assigned to it, as it was, in all cases, either the highest priority classifier able to produce an unambiguous response, or the highest priority classifier when no unambiguous response was produced.

Using this scheme, inaccurate classifiers are suppressed regardless of their priority. Suppose that C2 had been chosen to have the highest priority. Basins of attraction would be assigned first to C2. Many ambiguous responses would be produced in the class overlap region, resulting in an increasing number of basins of attraction being assigned to C1. Furthermore, the many

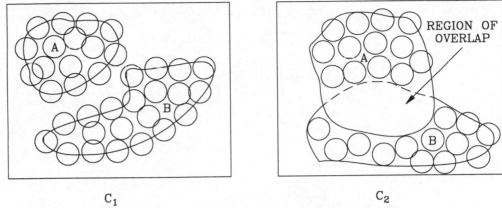

C_1 C_2

Figure 2-10. Disjoint and overlapping decision regions.

incorrect and confused responses from C2 would cause shrinkage of its basins in the region of class overlap. Once a basin has shrunk to a minimum size, the CSD has a mechanism which removes it. Furthermore, the CSD prevents the creation of basins of attraction in regions where they have repeatedly shrunk out of existence. As a result, C2 produces an increasing number of ambiguous responses. The CSD assigns basins of attraction to C1 in these cases, causing an effective reduction in the priority of C2 for training vectors in the overlap region.

During classification a similar priority reversal occurs. Assume that C2 has the highest priority and the network is fully trained. An incoming test vector is first tried on C2; if the result is ambiguous (which will often be the case due to the large overlap region), C1 is then tried. If C1 produces an unambiguous response, its response is used. In this way the classifier with the best classification ability is selected, regardless of the initial priorities.

Voting Methods

In some cases no classifier will produce an unambiguous response. Suppose there are three classes, A, B, and C which overlap in the classification spaces shown in Figure 2-11. If C1 produces responses for classes A and C, with C2 producing A and B responses, a vote count indicates that A is the most likely class.

It is often the case that multiple classifiers operating on different types of data will tend to make different errors. Thus, if there are three classifiers, each of which is in error 10% of the time, and if no two ever make the same error, the voting system will produce 100% classification accuracy. Of course this is seldom the case; nevertheless, significant improvements can be produced by voting.

This voting method can be extended to any number of classifiers. Furthermore, by setting the level of concurrence required, the conservatism of

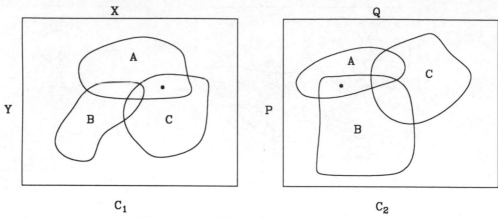

Figure 2-11. Two ambiguous responses.

the decision can be adjusted. For example, setting the system to require the agreement of all classifiers would produce the most accurate decisions. In this case many training vectors would not produce unanimous agreement and the system would frequently respond "unknown." If fewer agreeing votes were required, the system would produce more errors, but would make more decisions. Thus, a tradeoff between accuracy and throughput is possible. Here, accuracy is defined as the percentage of correct decisions, and throughput is the percentage of inputs that produces any nonambiguous decision. If the consequences of an incorrect decision are severe (a nuclear reactor safety system, for example), a conservative system is indicated. If, however, indecision is undesirable, one may opt for higher throughput.

A Classifier Hierarchy by Resolution

Classification decisions can often be made with coarse representations of the features. For example, the character in Figure 2-12 can be classified as the letter "A" despite the binary (black/white) image and the small number of pixels (image squares). Representing the character in this way requires only 25 bits, contained in a feature vector having 25 components with one bit per component, whereas, a high resolution image might require several million bits. The coarse resolution image requires far less memory, and, since the feature vector is shorter, much less computation to perform a classification.

In some cases a coarse representation is inadequate. It may be necessary to make fine distinctions that require a large feature vector with components having many bits. Figure 2-13 shows a case where a coarse representation makes it impossible to separate two objects; both intrude into the central pixel. Increasing the number of pixels as in Figure 2-14 makes the objects fully separable; each pixel contains portions of one object.

The NLS allows a hierarchy of classifiers which provides a range of resolutions for each feature set. Combined with the priority system of the pre-

Figure 2-12. Low resolution "A."

vious section, Figure 2-15 shows how a two-dimensional array of classifiers is constructed. Simple decisions are made through reference to the memory efficient, low resolution units; only when these produce an ambiguous response will the system resort to classifiers with progressively higher resolution. This strategy can yield major memory savings, reduce computation time, and improve classifier accuracy.

DISCUSSION

The NLS is a powerful classification system with many advantages. It has proven effective in a number of commercial applications, including the following:

1. Signal Classification
   Target Recognition of Sonar Pings
   Heartbeat Classification
2. Image Processing
   Real-Time 3-D Object Classification
   Industrial Parts Inspection
   Signature Verification
3. Character Recognition
   On-Line Handwriting Recognition
   On-Line Japanese Character Recognition
   Off-Line OCR of Handwritten Numerals
4. Speech Recognition
5. Financial pattern recognition
   Automated Mortgage Insurance Underwriting
   Mortgage Delinquency Prediction

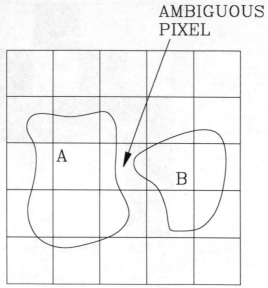

AMBIGUOUS
PIXEL

A

B

Figure 2-13. Nonseparable classes due to coarse representation.

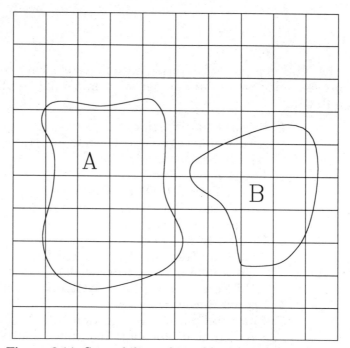

A

B

Figure 2-14. Separability achieved by increased resolution.

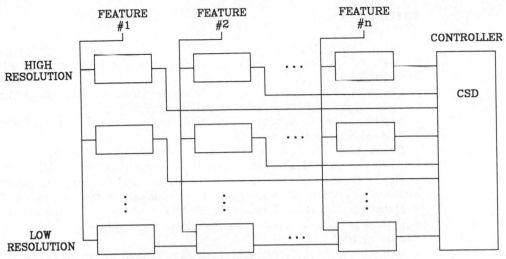

Figure 2-15. Two-dimensional array of classifiers.

Automated Securities Trading
Credit-Card Fraud Detection

A related paradigm called P-RCE has been introduced recently (Scofield and Reilly 1991). It is distinguished from RCE by its characteristic ability of learning the *a priori* class distributions in the areas of class territory overlap. It employs radius-limited and inner-product perceptrons in a three layer, feed-forward architecture that can be trained with real-time speeds using a nongradient descent, procedural learning algorithm.

A silicon implementation of P-RCE (Holler, Park, *et al.* 1992) has been announced and will be available from Intel as their part number 8016ONC. This chip allows for 256 inputs, 1024 internal layer cells, and 64 output layer cells. Full training and classification functionality will be implemented by on-chip logic, and the chip will achieve classification times of 100 microseconds (50 microseconds in the pipelined mode). Weight resolution is 5 bits. While this has been proven adequate for some applications, including classification of handprint classification, sea-trial active sonar signals and speech, it remains to be seen how well this relatively coarse weight quantization functions on a wide range of applications. In any case, the combination of P-RCE and a silicon implementation constitutes a powerful enhancement to this paradigm.

The NLS is proprietary and patented. Thus, unlike the many public domain algorithms, there is a cost associated with its use. One may well ask if the expense is justified. One factor in its favor is maturity. It is a complete and sophisticated system, representing years of thought and application experience on the parts of researchers such as Nobel Laureate, Dr. Leon Cooper and his co-workers at Brown University. While other methods may have lower initial cost, the total cost of development might be reduced, and perfomance improved by using RCE and NLS.

REFERENCES

Bachmann, C. M., L. Cooper, A. Dembo, and O. Zeitouni. 1987. A Relaxation Model for Memory with High Storage Density. *Proceedings of the National Academy of Science.* 21:7529–7531.

Cooper, L. N., C. Elbaum, and D. L. Reilly. 1982. Self Organizing General Pattern Class Separator and Identifier, U.S. Patent 4,326,259.

Dembo, A. and O. Zeitouni. 1987. ARO Technical Report, Brown University, Center for Neural Science, Providence, RI.

Holler, M. C., Park, J., Diamon, U., Santoni, S. C. The, M. Glier, and C. L. Schofield. 1992. Government Microcircuit Applications Conference, vol. XVIII, pp. 261–264.

Hopfield, J. J. 1982. Neural networks and physical systems with emergent collective computational abilities. *Proceedings of the National Academy of Science* 79:2554–2558.

Metropolis, N., A. W. Rosenbluth, M. N. Rosenbluth, A. Teller, and E. Teller. 1953. Equations of state calculations by fast computing machines. *Journal of Chemistry and Physics* 21:1087–1091.

Reilly, D. L., L. N. Cooper, and C. Elbaum. 1982. A Neural Model for Category Learning. *Biological Cybernetics* 45:35–41.

Scofield, C. L. and D. L. Reilly. 1991. Into Silicon: Real Time Learning in a High Density RBF Network. In Proc. IEEE International Conference on Neural Networks (July). Seattle, WA. New York: IEEE Press.

3

Probabilistic Neural Networks

PROBABILISTIC CLASSIFIERS

The Bayesian classifier and its outgrowth, the probabilistic neural network (PNN), have been used successfully to solve a diverse group of classification problems. These include vector-cardiogram interpretation (Specht 1967), radar/target identification (Huynen, Bjorn, and Specht 1969), reentry body discrimination (Bjorn and Specht 1967), and, more recently, hull-to-emitter correlations on radar hits (Maloney and Specht 1989). Although the PNN has not yet been fully evaluated relative to other techniques, if it lives up to its promise it may emerge as the method of choice for many difficult classification problems.

The PNN competes with the backpropagation algorithm (Rumelhart, Hinton, and Williams 1986). Backpropagation has been applied successfully to a wide range of applications, including the airport "bomb sniffer" (Shea and Lin 1989) that detects explosives in checked luggage. Compared with backpropagation, the PNN offers the following major advantages:

1. Rapid training: The PNN process is as much as five orders of magnitude faster than backpropagation. The days or weeks of iterative training of a backpropagation network are replaced by little more than reading in the training set.
2. With enough training data a PNN is guaranteed to converge to a Bayesian classifier (the usual definition of optimality), despite an arbitrarily complex relationship between the training vectors

and the classification. There is no such guarantee with back-propagation; long training periods can terminate in a local optimum that may be an unsatisfactory solution.

3. The PNN algorithm allows data to be added or deleted from the training set without lengthy retraining, whereas, any modification to a backpropagation training set will generally require a repetition of the entire training process. This characteristic of the PNN makes it more compatible with many real-world problems. As with human experience, network learning is often a continuous process. Additional input data collected during operation can improve the performance of the classifier—if it can be incorporated without major difficulties.

4. PNN provides an output indicating the amount of evidence upon which it is basing its decision. A backpropagation system provides no such confidence indication. Given an input that is quite unlike any it has been trained on, it may produce a totally erroneous answer.

The PNN overcomes many of the objections to backpropagation, yet retains its most important characteristics, including the following:

1. **Learning** The network is capable of learning the most complicated relationships between the training vectors and their correct classifications. Arbitrary nonlinear decision boundaries in a space of any dimensionality can be extracted solely from the training set without human intervention.

2. **Generalization** Inputs that are similar, but not identical to those in the training set will, within limits, be correctly classified. Also, erroneous, noisy, or incomplete training or data inputs do not have a disproportionate effect on the classification accuracy.

3. **Concurrency** The inherently parallel nature of the algorithms allows efficient use of multiprocessor systems. Since the classification time is almost exactly inversely proportional to the number of processors, arbitrary speed improvements can be achieved by adding hardware. With modular VLSI implementation, systems providing high performance/price ratios are feasible.

The PNN is based upon work done in the 60's (Specht 1966) at a time when limited computational power and memory made the method impractical for large problems. As a result, much early effort was dedicated to a polynomial approximation method that reduced the required computational resources (Specht 1967b). Modern computers with large, fast memories have made these considerations less significant. Nevertheless, under some circumstances the savings in memory and computation justify the additional complexity; the approximation method will be presented in a later section.

BAYESIAN CLASSIFIERS

The PNN is a direct outgrowth of earlier work with Bayesian classifiers. A study of this powerful method will illuminate the later discussion of the PNN. Bayes theorem provides a method for performing optimal classifications. Given enough information, it shows how to classify a new example with the maximum probability of success; no other method can do better. Due to its sound theoretical foundations, the Bayesian classifier is often used as a standard against which all other methods are evaluated.

A Lumber Sorting Example

With all of its power, the Bayesian classifier is conceptually simple and intuitively satisfying. Its principles can be illustrated by a lumber sorting example. Suppose that we wish to classify a piece of lumber (pine or oak), based solely on a measurement of its density (a one-component feature vector). From historical data, we know the fraction of the pieces that are oak, and the fraction that are pine (the *a priori* probabilities). Call these fractions h_{oak} and h_{pine}. Suppose we know, again from history, the probability that a piece of oak has the measured density. Call this probability f_{oak}, and the corresponding probability for pine f_{pine}. Now, compute the two products

$$h_{oak} \, f_{oak} \tag{3-1}$$

$$h_{pine} \, f_{pine} \tag{3-2}$$

An optimal classification can be made by assigning the piece to the class with the larger product.

Accounting for Losses

In some cases, erroneous decisions may have different consequences depending upon the nature of the misclassification. For example, it may be more costly to misclassify a piece of oak as pine than to classify pine as oak. Bayes theory provides a means for incorporating this information into the classification, thereby accounting for the different "losses" associated with each misclassification. Let l_{oak} represent the loss incurred by misclassifying a piece of oak as pine, and l_{pine} the loss if pine is classified as oak. An additional multiplicative term incorporates this information into the decision.

$$h_{oak} \, f_{oak} \, l_{oak} \tag{3-3}$$

$$h_{pine} \, f_{pine} \, l_{pine} \tag{3-4}$$

Again, the optimal decision assigns the sample to the class with the larger product.

The lumber example uses a single component feature vector representing density; however, the same equations apply regardless of the size of the vector. Also, only two categories were considered. The classifier is easily extended by determining h, f, and l for other types of wood, calculating the corresponding products, and placing the sample into the category with the largest product.

Gathering the Data

It has been assumed that h, f, and l were known. Finding h is usually easy. Records can be kept over a period of time indicating the percentage of the pieces that are of each type; these fractions are then the values for h. For example, if 10% of the pieces are oak, 70% are pine, and 20% are redwood, $h_{oak} = 0.1$, $h_{pine} = 0.7$, and $h_{redwood} = 0.2$.

Determining f involves a bit more work. Suppose that you have a set of bins for oak, a set for pine, and a set for redwood, with each bin labeled according to density. Figure 3-1 shows such a set of bins. Over a period of time, a large number of pieces of wood are placed into appropriate bins. Then,

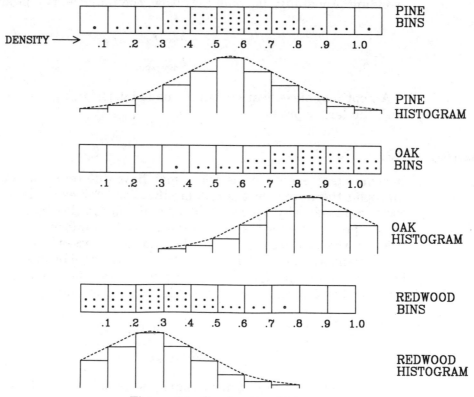

Figure 3-1. Constructing histograms.

the pieces in each bin are counted and a histogram is made as shown in the same figure.

If each bin is subdivided repeatedly (increasing the total number of bins toward infinity), and the number of samples collected are similarly increased, the histogram (after suitable scaling) approaches the dashed curve of Figure 3-1. This smooth curve is called the *probability density function* or *pdf*. To satisfy the mathematical definition, the curve must be scaled to make the area under the curve (the integral) equal to unity.

The probability of a piece of oak having a density value between points a and b on the horizontal axis is determined by finding the area under the curve between a and b through integration.

If h and l are assumed to be equal for all classes, the pdf curves of Figure 3-2 can be used to determine the classification that has the highest probability of being correct. One may think of placing a pin down through the stacked pdf curves, and reading off the value of each at that density. If, for example, the piece being classified has a density of 0.6, pine has the highest pdf and is the best choice. We shall see that this concept of "pinning" stacked pdf's can be extended to two and higher dimensions, even though visualization breaks down in spaces of high dimensionality.

A Three-Class Example With Losses

As a more complicated example, suppose that you have a piece of wood that you wish to classify. From historical data you know that 20% of the wood pieces have been pine, 50% oak, and 30% redwood. Thus, $h_{pine} = 0.2$, $h_{oak} = 0.5$, and $h_{redwood} = 0.3$. You know the density to be 0.8, and your pdf curves indicate that $f_{pine} = 0.5$, $f_{oak} = 0.7$, $f_{redwood} = 0.3$. For simplicity, assume that

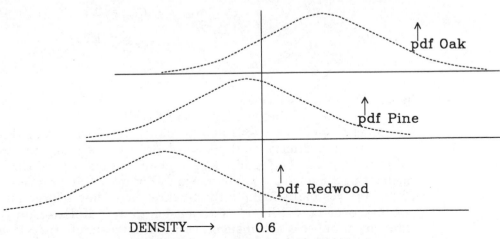

Figure 3-2. Probability density functions.

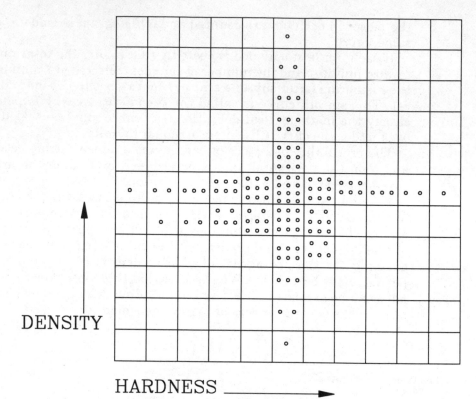

DENSITY

HARDNESS ⟶

Figure 3-3. Two-dimensional bins.

the loss for misclassifying a given type of wood is independent of how it is misclassified. Assume $l_{\text{pine}} = 1$, $l_{\text{oak}} = 5$, and $l_{\text{redwood}} = 2$. Thus,

$$h_{\text{pine}} \, f_{\text{pine}} \, l_{\text{pine}} = 0.1$$

$$h_{\text{oak}} \, f_{\text{oak}} \, l_{\text{oak}} = 1.75$$

$$h_{\text{redwood}} \, f_{\text{redwood}} \, l_{\text{redwood}} = 0.18$$

hence the best classification is oak.

Suppose instead that the arrangement of bins is two dimensional, graded for density along the x axis and hardness along the y axis (Figure 3-3). In this case a two-dimensional pdf can be constructed, and the corresponding value for f_{oak} can be found for each combination of hardness and density. Such a two-dimensional pdf is shown in Figure 3-4. In practice, classification often involves many factors; the feature vector has a large number of components, each of which adds a dimension to the pdf. Extending the pdf to an arbitrary number of dimensions is conceptually simple, but visualization and illustration break down.

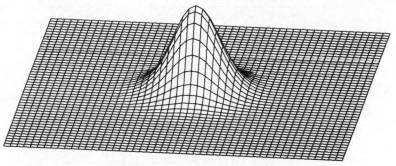

Figure 3-4. Two-dimensional pdf.

TERMINOLOGY

To add precision to the discussion, the following terminology will be used in the remainder of this chapter:

1. Training vector: A vector from the training set, used to establish the classification criteria of the classifier. The correct classification of this vector is known and is indicated by the value of an accompanying classification variable.
2. Test vector: A vector to be classified that is not in the training set.
3. Vector Component: A single value of a feature, either in a training vector or a test vector.
4. Vector Conventions: Vectors will be represented as upper-case bold letters; vector components as lower-case letters. Column vectors will be assumed unless otherwise indicated.

ESTIMATING THE PDF USING PARZEN WINDOWS

Bayesian classification requires a pdf for each class. In practice, it is often difficult to determine the pdf with high accuracy. There may be too few training vectors, and the data may be incomplete or it may be partially inaccurate. Some means are required to estimate the pdf from these sparse, real-world data sets. Fortunately, Parzen (1962) developed such a technique, commonly called the method of Parzen windows. Figure 3-5 shows how this is used for one feature and one class. The horizontal axis is calibrated in numerical values of the feature. For each sample in the training set (in that class) a unit area Gaussian curve is drawn centered at the value of the feature (curves for three feature values are shown in the top three boxes). All of the curves are then added to produce the composite curve in the lowest box. Parzen showed that with a large number of samples and suitable scaling the composite curve approaches the true pdf. While there is no general proof

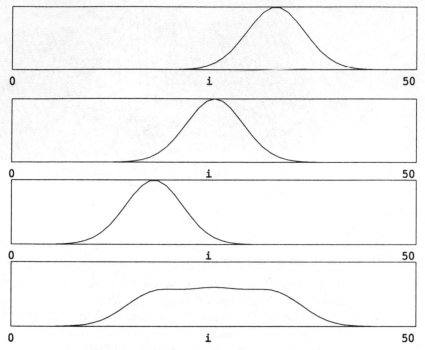

Figure 3-5. Three Gaussians and their sum.

that predicts the number of samples required to estimate the pdf with a specified degree of accuracy, good classification results are often obtained with a modest number of samples.

Training vectors generally have more than one component. If there are two components, a two-dimensional Gaussian is drawn for each training vector in a class, an example of which with three training vectors is shown in Figure 3-6. The sum of all such Gaussian curves taken at each point in the plane forms an estimate of the two-dimensional pdf of the training set. If there are n components, an n dimensional Gaussian is drawn for each training vector thereby extending the method to an arbitrary number of components in the feature vector.

It is not necessary to calculate the full pdf when using Parzen windows for classification; all that is needed is its value at the test vector point. The following equation expresses the method for finding the needed value, extended to the n-dimensional case:

$$f_a(\mathbf{X}) = 1/(2\pi)^{p/2}\sigma^p$$

$$(1/n_a) \sum_{i=1}^{n_a} \exp\left(-(\mathbf{X} - \mathbf{Y}_{ai})^t(\mathbf{X} - \mathbf{Y}_{ai})/2\sigma^2\right) \qquad (3\text{-}5)$$

where

$f_a(\mathbf{X})$ = the value of the pdf of class A at point $\mathbf{X}$
i = training vector number
p = number of components in the training vector
σ = smoothing variable
n_a = number of training vectors in class A
$\mathbf{X}$ = the test vector to be classified
$\mathbf{Y}_{ai}$ = ith training vector from class A
t = vector transpose

While this formula may appear complicated, the idea is simple: add up the values of the n-dimensional Gaussians, evaluated at the training vector point in n-dimensional space, and scale the sum to produce the estimated probability density at that point. As the number of training vectors (and their Gaussians) increases, the estimated pdf approaches the true value.

Determining σ

The smoothing constant σ, the standard deviation of the Gaussian, must be selected to provide an appropriate width for the curve. If σ is small ($\ll 1$), each Gaussian is sharply peaked. Figure 3-6 shows the pdf produced by three Gaussians with $\sigma = 0.5$. As σ is increased, the pdf is smoothed. Figure 3-7 shows the pdf with $\sigma = 1.0$. If σ is made larger the Gaussian functions are spread and flattened, producing a still smoother pdf estimate as in Figure 3-8 where $\sigma = 2.0$. Since all three pdf estimates were produced from the same training set, which should be used? There is no certain answer. Fortunately, classification accuracy has been found to be relatively insensitive to the value of σ (Specht 1990). Specht (1967) showed that as σ approaches 0, a nearest

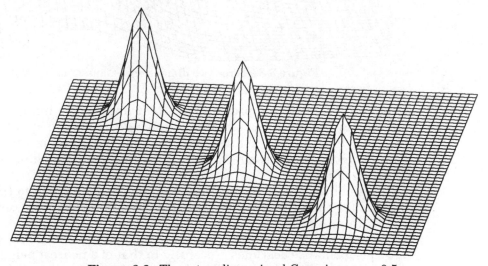

Figure 3-6. Three two-dimensional Gaussians, $\sigma = 0.5$.

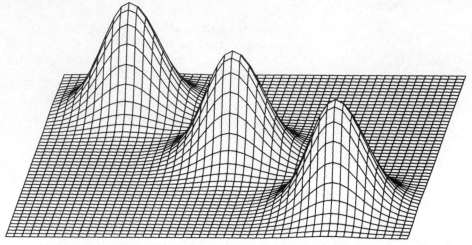

Figure 3-7. Three two-dimensional Gaussians, $\sigma = 1.0$.

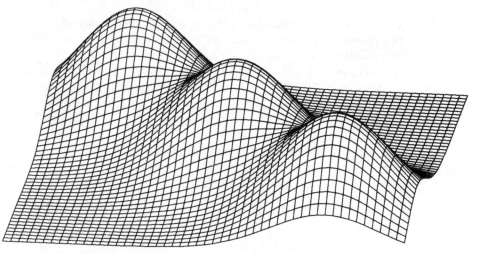

Figure 3-8. Three two-dimensional Gaussians, $\sigma = 2.0$.

neighbor classifier is approximated. As it approaches infinity, the decision boundaries approach hyperplanes, limiting the classifier to functions that are linearly separable. While either extreme will produce acceptable classification under some circumstances, some intermediate value for σ is generally superior.

Reversion to a nearest neighbor classifier adds greatly to the robustness of the algorithm. Real-world training sets are often sparse in certain regions. The training vectors are so far apart that there is inadequate overlapping of the Gaussians to produce an accurate estimate of the actual pdf. In these cases performance degrades gracefully to that of a nearest neighbor classifier rather than failing outright. If, of course, the data set is generally sparse, there is little advantage to the method of Parzan windows, and a simpler nearest neighbor classifier may produce equivalent performance.

Between training vector points nothing is known about the pdf, other than the definitional requirement that it be nonnegative; everything else is supposition. The Parzen windows estimator functions well with little data because of the assumption that the true pdf is smooth enough to be approximated by a sum of a reasonable number of Gaussians, an empirically observed characteristic of many naturally occurring distributions, but not a law of nature.

Duda and Hart (1973) present a technique for selecting σ. In their method, a separate value of σ is calculated for each training vector, such that its Gaussian is spread until its value exceeds a predetermined level at a specified number of other training vector points. The resulting Gaussian may be thought of as enclosing these points. Thus, a Gaussian will be broad (large σ) in regions where there are few training vectors. Where the density of training vectors is high, a small value of σ results, thereby avoiding excessive smoothing of the pdf. While this method is appealing, it may not always be justified, due to the previously discussed insensitivity to the value of σ. Furthermore, it destroys the algorithm's property of reversion to a nearest neighbor classifier in regions where data is sparse, an excessive price to pay in many cases.

Two Category Classification

If vectors are to be separated into two classes, the following decision equations apply

$$d(X) = \Theta_a \quad \text{if } h_a l_a f_a(X) > h_b l_b f_b(X) \tag{3-6}$$

$$d(X) = \Theta_b \quad \text{if } h_a l_a f_a(X) < h_b l_b f_b(X) \tag{3-7}$$

where

$d(X) =$ the decision on test vector X
$\Theta_a =$ class A
$h_a =$ the probability of occurrence of training vectors from class A
$l_a =$ the loss from erroneously placing a vector into class B when it belongs in class A
$f_a(X) =$ the probability density function for class A

Θ_b, h_b, l_b, and $f_b(X)$ have the same definitions except that they apply to class B.

Multi-Category Classification

The multicategory classifier decision may be expressed as follows

$$\text{if } \quad h_r l_r f_r \geq h_s l_s f_s \text{ for all classes of } r \text{ not equal to } s,$$

$$\text{then class } r \text{ is the best choice} \qquad (3\text{-}8)$$

It is important to note that the loss factor, l_x is not contained in the statistics of the training set; it is determined by the consequences of misclassification and must either be calculated or subjectively estimated. In general, each class has a different misclassification loss for each other class, yielding a loss matrix. To avoid the complexity this entails, all losses for a given class will be assumed to be equal and positive, therefore, only a single value of l_s will be associated with each class.

If the training set is large and representative, variable h_a may be estimated as the relative frequency of vectors in each class. This is easily calculated by counting the number of times that a vector in that class occurs in the training set, then dividing the count by the total number of training vectors.

In this case, the following equation applies

$$h_a = n_a / n_{\text{total}} \qquad (3\text{-}9)$$

where n_a is the number of training vectors in class A, and n_{total} is the total number of training vectors.

Using this estimate, the classification criterion may be simplified substantially. Substituting Equation (3-9) into Equations (3-6) and (3-7) [(or 3-8)], the denominator of Equation (3-9) has no effect upon the decision, as it is the same for all classes and may, therefore, be dropped. Also note that n_a in Equation 3-9 cancels the $1/n_a$ in Equation (3-5). Likewise, the other constant multipliers before the summation do not affect the decision and may be dropped. This results in the following criterion for the multicategory case

$$D(X) = \Theta_r \text{ if}$$

$$l_r \sum_{i=1}^{n_r} \exp\left[-(\mathbf{X} - \mathbf{Y}_{ri})^t(\mathbf{X} - \mathbf{Y}_{ri})/2\sigma^2\right]$$

$$\geq l_s \sum_{i=1}^{n_s} \exp\left[-(\mathbf{X} - \mathbf{Y}_{si})^t(\mathbf{X} - \mathbf{Y}_{si})/2\sigma^2\right]$$

$$\text{for all classes of } r \text{ not equal to } s \qquad (3\text{-}10)$$

THE POLYNOMIAL DISCRIMINANT FUNCTION

The classifier described above using Parzen windows employs the entire training set to perform each classification. As a practical matter, this requires storage of the entire training set in fast random access memory. Thus, both the storage requirements and the computational load are proportional to the number of examples in the training set. If the training set is large, impractical amounts of memory and computation may be required. The rapid increase in memory capacity and computation rate in digital computers is reducing the number of applications where this is a significant problem. Nevertheless, classifiers operating with very large training sets can benefit from a more compact and efficient representation of the pdf.

Since the pdf generated by the Parzen window technique is simply a function on n-dimensional space, it may be approximated by a polynomial in n variables. Storage requirements are then reduced to the coefficients of the polynomial rather than the entire training set. Thus, calculating the estimated pdf requires only the evaluation of the polynomial. Since the number of coefficients is related to the desired accuracy of the approximation, storage and calculation time is independent of the size of the training set. Experience has shown that a relatively small number of coefficients is sufficient for many applications, and major reductions in both memory and computation time may be achieved.

The selection of polynomials as the approximating functions is somewhat arbitrary; linear combinations of a wide variety of orthogonal basis functions may be used instead. There is no clear choice regarding which functions to use, however, the Taylor expansion using polynomials (Specht 1966) has been well developed, and successfully applied. It will be the sole method presented here.

To apply this method, coefficients of the polynomial are calculated for each category. These coefficients are used to approximate the estimated pdf produced by the Parzen windows method. Thus, calculating the value of the pdf for a class requires only the evaluation of its polynomial.

It may seem strange to approximate an estimated pdf with another approximating function. In fact, it is advantageous, as the Parzen windows method acts as an interpolator, smoothing the pdf prior to the polynomial approximation. In other methods where the approximation is made directly on the training data, overfitting problems can result, thereby producing errors at points between actual training vectors.

The objective is to approximate the function of Equation (3-5) (repeated here for reference).

$$f_a(\mathbf{X}) = 1/[(2\pi)^{p/2}\sigma^p]\,(1/n_a)\sum_{i=1}^{n_a}\exp\left[-(\mathbf{X}-\mathbf{Y}_{ai})^t(\mathbf{X}-\mathbf{Y}_{ai})/2\sigma^2\right] \quad (3\text{-}11)$$

Expanding the argument of the exponential, this can be written as follows

$$F_a(X) = 1/[(2\pi)^{p/2} \sigma^p] \, (1/n_a) \sum_{i=1}^{i=n_a} \exp \{-[(x_1 - y_{ai1})^2$$

$$\cdots + (x_j - y_{aij})^2 + \cdots + (x_p - y_{aip})^2]/(2\sigma^2)\} \qquad (3\text{-}12)$$

where

x_y = is component y of the test vector being classified
y_{aij} = is the jth component of the ith vector in category A

Performing the indicated multiplications in the exponential, and separating it into the product of two exponentials

$$f_a(X) = 1/[(2\pi)^{p/2} \sigma^p] \, (1/n_a)$$

$$\cdot \sum_{i=1}^{i=n_a} \exp \{- [x_1^2 + \cdots + x_j^2 + \cdots x_p^2]/(2\sigma^2)\}$$

$$\cdot \exp [(-2x_1 \, y_{ai1} + y_{ai1}^2 - \cdots -2x_j \, y_{aij} + y_{aij}^2$$

$$- \cdots -2x_p y_{aip} + y_{aip}^2)/(2\sigma^2)] \qquad (3\text{-}13)$$

But

$$(x_1^2 + \cdots + x_j^2 + \cdots x_p^2) = \mathbf{x}^t\mathbf{x} \qquad (3\text{-}14)$$

the squared magnitude of the test vector $\mathbf{X}$, a column vector.
For compactness, define

$$B_{ai} = (-1/2) \sum_{j=1}^{p} y_{aij}^2$$

$$= (-1/2) \, (\mathbf{Y}_{ai}^t \, \mathbf{Y}_{ai}) \qquad (3\text{-}15)$$

Substituting Equations (3-14) and (3-15) into Equation (3-13) yields

$$f_a(X) = 1/[(2\pi)^{p/2}\sigma^p] \exp [- (\mathbf{X}^t\mathbf{X})/(2\sigma^2)](1/n_a)$$

$$\cdot \sum_{i=1}^{m} \exp \{(x_1 \, y_{ai1} + \cdots + x_j \, y_{aij} + \cdots + x_p y_{aip}) + B_{ai}]/\sigma^2\}$$

$$(3\text{-}16)$$

Terms on the first line of Equation (3-16) are either constants or relate to the test vector, hence, they do not affect the approximation of the pdf. Concentrating therefore, on the second line of Equation (3-16), applying the Taylor expansion of the exponential function and the multinomial theorem produces the following results

$$\sum_{i=1}^{m} \exp\left[(x_1 y_{ai1} + \cdots + x_j y_{aij} + \cdots + x_p y_{aip}) + B_{ai})/\sigma^2\right]$$

$$
\begin{aligned}
= \sum_{i=1}^{m} &\left[\exp\left(B_{ai}/\sigma^2\right)\right]\left[1 + (x_1 y_{ai1} + \cdots + x_p y_{aip}/\sigma^2)\right] \\
&+ (x_1^2 y_{ai1}^2 + 2x_1 x_2 y_{ai1} y_{ai2} + 2x_1 x_3 y_{ai1} y_{ai3} \cdots)/(2!\sigma^4) \\
&+ (x_1^3 y_{ai1}^3 + 3x_1^2 x_2 y_{ai1}^2 y_{ai2} + 6x_1 x_2 x_3 y_{ai1} y_{ai2} y_{ai3} + \cdots)/(3!\sigma^6) \\
&+ \cdots + [h!/(z_1! z_2! \cdots z_p!)] x_1^{z1} x_2^{z2} \cdots x_p^{zp} y_{ai1}^{z1} y_{ai2}^{z2} \\
&\cdots y_{aip}^{zp}/(h!\sigma^{2h}) + \cdots]
\end{aligned}
$$

(3-17)

where z_j is the nonnegative integer exponent of x_j, and $z_1 + \cdots z_j \cdots z_p = h$.

Equation (3-16) can now be expressed as

$$f_a(X) = 1/[(2\pi)^{p/2}\sigma^p] \exp\left[-(X^t X)/(2\sigma^2)\right] P^A(X) \tag{3-18}$$

where

$$
\begin{aligned}
P^A(X) = D_{0\cdots 0}^A &+ D_{10\cdots 0}^A x_1 + D_{010\cdots 0}^A x_2 \\
&+ \cdots + D_{0\cdots 01}^A x_p + D_{20\cdots 0}^A x_1^2 \\
&+ D_{110\cdots 0}^A x_1 x_2 + \cdots + D^A z_1 z_2 \\
&\cdots z_p x_1^{z1} x_2^{z2} \cdots x_p^{zp} + \cdots
\end{aligned}
$$

and $P^A(X)$ is the polynomial approximation for vectors from category A; such a polynomial is required for each category.

Recognizing the coefficients $Dz_1 z_2 \cdots z_p$ of $x_1^{z1} x_2^{z2} x_p^{zp}$ in Equation (3-17),

$$Dz_1 z_2 \cdots z_p = 1/(z_1! z_2! \cdots z_p!\, \sigma^{2h})\,(1/n_a) \sum_{i=1}^{n_a} y_{ai1}^{z1} y_{ai2}^{z2} \cdots y_{aip}^{zp} \exp\left(B_{ai}/\sigma^2\right)$$

(3-19)

where

$$h = z_1 + z_2 \cdots z_p,$$

The equations are complicated, but when translated into a digital computer program they provide a means for approximating the pdf to any desired accuracy, simply by including enough terms. If the number of terms is small, a considerable reduction in the storage and computational load can be realized. Fortunately the functions are often smooth, and low degree (2 or 3) polynomials will suffice to achieve a satisfactory accuracy in the pdf approximation.

A Numerical Example

Suppose that we wish to approximate $f(x)$ for a given class using a second-degree polynomial. Using Equation (3-18), with the subscript indicating the class suppressed, the following function must be evaluated

$$f(\mathbf{X}) = 1/[(2\pi)^{p/2}\sigma^p]\, \exp\left[-(\mathbf{X}^t\mathbf{X})/(2\sigma^2)\right] P(\mathbf{X}) \qquad (3\text{-}20)$$

Assume that there are two training vectors, each having two components

$$\mathbf{Y}_1 = [-1,\, 1]^t$$

$$\mathbf{Y}_2 = [1,\, -1]^t \qquad (3\text{-}21)$$

and we wish to evaluate the function at the following test vector

$$\mathbf{X} = [1,\, 1]^t$$

Then we must find

$$P(\mathbf{X}) = D_{00} + D_{10}x_1 + D_{01}x_2 + D_{20}x_1^2 + D_{11}x_1x_2 + D_{02}x_2$$

where from Equation 3-19

$$D_{z1z2\cdots zp} = 1/(z_1! z_2! \cdots z_p!\, \sigma^{2h})\, (1/n_a) \sum_{i=1}^{n_a} y_{i1}^{z1} y_{i2}^{z2} \cdots y_{ip}^{zp} \exp(B_i/\sigma^2) \quad (3\text{-}22)$$

Thus

$$D_{00} = \tfrac{1}{2}\left\{[\exp(B_1/\sigma^2) + \exp(B_2/\sigma^2)]\right\}$$

where

$$B_1 = (-1/2)\mathbf{Y}_1^t\mathbf{Y}_1 = -1$$

$$B_2 = (-1/2)\mathbf{Y}_2^t\mathbf{Y}_2 = -1$$

therefore, assuming $\sigma = 1$

$$\exp(B_1/\sigma^2) = 0.3678$$

$$\exp(B_2/\sigma^2) = 0.3678$$

and

$$D_{00} = 0.3678$$

similarly

$$D_{10} = (1/2\sigma^2)[\, y_{11} \exp\,(B_1/\sigma^2) + y_{21} \exp\,(B_2/\sigma^2)]$$

$$= 0$$

$$D_{01} = (1/2\sigma^2)[\, y_{12} \exp\,(B_1/\sigma^2) + y_{22} \exp\,(B_2/\sigma^2)]$$

$$= 0$$

$$D_{20} = (1/2\sigma^4)(1/2)[\, y_{11}^2 \exp\,(B_1/\sigma^2) + y_{21}^2 \exp\,(B_2/\sigma^2)]$$

$$= 0.1839$$

$$D_{11} = (1/\sigma^4)(1/2)[\, y_{11}y_{12} \exp\,(B_1/\sigma^2) + y_{21}y_{22} \exp\,(B_2/\sigma^2)]$$

$$= -0.3678$$

$$D_{02} = (1/\sigma^4)(1/2)[\, y_{12}^2 \exp\,(B_1/\sigma^2) + y_{22}^2 \exp\,(B_2/\sigma^2)]$$

$$= 0.1839$$

thus

$$P(\mathbf{X}) = 0.3678 + 0.1839 - 0.3678 + 0.1839 = 0.3678$$

and

$$f(\mathbf{X}) = (1/2\pi)[(-\mathbf{X}^t\mathbf{X})/2\sigma^2)P(\mathbf{X}) = 0.0215$$

Comparing this result to the function we are approximating

$$f(\mathbf{X}) = 1/[(2\pi)^{p/2}\sigma^p]\,(1/n) \sum_{i=1}^{n_a} \exp\,[-(\mathbf{X} - \mathbf{Y}_i)^t(\mathbf{X} - \mathbf{Y}_i/2\sigma^2)]$$

$$= 0.0215$$

showing perfect agreement at this point.

It is important to remember that the polynomial is an approximation; at various points it will deviate from the function, and may cause classification errors. While the approximating function in the numerical example above is quite accurate at most points, it has an error of 0.02818 occurring at the point $(-1.5, 1.5)$. Since the value of the function is 0.062129 at this point, an error of over 45% results.

The accuracy of the approximation may be improved by increasing the degree of the polynomial. This can only be done at the expense of increased storage requirements and computation time. Since the number of coefficients rises exponentially with the degree of the polynomial, it is important to use the lowest degree which yields acceptable accuracy.

PROBABILISTIC NEURAL NETWORKS

The many advantages offered by artificial neural networks have prompted an effort to recast the Bayesian classifier into this general model. The relationship to conventional neural networks may be seen most clearly if both the training vectors and test vectors are normalized. They are set to have length of unity by dividing each vector by the square root of the sum of the squares of its components. Note that normalization is assumed here for clarity of exposition; it may indeed be disadvantageous in cases that will be described. In the normalized case (ignoring loss terms), the exponential terms in Equation (3-10) may be simplified, as $(\mathbf{X} - \mathbf{X}_{Ri})^t(\mathbf{X} - \mathbf{X}_{Ri})$ and may be expressed as

$$(\mathbf{X}^t\mathbf{X} - 2\mathbf{X}^t\mathbf{X}_{Ri} + \mathbf{X}_{Ri}^t\mathbf{X}_{Ri}) \tag{3-23}$$

but $\mathbf{X}^t\mathbf{X} = \mathbf{X}_{Ri}^t\mathbf{X}_{Ri} = 1$ due to normalization, hence this expression becomes

$$-2(\mathbf{X}^t\mathbf{F}_{Ri} - 1)$$

therefore

$$D(\mathbf{X}) = \Theta_R \text{ if}$$

$$\sum_{i=1}^{nR} \exp\left[(\mathbf{X}^t\mathbf{X}_{Ri} - 1)/\sigma^2\right] \geq \sum_{i=1}^{nS} \exp\left[(\mathbf{X}^t\mathbf{X}_{Ri} - 1)/\sigma^2\right] \tag{3-24}$$

The network of Figure 3-9 accomplishes the classification for a two-class PNN. An input vector $\mathbf{X} = (x_1 \ x_2 \cdots x_n)$ to be classified is applied to the neurons of the *distribution layer*. This layer serves merely as a connection point; the neurons perform no computation.

The set of weights entering a *pattern layer* neuron represent a specific training vector; each weight has the value of a component of that vector. Furthermore, the pattern layer neurons are grouped by the known classification of its associated training vector. Each pattern layer neuron sums the weighted inputs from every distribution layer neuron, then applies the non-

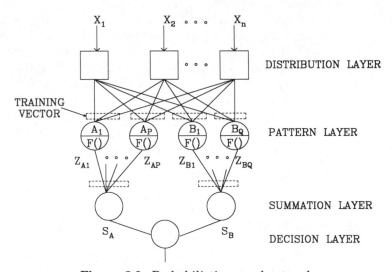

Figure 3-9. Probabilistic neural network.

linear function $f(\cdot)$ to that sum to produce the output Z_{ci}, where the first subscript, c, indicates the class of the associated training vector, and the second identifies the pattern layer neuron computing that class.

Since the set of weights associated with a given pattern neuron represent a training vector $\mathbf{X}_{Ri} = (x_{R1}\ x_{R2} \cdots x_{Rn})$, the pattern neuron computes $x_{R1} x_1 + x_{R2} x_2 + \cdots x_{Rn} x_n = \mathbf{X}_{Ri}^t \mathbf{x}_i$, the dot product needed to implement Equation (3-11). Z_{ci} is then formed by subtracting 1, dividing by σ^2, and applying the exponential function. Thus, the resulting output is

$$\mathbf{Z}_{ci} = \exp\left[(\mathbf{X}_{Ri}^t \mathbf{X}_i - 1)/\sigma^2\right]$$

Each neuron in the *summation layer* receives all pattern layer outputs associated with a given class. If ten neurons in the pattern layer each computed the exponential function for class 1, all ten pattern layer outputs would be summed by a single summation layer neuron. Thus, the output of each summation layer neuron is:

$$S_c = \sum_{i=1} \exp\left[(\mathbf{X}^t \mathbf{X}_{Ri} - 1)/\sigma^2\right] \tag{3-25}$$

This is exactly the form needed to implement Equation (3-10).

In the decision layer, each neuron forms a comparison, outputting a one, if S_a is greater than S_b, and zero otherwise, thereby indicating the class of the current input vector. This technique can be easily extended to an arbitrary number of classes by adding a group of pattern layer neurons and a summation layer neuron for each class. A mechanism must then be provided to determine which summation layer neuron has the maximum output. For example, an array of decision layer neurons could be used to form all possible pair-wise comparison decisions, and an output logic layer could then decide upon the classification.

DISCUSSION

The PNN approach offers many advantages. It trains virtually instantaneously, it is robust in the presence of noise, and it offers a unique guarantee. It approaches Bayesian optimality if the training set is sufficiently large. Nevertheless, some factors must be considered before selecting it for an application.

The dot product version of the PNN described above uses normalized training and test vectors. This means that colinear vectors will become indistinguishable. In many cases this is not a problem; the classification decision is based on the relative pattern that is not lost in the normalization process. If however, each component of a vector represents a pixel in an image, and another vector represents the same image at a different illumination level, the two vectors could not be separated after normalization. Note that there is no compelling reason to normalize these vectors, PNN functions as well or better if the difference function of Equation (3-10) is used instead of the dot product of Equation (3-25), and the concern with colinear vectors disappears.

The amount of computation required to do a classification with the PNN is roughly proportional to the size of the training set. Also, storage requirements go up at the same rate. This can become a severe problem with large training sets, but may be alleviated through the use of the polynomial discriminant functions method described above. As previously discussed, this method of approximation is not without its problems. The degree of the polynomial must be selected to approximate the function with adequate accuracy without creating excessive storage or computational loads. Unfortunately, the required degree is problem dependent; highly irregular pdf's require a high-degree polynomial. Since little is known in advance regarding the shape of the pdf, selecting an optimal degree requires care, judgment, and some experimentation.

Some object to the PNN method due to its lack of biological plausibility; the exponential neuron response is atypical if not nonexistent in the brain. To those engaged in modeling the central nervous system, this is a serious disadvantage. For the pragmatic engineer, bent on solving a difficult classification problem, biological considerations are not on the priority list.

Still another objection relates to the lack of modernity. PNN is, after all, a variation on the Bayesian classifier using Parzen windows, both well known and seasoned techniques. Casting the problem so that it can be computed in a fully concurrent manner by a large number of simple processors is a nontrivial achievement. With the low cost and staggering complexity of VLSI circuits, highly parallel processing hardware is readily available. Unfortunately most algorithms do not make efficient use of these parallel processing systems. For all of recorded history, serial processing methods have been dominant, perhaps representing the common mode of human thought. If we are to realize the potential of our hardware, fully parallel algorithms must be devised. PNN is such an algorithm.

REFERENCES

Bjorn, T. and D. F. Specht. 1967. Discrimination between re-entry bodies in the presence of clutter using the polynomial discriminant method of pattern recognition. LMSC-B039970, Lockheed Missiles and Space Co.

Duda, R. O. and P. E. Hart. 1973. *Pattern Classification and Scene Analysis*. New York: Wiley.

Huynen, J. R., T. Bjorn, and D. F. Specht. 1969. Advanced radar target discrimination technique for real-time application. LMSC-D051707, Lockheed Missiles and Space Co.

Maloney, S. P. 1989. The Use of Probabilistic Neural Networks to Improve Solution Times for Hull-To-Emitter Correlation Problems. *International Joint Conference on Neural Networks*, vol. 1, pp. 289–294. New Jersey: IEEE Press.

Parzen, E. 1962. On estimation of a probability density function and mode. *Ann. Math. Stat.*, 33:1065–1076.

Rumelhart, D. E., G. E. Hinton, and R. J. Williams. 1986. Learning internal representations by error propagation. In: *Parallel Distributed Processing*, vol. 1, pp. 318–362. Cambridge, MA: MIT Press.

Shea, P. M. and V. Lin. 1989. Detection of explosives in checked airline baggage using an artificial neural system. *International Joint Conference on Neural Networks*, vol. 2, pp. 31–34. New Jersey: IEEE Press.

Specht, D. F. 1966. *Generation of Polynomial Discriminant Functions for Pattern Recognition*. Ph.D. dissertation, Stanford University, Stanford, CA; also available from Stanford Electronics Labs, Stanford, CA, Rept. SU-Sel-66-029, Tech. SEL Rept. 6764-5, and Defense Documentation Center Rept. AD 487 537.

Specht, D. F. 1967. Vectorcardiographic diagnosis using the polynomial discriminant method of pattern recognition. *IEEE Transactions on Bio-Medical Engineering*. BME-14, pp. 90–95.

Specht, D. F. 1967b. Generation of polynomial discriminant functions for pattern recognition. IEEE *Transactions on Electronic Computers*, EC-16, pp. 308–319.

Specht, D. F. 1988. Probabilistic Neural Networks for Classification, Mapping, or Associative Memory. *Proceedings of the IEEE International Conference on Neural Networks*, vol. 1, pp. 525–532. New York: IEEE Press.

Specht, D. F. 1990. Probabilistic neural networks. *Neural Networks*. 3(1):109–118.

4

Sparse Distributed Memory

INTRODUCTION

Human intellect consists largely of the ability to sense characteristics of our environment, encode these, store and retrieve these encodings as memories; produce related memories where each leads to the next, and to combine memories into abstract concepts and generalizations. Thus, a complete theory of memory would constitute a large part of a comprehensive theory of mind and intelligence.

Kanerva's sparse distributed memory (SDM) is nothing less than an ambitious attempt to produce such a theory. Inspired by observations of human memory, he expresses his concepts in the concrete terms of computer hardware. By so doing, SDM has become both a profound conceptual system and a hardware implementation compatible with modern VLSI integrated circuits.

SDM may be viewed as a useful computational paradigm, quite independent of biological associations. Such an approach may produce implementations of substantial practical significance, however, a deeper understanding will result through an appreciation of the correspondences to human mental functions which motivated SDM, as these may be expected to provide inspiration for its improvement and expansion.

HUMAN MEMORY

Much more than the simple storage and recall mechanism of a digital computer that bears the same name, human memory has the ability to store relationships as well as data, thereby allowing the construction of an accurate internal model of the external environment. This model is developed automatically as a result of sensory inputs as well as purely internal mental experiences. Through reference to the model we can recognize familiar objects, sequences, and classes by comparing sensory features to those previously stored.

The power of human recall comes from its ability to generalize, abstract, and associate related data,[1] as well as the simple storage and retrieval of huge amounts of data. Since these attributes were the design objectives for SDM, each will be treated in more detail.

Generalization

It is rare that a datum stored in the model corresponds exactly to a current sensory input. Objects, people, and concepts are in a constant state of change. Fortunately, human memory generalizes; correct recognition is performed despite the inevitable deviations between current perceptions and stored data. This allows us to recognize the Mississippi River as having the same identity in the spring as in the fall, despite variations in many features.

Abstraction

Often we recall a datum representing a group of experiences, but not exactly any specific instance. For example, the word "cat" may produce a mental image that is the composite of all cats we have seen, but not a precise replica of any one of them. This ability to produce representative prototypes of classes, along with appropriate names, provides a mental shorthand which vastly increases our intellectual ability; we can now use a single datum to think of a large group. Consider how hopelessly inefficient it would be if we had to recall every dog and cat we have ever seen to express the concept that dogs chase cats!

Association

Sensory experiences rarely occur as isolated examples; life is a sequence of related perceptions. A useful model must store these along with the relational links that tie one to the next, thereby allowing the chain to be accessed and recalled in the correct order. For example, hearing a few bars of a tune will often allow us to hum it to completion.

This capability allows prediction. Given a set of current sensory inputs, it is possible to access a similar situation from the past (or the abstracted com-

---

[1]To avoid the ambiguity resulting from the use of the term "memory," both as the thing stored and the storage mechanism itself, the term datum (data if plural) will be substituted for the stored information.

posite of many situations), and follow a chain of recollections to the likely outcome.

We can consider various courses of action, anticipate their consequences, and select the one that is most desirable. This mental experimentation can be done quickly, privately, and safely. Through experience, we store more sequences, and we become increasingly able to select actions leading to desirable outcomes. This ability of hypothesis selection, combined with the regular application of associative memory, is often called wisdom.

FOUNDATIONS OF SPARSE DISTRIBUTED MEMORY

SDM as described by Kanerva (1986a,b, 1988) is a system that reproduces important functions of human memory. Although not originally modeled after specific anatomical structures, later studies have shown striking correspondences with the neuroanatomy of the cerebellum. Since the detailed functions of this organ are poorly understood, it is not possible to conclude that it actually functions as SDM.

In formulating SDM, Kanerva constructed a system that is not only functionally similar to human memory, but may also be structurally similar. It not only duplicates <u>what</u> the brain does, but perhaps also <u>how</u> it does it; at the very least SDM does not use mechanisms that are biologically impossible. This is a significant accomplishment considering the fragmentary nature of our understanding of the brain's operation. In so doing Kanerva was obliged to infer a great deal about the actual biological mechanisms.

There are two extreme approaches (plus many intermediate alternatives) to making such inferences about a large complex system, both of which may be regarded as reverse engineering. Given a functioning system, attempts to deduce its intended purpose and design generally follow one of the following patterns:

1. Reductionist: Dissect an incomprehensible system into ever smaller components until a level of complexity is reached where understanding becomes possible. Despite its success in many areas of science, this method has not been fruitful in explorations of the human mental functions. Our ever increasing knowledge about the detailed operation of the neuron has not lead to an understanding of overall functions of the brain. This is due to the near impossibility of deducing how a huge number of neurons can be connected to account for the observed human mental capabilities. In other words, the essence of the brain is not implicit in the neuron, but rather exists in the pattern of interconnections and interactive dynamics.

   As an example, one would never be able to understand the functioning of a digital computer through only an increasingly microscopic examination of its constituent integrated circuits.

The same computational functions could be implemented by Josephson junctions, vacuum tubes, or even magnetic amplifiers. Thus, the essence of the computer's architecture is not to be found in the details of the components. Rather, it exists in the conceptual organization of the entire structure.

Trying to produce a computer from random connections of components would also be futile. There are simply too many combinations to be tried; the probability of success is vanishingly small. Early hopes of doing useful computation with randomly connected artificial neural networks were frustrated by this reality.

2. Holistic: Observe the overall system function and hypothesize mechanisms that might produce it. This approach has a major advantage in that an experienced human can draw upon memories of similar functions whose mechanisms are understood. Since nature tends to use and reuse a small number of techniques, it is likely that an appropriate system can be recalled, either directly or by analogy, and that the underlying mechanisms will be similar. This approach has a weakness in that the system constructed using these mechanisms may not observe the constraints of the system being studied. In the case of the brain, such systems may not be biologically plausible, relying upon mechanisms that have not been observed in the brain, and that may in fact be biologically impossible.

Kanerva has chosen the holistic approach while retaining biological plausibility. His implementation uses conventional computer hardware components such as address decoders and counters. Nevertheless, the structure violates no biological principles, and as previously discussed, may model the function of the cerebellum.

OVERVIEW

SDM is a system with many of the desirable characteristics of human memory. In addition to the simple read/write function of ordinary computer memory, SDM generalizes, abstracts, and recalls sequences of recorded data. Making use of the statistical properties of vector spaces, it provides an address space that is much larger than the amount of physical memory, hence, the term "sparse" in its name.

Data and Address Representation

SDM represents a pattern to be memorized (and subsequently recalled) as a binary vector; each vector component may take on only the values 0 or 1. A component value of 1 indicates the presence of a feature; a 0 its absence. The theory is easily extended to include components with a broader range of values, however, binary vectors will be assumed for the sake of simplicity.

A vector can represent either an address in memory, or the data stored at that address or at a different address (called autoassociative and heteroassociative, respectively). For example, a vector representing a dog might have nine components, one each for large, medium, small, black, brown, gray, long tail, short tail, no tail. The vector [0, 0, 1, 1, 0, 0, 0, 0, 1] would then describe a small black dog with no tail. This vector could represent an address in memory at which the same vector is stored as data. Extending the vector would allow the representation of every characteristic of every dog. The method of representation is perfectly general if not compact.

It is important to note that a feature vector is not an ordinal binary number. That is, [1, 0, 0] is not the binary number 100. Since there is no natural first, second, or third vector component, traditional binary arithmetic operations cannot be applied to them. A detailed discussion of operations on these vectors will be discussed later, however, it will be useful to define the concept of *difference* and *distance* between two such vectors.

First, the *difference* between two such vectors is itself a vector having a 1 in each bit position where the two vectors differ. This may be recognized as the exclusive–or function on the two vectors. The *distance* between the two vectors is then the number of 1's in the difference vector. For example, the difference between [1 0 1 0] and [1 1 0 0] would be [0 1 1 0] and the distance between the two vectors would be 2. This is called the Hamming distance, and equals the number of bit positions in which the two vectors disagree.

Best Match Operation

SDM can input a feature vector and produce the nearest vector that has been previously stored. A fixed number of physical memory locations at fixed addresses are assumed to exist. When a feature vector is stored to an SDM, it is interpreted as an address and it is stored simultaneously to all memory addresses within a specified distance. This differs sharply from the conventional digital computer where data is stored to only a single location at a time. For example, our dog feature vector [0, 0, 1, 1, 0, 0, 0, 0, 1] might be stored to all locations within a Hamming distance of 2. Thus, locations written with the feature vector would include 100100001, 001010001, 001100111, and so on.

Another unusual characteristic of SDM is that each memory location remembers, in effect, everything that has ever been stored in it. This differs from ordinary computer memory where storing in a memory location overwrites and obliterates anything previously stored there. An SDM system could be implemented by putting a number of storage registers at each memory location. We shall see that SDM requires memorization of only the number of 1's minus the number of 0's stored in each bit position, not their individual values. Therefore, the implementation may be greatly simplified by placing a digital counter at each bit position of each memory location (Figure 4-1). If a 1 is stored in a specified bit position at a given memory location, the associated counter is incremented, whereas, storing a 0 decrements the counter.

The SDM retrieval operation is equally unusual. Here, a feature vector is applied, interpreted as an address, and data from a group of locations are retrieved simultaneously. The group comes from all addresses that are within a specified distance from the feature vector. The data retrieved from each location consists of the contents of all of its counters (one counter for each bit position). Since data from many locations is retrieved simultaneously, each of which produces the contents of several counters, some means are required to convert this data to the desired binary output vector. The following algorithm accomplishes this objective:

1. Pick the first bit position.
2. Sum the counters at this bit position for all locations read. Call this SUM.
3. If SUM is greater than zero, set the corresponding bit in the output vector to 1; otherwise set it to 0.
4. Repeat steps 2 and 3 for each bit position.

The mathematical justification for this calculation will be developed later, but in a qualitative sense the resulting binary output vector is the average of all stored vectors which are similar (close) to the feature vector. In this way a memory may be correctly retrieved given a partially incorrect or incomplete feature vector. This bears an important similarity to human

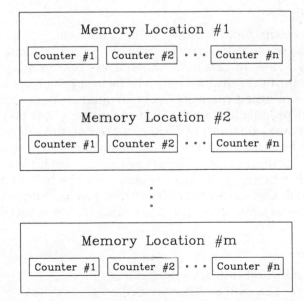

Figure 4-1. Digital counters in each memory location.

memory that can correctly identify a person from a partial view of a face, or interpret a sentence where 30% of the letters have been removed.

Note that there need be no physical memory address exactly equal to the input feature vector. The memory operates to produce data from the set of addresses that are sufficiently similar to the feature vector, none of which must be identical to it. Furthermore, writing to memory is done also on the basis of address similarity. In this way a small, fixed number of evenly distributed memory locations, can suffice to cover a much larger address space. In a conventional memory, a feature vector of 1000 bits interpreted as an address would require 2^{1000} memory locations, an unthinkably large memory. It will be shown that SDM requires only 2^{20} locations to produce useful storage capabilities, hence, the name, "sparse distributed memory."

Memory Capacity

If too many data items are stored in an SDM they can overlap and interfere. Clearly, memories retrieved from a set of locations may include vectors stored to other addresses. If too many feature vectors are stored, the resulting output vectors can be incorrect. While not intuitively obvious, the characteristics of the vector space allow remarkably dense storage before the memory capacity is exceeded, a topic that will be treated in more detail in subsequent sections. For now, note only that storing the same vector repeatedly will increase its contribution when a nearby vector is retrieved. The analogy to human learning is striking; repeatedly memorizing data increases the probability of correctly remembering it in the future.

Iterative Best Match

When the input feature vector is not exactly like any stored vector, the SDM can generalize; it may be used to find the best stored match through repeated retrievals. In this case, the address represented by the feature vector must be similar to that with which the best match was stored. (These concepts will be explained quantitatively in later sections.) The first memory retrieval will produce an output vector that may not be the best possible match. If, however, this output vector is used as the address for a second retrieval, it can be shown that the resulting output vector will be closer to the best match (if maximum storage limits are not exceeded). By repeating this process until no further improvement is observed, the best matching stored vector will be found. Convergence occurs within a small number of iterations (typically ten or fewer), and is fastest if the initial feature vector is close to the best match.

Retrieving Sequences

Humans often memorize sequences, yet find themselves unable to recall the same data in a different order. If you have memorized the Gettysburg Address, you would probably be unable to recite it backwards, or with the words in alphabetical order. Obviously, a word serves as a cue to the next word in the sequence; the entire word sequence is represented as a chain of associated stored data items.

It is possible to use SDM to recover a stored sequence of related vectors, given a feature vector close to any vector in the sequence. Given a feature vector representing a few notes of music, a sequence of vectors may be read that produces the remainder of the piece. The memory architecture and the read/write methods are identical; only the data written must change to represent the associations.

In the best match case, a vector to be written is used both as the address and the data to be stored, thereby storing each vector into the set of addresses close to itself. In contrast, if the memories are to be retrieved as a sequence, then the first feature vector will be used as the address for the first storage, but the data stored will be the next vector in the sequence. The second memory storage uses the second vector in the sequence as the address and the third vector as the data. This pattern is repeated up to the end of the sequence.

To read the entire sequence, the first vector is applied as the initial address. Each vector retrieved is then used as the address for the subsequent retrieval, and the remainder of the sequence is produced in order. Alternatively, any vector in the sequence can be used to start the output at an intermediate point, thereafter producing the remainder of the sequence. Note that the reading procedure is identical to that for finding the best match through iteration; the difference lies in the manner in which the data is written.

So far, the function described could be performed in a conventional computer memory by creating a linked list of records, each of which contains a pointer to (the address of) the next record in the sequence. SDM has an important additional capability; the initial vector used for retrieval need not be precisely like any in the sequence. Correct retrieval requires only that it be close to a vector in the sequence. If it is, the sequence will converge to the one stored. Like the best match case, convergence is rapid, usually occurring within fewer than ten memory reads.

MATHEMATICS OF THE VECTOR SPACE

The preceding qualitative discussion, while correct, provides only a limited insight into the principles which allow the SDM to function. The remainder of the chapter will develop the mathematical foundation that is necessary to understand the method more fully. Fortunately, a great deal of illumination can be provided by a few simple concepts, once some preliminary ideas are established. For a more complete and rigorous treatment see Kanerva's excellent book (Kanerva 1988).

Geometric Interpretation of Binary Vector Spaces

As we have seen, the vectors used in SDM have components that are either 0 or 1; these will be called binary vectors. We may visualize a binary vector as a point in space as in Figure 4-2(a). Here the vectors [0, 0], [0, 1], [1, 0], and [1, 1] are shown. Since each vector has two components, it may be drawn in two-dimensional space, each vector representing a vertex of a unit square. Figure 4-2(b) shows eight three-dimensional vectors, each defining a vertex of a unit cube. Similarly, binary vectors having any number of components may be defined. Even though illustration and visualization fail, the pattern may be extended to show that a vector having n components defines a vertex of a unit hypercube in n-dimensional space. Such a space consists of 2^n unique vectors.

Vector Difference

We have seen that the difference between two binary vectors is itself a vector, each component of which is 0 in bit positions where both vectors agree, and 1 where they differ. This constitutes a bitwise exclusive–or of the two vectors.

In more conventional mathematical terms, this operation may be viewed as component-by-component subtraction, where the special rule, $0 - 1 = 1$, is required for closure, as -1 is not included in this number system.

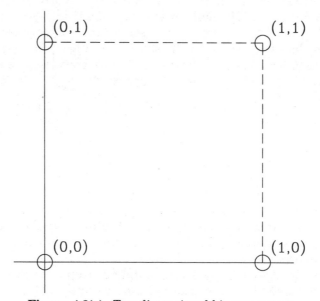

Figure 4-2(a). Two-dimensional binary vectors.

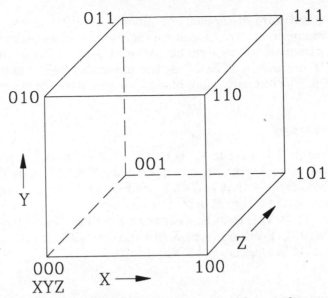

Figure 4-2(b). Vectors form a three-dimensional hypercube.

Norm of a Vector

The size or norm of vector **X**, written $\|\mathbf{X}\|$, is easily found by counting the number of 1's in the vector. Conceptually, it is the size of the difference vector with the origin vector that consists of all 0's.

Vector Distance

The distance between two vectors is computed by summing the number of 1's in the difference vector, or more directly by counting the number of bit positions in which the two vectors differ.

This method of defining distance is commonly called the Hamming distance (after Richard Hamming who developed the idea at Bell Labs). It may be interpreted geometrically as the minimum number of edges that must be traversed to go from one vertex of the unit hypercube to another.

Equivalently, distance may be defined as the norm of the vector difference, that is

$$d(\mathbf{X}, \mathbf{Y}) = \|\mathbf{X} - \mathbf{Y}\| = |x_1 - y_1| + |x_2 - y_2| + \cdots + |x_n - y_n|$$

using the so-called city block metric.

Binary Vectors Versus Binary Numbers

It is important to note that a binary vector so defined is not a binary number. A binary number with n bits defines a point on a one-dimensional line with a maximum distance from the origin of 2^{n-1}, whereas a binary vector with n components represents a point in n-dimensional space, a vertex of an n-dimensional hypercube. A solid grasp of this concept is essential to an understanding of SDM, as the algorithm relies upon the unusual properties of high-dimensionality binary vector space for its operation.

Vector Between Two Vectors

Vector **Y** is said to lie between vectors **X** and **Z** if and only if the distance from **X** to **Y** plus the distance from **Y** to **Z** equals the distance from **X** to **Z**. This implies that each bit position of **Y** agrees with the corresponding bit position of either **X** or **Z**. For example, if **Y** = [1, 1, 0, 1], **X** = [0, 1, 0, 0], and **Z** = [1, 0, 1, 1] then **Y** is between **X** and **Z**. This is true because in bit positions 1 and 4, **Y** differs from **X** but agrees with **Z**; in positions 2 and 3, **Y** differs from **Z** but agrees with **X**.

Distribution of Distances

The distribution of vectors in the binary vector space is highly nonintuitive. It may be derived by calculating the probability of finding a vector exactly d bits away from a given vector. Since this is related directly to the number of ways to complement d bits of an n-bit vector, the answer is found from the binomial distribution: $(d; n, 0.5) = \{n!/[d!(n - d)!]\}(0.5)^n$. This distribution has a mean of $n/2$ and variance $n/4$. This is well approximated by the normal distribution, with the same mean and variance (standard deviation = $n^{0.5}/2$).

From this distribution a surprising result emerges; given any vector in a high dimensional space, all other vectors are almost exactly $n/2$ bits away! For example, if $n = 1000$, only a millionth of the possible vectors are closer than 422 bits or further away than 578 bits. For larger values of n, the effect becomes still more pronounced. If two-dimensional Euclidian space were distributed this way, the situation would look like Figure 4-3, where from the standpoint of the central vector, nearly all others are clustered around the perimeter of circle with radius $n/2$. Furthermore, the same distribution of distances will be observed, regardless of the vector selected for the central vector.

If this situation existed in our familiar three-dimensional Euclidian space, measuring the distance to all of the stars from earth would show that the vast majority would occupy a thin shell. However, from the standpoint of an observer on any star in the shell, nearly all other stars would be in a shell of the same diameter!

This distribution has important consequences for SDM, where both storing and retrieving are done over a set of vector locations within a specified distance d of an input vector. If d is somewhat less than $n/2$, quite similar to the input vector will dominate the data retrieved. Thus, with this unusual

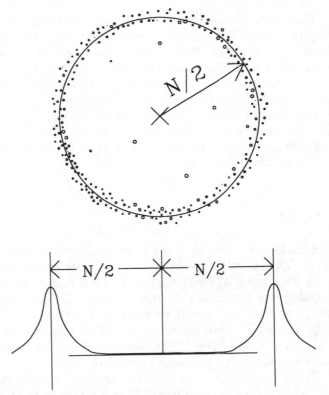

Figure 4-3. Analogous distribution in two-dimensional space.

distribution the interference between vectors using the same memory space is minimal, provided that the dimensionality of the vector space is high.

Distribution of Vectors in a Hypersphere

In SDM, both storage and retrieval operations activate the set of memory locations within a distance d of an input vector. Equivalently, these locations may be thought of as occupying a hypersphere of radius R, with the input vector at the center. At this point a word of caution is appropriate. The binary vector space has unusual properties; analogies with three-dimensional Euclidean space may produce incorrect assumptions. For example, a hypersphere in binary vector space is not convex, and the minimal length path between points is not unique!

The number of vectors in a hypersphere of radius R about a point x can be approximated by the normal distribution $(N)\{F[(R - n)/2]/(n/4)^{0.5}\}$, where

n = the number of components in a vector
$N = 2^n$, the total number of vectors in the space
F = the normal distribution.

This distribution implies that the accurate retrieval of a stored vector requires little knowledge of its components. Suppose, for example, that the desired vector has 1000 components (1000-dimension space), only 595 components of which are known with certainty, with no information about the others. Assume that ten thousand random vectors have already been written to the SDM. In this case the probability of retrieving the correct vector is better than 0.5, with the chances for success going up exponentially as the number of known components increases. This is consistent with our observations of human memory; little correct data are required to perform an accurate identification.

IMPLEMENTING THE SDM

The SDM involves many memory locations in each storage or retrieval operation. The set of locations stored to or retrieved from exists within a distance R of the input address vector. Each memory location requires an address decoder to determine if it should respond to a memory reference. A conventional address decoder does not perform the desired function. It responds to only a single address, whereas SDM requires a response to a range of addresses around the input address. This is a function performed nicely by both artificial and biological neurons.

Figure 4-4 shows an address decoder neuron with fixed weights representing its location address. The NET output of the neuron produces the weighted sum of the inputs, i.e,

$$NET = x_1 w_1 + x_2 w_2 + \cdots x_n w_n$$

The NET signal is compared to the threshold T, thereby producing the signal OUT according to the function

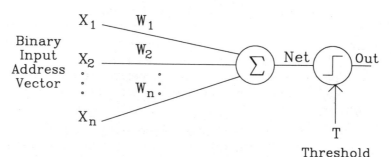

Figure 4-4. Decoder neuron.

$$\text{OUT} = 1 \quad \text{if NET} \geq T$$

$$\text{OUT} = 0 \quad \text{if NET} < T$$

Thus, OUT is 1 when the input address is within the desired range of the location address and 0 for all other input addresses. A threshold, T, determines the range of input addresses over which OUT is 1.

Weights are chosen to produce a maximal response to one location address. These are bipolar, having values of $+1$ or -1. Each weight, w_i, is given the value $+1$ if there is a 1 in the corresponding position x_i of the location address vector, or -1 if x_i is 0. Let $S = $ the number of weights with the value $+1$.

If the threshold, T, is chosen to be equal to the neuron's response to the location address vector, i.e., if $T = S$ the decoder responds to only a single address. As T is reduced, the neuron responds to all addresses within a Hamming distance of $S - T$ of the location address (bits differing in $2 - T$ or fewer locations). This distance is called the neuron's *response region*.

As an example, suppose that the location address is [1, 0, 0, 1]. The weights would be set to [1, -1, -1, 1], producing a NET output of 2 if an input address of [1, 0, 0, 1] is applied. If the threshold T is set to 2, no other address will produce a 1 on OUT. The NET output for each input vector is shown in Table 4-1.

Note that NET has a maximum value, S, equal to the sum of the positive weights and a minimum value, s, equal to the sum of the

TABLE 4-1 NEURON ADDRESS DECODER
RESPONSE, WEIGHTS = [1, -1 -1, 1]

Address Vectors	NET	Threshold		
		T = 2 OUT	T = 1 OUT	T = 0 OUT
0 0 0 0	0	0	0	1
0 0 0 1	1	0	1	1
0 0 1 0	-1	0	0	0
0 0 1 1	0	0	0	1
0 1 0 0	-1	0	0	0
0 1 0 1	0	0	0	1
0 1 1 0	-2	0	0	0
0 1 1 1	-1	0	0	0
1 0 0 0	1	0	1	1
1 0 0 1	2	1	1	1
1 0 1 0	0	0	0	1
1 0 1 1	1	0	1	1
1 1 0 0	0	0	0	1
1 1 0 1	1	0	1	1
1 1 1 0	-1	0	0	0
1 1 1 1	0	0	0	1

negative weights. If the threshold T is greater than S then OUT is always zero. If T is less than s, OUT is always one. Letting $T = S - D$, where D is the distance (number of differing bits) between the target address and another address, the decoder responds with a NET output of 1 to any input vector within a Hamming distance D of the location address. By correct selection of T, i.e., $T = S - R$, the neuron can be adjusted to respond to only those vectors within the desired response region.

Note that the number of vectors included in the response region is a highly nonlinear function of D. As previously discussed, if the dimensionality, n, of the space is large, nearly all of the vectors lie at approximately the distance $n/2$ from a given vector. Hence, increasing D from zero at first causes the response region to grow slowly. As D approaches $n/2$ the response region grows rapidly, quickly including nearly all of the address space.

CONVERGENCE AND MEMORY CAPACITY

The iterated reading method of SDM uses the data fetched from a memory location as the address of the next read. This process will only converge to the correct data if the initial address is sufficiently close to where the desired data was written, that is within its convergence range, and if the number of stored vectors has not exceeded the capacity of the system. Convergence range and memory capacity are closely related issues, and will be considered together in the following paragraphs. Formulas to calculate each will be presented with a discussion adequate to permit their use. For a detailed derivation of the formulas see Kanerva's book (Kanerva 1988).

An SDM, like any memory, has a limit on the number of vectors that may be written and accurately recovered. In an ordinary computer memory with N locations, exactly N items may be written and read with perfect accuracy. With SDM that limit can only be expressed statistically, as the effect of interfering stored vectors depends upon where they are written.

If a desired data vector, called the *target*, has been written to an SDM, a sequence of memory reads converges to it only if the initial address is sufficiently close to the target. The distance where convergence is as likely as

TABLE 4-2 MEMORY CAPACITY FOR EACH 1000
PHYSICAL LOCATIONS

n = Number of Vector Components	C = Memory Capacity
100	165
200	137
500	113
1000	97
2000	88
5000	75

divergence is called the *critical distance.* If the initial distance D is substantially less than the critical distance, convergence is rapid. As D approaches the critical distance, convergence time approaches infinity. Capacity is defined as the number of stored vectors that make the critical distance equal to zero, and may be estimated as follows

$$C = N/\{F^{-1}[1/(2^{1/n})]\}^2$$

where

C = memory capacity
N = number of physical memory locations
n = number of components in the stored vector
$F^{-1}[.]$ = the inverse of the cumulative probability function of the standard normal deviate (best obtained from a table)

Table 4-2 shows the memory capacity per thousand physical memory locations as a function of the number of components in the vector. Since there is a linear relationship between physical memory locations and memory capacity, the table can be used to estimate capacity for larger and smaller physical memories.

From this table it may be seen that the capacity for 1000 component vectors is roughly 10% of the number of physical memory locations. Note that this is a statistical estimate assuming a random uniform distribution of vectors and the storing of each vector once. "Clumping," a common phenomena in data sets, can reduce this capacity substantially. Also, since a memory at this capacity limit will fail to converge 50% of the time, operation at this point is usually infeasible.

Since each physical memory location requires n counters, the required capacity of these counters will have a major impact on the hardware requirements. It has been shown (Kanerva 1988) that with random data the mean count in any counter is 0 (because 1's and 0's are equally likely) and the standard deviation is $(pC)^{1/2}$, where p is the fraction of the physical memory locations accessed in a single write, and C is the memory capacity. For $N = 1,000,000$, $n = 1000$, $p = 0.001$, and the memory filled to capacity C of roughly 100,000, the standard deviation of the counter contents is 10. Therefore, counters with a capacity of $-40-+40$ will have a small probability of overflow. If the memory is not filled to capacity (the usual case) still smaller counters will suffice.

RELATED RESEARCH

The potential offered by SDM has prompted a number of researchers to explore its characteristics and applications. The following references are by no means exhaustive; they are intended to indicate the high degree of interest in this method and the breadth of its application.

Keeler (1986) compares SDM to Hopfield networks, showing the capacity of the SDM to be independent of the dimension of the stored vectors, unlike Hopfield nets where it is a fraction of that dimension. However, he also shows that the total number of stored bits per matrix element is the same.

A hardware implementation of SDM is discussed in Keeler and Denning (1986) involving a resistive network for rapid address decoding and a systolic array for high-throughput read and write operations.

Rogers (1989) explores the use of SDM in the overcapacity region where associative memory behavior breaks down. He shows that, in this case, the SDM can be used for statistical prediction. He suggests a variant of SDM which weights the locations differently depending upon their contents, thereby doubling the capacity of an SDM when used as an associative memory. He also suggests improvements based on Holland's genetic algorithms (see Chapter 5). Continuing in this direction he (Rogers 1990) describes a hybrid system called genetic memory that combines SDM and genetic algorithms. He demonstrates a system that interprets weather data to predict rain and that reconfigures the location addresses using a genetic algorithm.

Anderson (1990) shows that SDM approximates a multidimensional conditional probability integral. He shows that valid responses can be expected only when the training set is adequate to provide good estimates of the underlying joint probability density functions. He draws a parallel between an inadequate data set and an undersampled system which produces distortion due to aliasing.

DISCUSSION

SDM is an interesting algorithm with many possibilities. Some may object to the hardware implications. Indeed, a memory with 1,000,000 locations, each of which has 1000 digital counters, is beyond the current limits of economical implementation. With VLSI complexity doubling approximately every three to four years, the hardware may not pose a serious problem in the not too distant future.

The rather modest memory capacity per hardware element of SDM appears to limit its application. This issue has been explored in Chou (1988) where he demonstrates that the capacity of the SDM is exponential. One may hope that further explorations and extensions of the theory will increase the memory capacity limit, and preliminary experiments indicate that this is, indeed the case.

Kanerva has made a major contribution by exploring the nonintuitive properties of high dimensional space. Because such spaces are outside our physical experience, it is difficult to create conceptual systems that depend upon their properties. Kanerva's mathematical–statistical approach makes the characteristics understandable, if not intuitively compelling.

The human brain operates in a space of tremendous dimensionality. Perhaps our difficulty in understanding the brain's principles of operation is traceable to our limited intuition regarding the properties of such spaces. In Kanerva (1988), striking parallels are drawn between the gross anatomy of the cerebellar cortex and the architecture of an SDM, with the implication that the human cerebellum could be a memory with 10^{11} locations, each with several hundred counters for storing data. The SDM may provide a conceptual framework that will lead to an improved understanding of the brain, or perhaps show a method for studying this perplexing organ.

REFERENCES

Albus, J., P. Kanerva, E. Loebner. 1989. Cerebellar Models of Associative Memory. In *Three Papers from IEEE Compcon Spring '89*, ed. Michael R. Raugh. RIACS Technical Report 89.11. Research Institute for Advanced Computer Science, NASA Ames Research Center.

Anderson, C. H. 1989. A Conditional Probability Interpretation of Kanerva's Sparse Distributed Memory. *Proceedings of the International Joint Conference on Neural Networks*, vol. 1, pp. 415–417. New Jersey: IEEE Service Center.

Chiueh, T, and R. M. Goodman. 1991. The Kanerva Memory is Stable. *Proceedings of the International Joint Conference on Neural Networks*, vol. 2, pp. 267–271. New Jersey: IEEE Service Center.

Chou, P. A. 1988. The Capacity of the Kanerva Associative Memory is Exponential. In *Neural Information Processing Systems*, ed. D. Z. Anderson, pp. 184–191. New York: American Institute of Physics.

Kanerva, P. 1986a. Parallel Structure in Human and Computer Memory. In *Neural Networks for Computing*, ed. J. S. Denker, pp. 247–258. New York: American Institute of Physics.

Kanerva, P. 1986b. Parallel Structures in Human and Computer Memory. RIACS Technical Report TR-86.2. Research Institute for Advanced Computer Science, NASA Ames Research Center.

Kanerva, P. 1988. *Sparse Distributed Memory*. Cambridge: MIT Press.

Keeler, J. D. 1986. Comparison Between Sparsely Distributed Memory and Hopfield-Type Neural Network Models. RIACS Technical Report 86.31. Research Institute for Advanced Computer Science, NASA Ames Research Center.

Keeler, J. D. and P. J. Denning. 1986. Notes on Implementation of Sparsely Distributed Memory. RIACS Technical Report 86.15. Research Institute for Advanced Computer Science, NASA Ames Research Center.

Rogers, D. 1989. Statistical Prediction with Kanerva's Sparse Distributed Memory. In *Advances in Neural Information Processing Systems 1*, ed. D. Touretzky. San Mateo, CA: Morgan Kaufmann.

Rogers, D. 1990. Predicting Weather Using a Genetic Memory: A Combination of Kanerva's Sparse Distributed Memory with Holland's Genetic Algorithms. In *Advances in Neural Information Processing Systems 2*, vol. 1, pp. 455–464, ed. D. Touretzky. San Mateo CA: Morgan Kaufmann.

Surkan, A. J. 1989. Fast Trainable Pattern Classification By a Modification of Kanerva's SDM Model. In *Advances in Neural Information Processing Systems 2*, pp. 347–349, ed. D. Touretzky. San Mateo CA: Morgan Kaufmann.

5

Genetic Algorithms

WHY GENETIC ALGORITHMS?

Nature has demonstrated the power of genetics. Through this ubiquitous mechanism an array of intelligent, self-organizing, self-repairing, self-motivating organisms have been produced. Those attempting to duplicate the performance of these biological systems, even in part, can ill afford to ignore how they developed; evolution may be the only way that such performance can be achieved.

Genetic algorithms are a means by which machines can emulate the mechanisms of natural selection. This involves searching high-dimensional spaces for superior, if not optimal, solutions. The algorithms are simple, robust, and general; no knowledge of the search space is assumed. They are computationally intensive, therefore, some may feel that they are impractical. In the long run, this is probably not a valid objection. These algorithms, like neural networks, are parallel in nature; their execution rate increases almost linearly with the number of processors. As techniques become proven and standardized, it will become practical to develop VLSI hardware that can exploit this inherent parallelism.

There is a growing recognition that genetic algorithms have a close relationship with artificial neural networks. This has resulted in significant efforts to unite these techniques in a system where each complements the other (Belew and Gherrity 1989; Harp, Caudell, and Dolen 1989; Davis 1989; Miller, Todd, and Hegde 1989; Oosthuizen 1989; Whitley and Hanson 1989).

In addition to the fact that both methods are applied to similar problems, there appear to be common principles underlying their operation. As these commonalities are explored by continuing research, applications may be expected in which the techniques are seamlessly integrated into systems.

FUNDAMENTALS OF GENETIC ALGORITHMS

Conventional optimization techniques are based upon adjusting the parameters of a model to produce a desired result. For example, training an artificial neural network involves modifying its weights so that it produces the desired relationship between inputs and outputs. Thus, one solution is maintained and iteratively optimized.

Genetic algorithms have been developed which perform optimization with techniques modeled on biological genetics and natural selection (Holland 1975, Goldberg 1989). These operate by maintaining and modifying the characteristics of a *population* of solutions (individuals) over a large number of generations. This process is designed to produce successive populations having an increasing number of individuals with desirable characteristics. Like nature's solution, the process is probabilistic but not completely random. As we shall see, the rules of genetics retain desirable characteristics by maximizing the probability of proliferation of those solutions (individuals) who exhibit them.

Optimization Versus Improvement

Like calculus-based methods of optimization that find the maximum value of a function, genetics seeks continuous improvement of a population. The results may, however, be quite different. Rather than producing optimal populations, individuals produced through genetics need only be superior to other individuals in the population for them to survive, procreate, and pass their genes to the next generation. This is consistent with the criteria for success in most human endeavors. For example, it is not necessary that an army be optimal; to win the war it must only be better than the enemy. Thus, genetic optimization can become "stuck" in a nonoptimal solution, awaiting a chance mutation.

A bit of black humor will illustrate this point. As the story goes, Sam and Ed are on a camping trip when they see a charging bear. Sam immediately starts to lace up his running shoes.

Ed says, "Sam, don't bother; you'll never outrun that bear."

Sam replies, "I don't have to outrun the bear. I only have to outrun you."

Coding

Genetic algorithms operate on a coding of the parameters, rather than the parameters themselves. Just as the strands of DNA encode all of the characteristics of a human in chains of amino acids, so the parameters of the problem must be encoded in finite length strings. While a string might be a sequence of any symbols, the binary symbols "0" and "1" are often used. The nature of the encoding is critical. As in artificial neural networks, the technique of knowledge representation can make or break an application. As we shall see, selection of the coding method is not straightforward.

Genetic Optimization

Optimization is performed on a set of strings, where each string is composed of a sequence of characters. Given an initial population of strings, a genetic algorithm produces a new population of strings according to a set of genetic rules. This constitutes one generation. The rules are devised so that the new generation tends to have strings that are superior to those in the previous generation, measured by some objective function. Successive generations of strings are produced, each of which tends to produce a superior population.

Optimizing a population rather than a single individual contributes to the robustness of these algorithms. Even if the genetic process inadvertently acts to lose a desirable characteristic in one string, it may be safely retained in other members of the population, thereby allowing it to appear more frequently in later generations.

Note that genetic algorithms operate without any knowledge of the search space. Unlike the gradient search techniques commonly used in artificial neural networks, no derivatives are calculated. Superior strings are selected solely by their objective function, hence, the procedure is completely general: Any problem for which an objective function can be defined is a candidate for genetic optimization.

Genetic search algorithms use probabilistic rules to produce a new generation. This does not mean that they perform a completely random search; the rules are devised to lead quickly to areas of the search space where improvement is likely. Simulated annealing (Metropolis *et al.* 1953) uses this concept of "guided randomness" to produce optimal solutions, although the mechanisms are quite different.

A Simple Example of Genetic Optimization

A numerical example of a simple genetic algorithm will be used to illustrate how this method performs optimization. The chosen problem is to minimize the value of a string of 1's and 0's treated as a binary number. While this is a trivial problem, it will serve to illustrate the operation of the algorithm without the obscuring effects of a complicated objective function.

The genetic algorithm performs minimization in the following steps:

1. Initialization
2. Reproduction
3. Crossover

4. Mutation

5. Repeat steps 2–4

Each step will be explained as it is performed.

Initialization

First, an initial population of strings must be produced. One simple way is to make each string a random binary number—a sequence of 1's and 0's. Each position in the string is given as its weight an appropriate power of two. For example, a string and its weights might be the following

128 64 32 16 8 4 2 1 Weights

1 0 1 0 1 1 0 1 String

The string may be converted to its decimal equivalent by adding the weights over the 1's. In this case that sum would be

$$128 + 32 + 8 + 4 + 1 = 173$$

In guiding the course of genetic evolution, there is always an objective function to be maximized. In a human it might be the weighted sum of a large set of characteristics, such as strength, speed, intelligence, etc. In this example, the function chosen will be the reciprocal of the decimal equivalent of these binary numbers. The six strings in Table 5-1 were chosen at random.

Reproduction

In this step the current population is used to produce a second generation of strings that, on the average, have a higher objective function. This is done by conducting a series of random trials in which each string is copied to the

TABLE 5-1 INITIAL STRING POPULATION

j String Number	Binary String	Decimal Value	O_j Objective Function	F_j Fraction of Total
1	011010	26	0.0385	0.142
2	001011	11	0.0909	0.334
3	110110	54	0.0185	0.068
4	010011	19	0.0526	0.194
5	100111	39	0.0256	0.094
6	010110	22	0.0455	0.168
Total			0.2716	1.00

next generation a number of times that is proportional to the value of its objective function relative to that of the other strings.

In Table 5-1 the objective function has been calculated for each binary string. In the last column, the fractional objective function of each string is shown. It was calculated as the ratio of each objective function to the sum of all objective functions. This may be expressed as

$$F_j = O_j \bigg/ \sum_i O_i$$

where

F_j = the fractional objective function for string j
O_i = the objective function for string i

In the reproduction phase, each string is copied to the second generation a number of times that is proportional to its fractional objective function, F_j. To visualize how this is done, imagine the "wheel of fortune" shown in Figure 5-1. Here, each string is assigned a segment size that is proportional to its fractional objective function. For each spin of the wheel (a trial) a string is copied to the breeding population if the wheel stops with the pointer in its segment.

Thus, on the average, string #1 will be copied 0.142 times for each trial. In order to maintain a breeding population that is approximately the same from generation to generation, there will be six trials (spins) to determine the second generation. In six trials string #1 will be reproduced 6×0.142

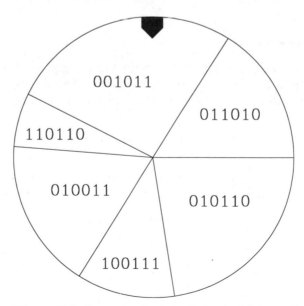

Figure 5-1. Reproduction of a "wheel of fortune."

or 0.710 times on average. Rounding this to the nearest integer, it is included one time in the second generation.

Using these probabilities, the same computation and rounding method, and the number of copies, the following breeding population was produced for the second generation

$$011010$$
$$001011$$
$$001011$$
$$010011$$
$$100111$$
$$010110$$

Note that string #2 had the highest objective function, it has two copies in the second generation. String #3 with the lowest objective function has no copies; it has evolved to extinction. On the average, strings with a high objective function will have more copies in the subsequent generation, however, it is possible (though improbable) to get many copies of a string with a low objective function.

Crossover

This process is intended to simulate the exchange of genetic material that occurs during biological reproduction. Here, pairs in the breeding population are mated randomly. For simplicity we will mate adjacent pairs. For each pair, a random integer from 1–6 is chosen. This indicates how many bits on the right end of each string should be exchanged between the two mated strings.

For example, consider mated strings #1 and #2. Suppose the random integer 2 was selected indicating that the last two bits on their right end should be exchanged. Crossover produces the following two strings

$$\left\{ \begin{array}{c} 011010 \\ 001011 \end{array} \right\} \xrightarrow{\text{crossover}} \left\{ \begin{array}{c} 011011 \\ 001010 \end{array} \right\}$$

This process is continued over the remaining two pairs, assuming random bit exchange integers of 4 and 3 were chosen. The results are shown in Table 5-2.

Mutation

A surprisingly small role is played by mutation. Biologically, it randomly perturbs the population's characteristics, thereby preventing evolutionary

TABLE 5-2 STRING POPULATION AFTER ONE GENERATION

String Number	Binary String	Decimal Value	Objective Function	Fraction of Total
1	011011	27	0.037	0.064
2	001010	10	0.10	0.174
3	000011	3	0.333	0.578
4	011011	27	0.037	0.064
5	100110	38	0.0263	0.046
6	010111	23	0.043	0.075
Total			0.576	1.00

dead ends. Most mutations are damaging rather than beneficial; therefore, rates must be low to avoid the destruction of species. In the simulation we will assume a mutation rate of one bit per thousand, where a mutation acts to reverse the value of a single bit. Since we have only 36 bits in our population, the probability of a mutation is only 0.036; therefore, no bits are reversed in the simulation.

As a result of performing these five steps, the population shown in Table 5-2 is produced.

Note that the total objective function has more than doubled, largely because of the evolution of string #3, that is likely to have many offspring. The reproduction phase has now produced the following breeding population

001010

000011

000011

000011

000011

010111

After crossover with random numbers of 3, 5, and 1 (again without mutation), the population in Table 5-3 is produced.

Again the total objective function has more than doubled, and a superior string #2 has been produced. Note that it is coincidental that the number of strings in the population has not changed in this simulation. In general, a breeding population may shrink or grow over successive generations.

These processes of reproduction, crossover, and mutation are repeated until the objective function has reached an acceptable value. Note that the rapid convergence is typical of this method; only a few generations are required to achieve substantial improvements.

TABLE 5-3 STRING POPULATION AFTER TWO
GENERATIONS

String Number	Binary String	Decimal Value	Objective Function	Fraction of Total
1	001011	11	0.091	0.0557
2	000010	2	0.5	0.306
3	000011	3	0.333	0.204
4	000011	3	0.333	0.204
5	000011	3	0.333	0.204
6	010111	23	0.043	0.026
Total			1.633	1.000

Evaluating the Example

It may happen that rapid improvement will cease, even though the objective function is not as high as possible. In the simulation above this would result if all strings assumed the value 000011. This nonoptimal result could only be improved by waiting for a favorable mutation. Since mutations are infrequent and usually damaging, improvement could require a great many generations. A substantial research effort has focused on overcoming this problem of stabilizing at a poor solution for long periods. Still, it is typical of the way that nature works under similar circumstances. Species may become trapped in highly nonoptimal adaptations for millennia, provided that no better adapted organisms arise to usurp their ecological niches.

To review, the example has shown how the genetic algorithm performs optimization. First, reproduction makes it likely that better strings will have more offspring in the next generation. Next, crossover exchanges substrings from the better strings. The rationale for crossover is more subtle, but it makes sense that combining portions of good strings will tend to produce still better strings. Finally, mutation is the method of last resort. Its effects must be small if they are not to destroy a population, as they are usually harmful. Therefore, improvements often require many generations to appear from this process.

The example is suggestive but hardly conclusive evidence for the general effectiveness of the genetic algorithm. For example, it has not been shown that the optimization process is reliable and robust. In particular, the effects of crossover are obscure. Putting these techniques on a sounder mathematical foundation will be the objective of the next section.

THEORETICAL FOUNDATIONS

Terminology

As with any technology, a set of specialized terminology has been developed to describe the unique concepts. Since these terms are widely used by genetic algorithm researchers, learning a few definitions will ease access to the large and rapidly growing literature on this subject.

The concept of a *schema* (the plural is *schemata*) is central to genetic algorithm theory. This idea will be fully developed, in a later section. For now, consider a schema to be a special kind of string.

We have seen that strings can be produced from sequences of "0" and "1" symbols. Such strings are said to be produced from the alphabet $A = \{0, 1\}$. Each symbol in a string is identified by its *bit position*, where bit position 1 is furthest to the left.

A schema is a string that is constructed from the augmented alphabet A' = $\{0, 1, *\}$, where $*$ indicates a don't care or wild card position. A string which matches a schema in all of its *definite* bit positions (those holding a 0 or a 1) is said to *represent* the schema. Note that schema bit positions holding $*$ are ignored for this comparison. Suppose the schema of length 8 is defined

$$S = * \ 1 \ * \ 0 \ * \ * \ 0 \ 0$$

The following strings A, B, and C all represent this schema

$$A = 1 \ 1 \ 0 \ 0 \ 1 \ 0 \ 0 \ 0$$
$$B = 0 \ 1 \ 1 \ 0 \ 0 \ 0 \ 0 \ 0$$
$$C = 1 \ 1 \ 1 \ 0 \ 1 \ 1 \ 0 \ 0$$

The *order* of a schema S, symbolized $o(S)$, is the number of definite bit positions. By this definition the schema S from the example above is of order 4.

The *defining length* of a schema S, $\delta(S)$, is the distance between the leftmost and rightmost bit positions holding either a 0 or a 1. These are called *specific positions*. For example, schema S above has a defining length of 6. Similarly, a schema such as $* \ * \ 1 \ 0 \ * \ * \ * \ *$ has a defining length of 1. Defining length is calculated by subtracting the bit position b_r of the rightmost 1 or 0 from the bit position of the leftmost, b_l.

Schemata

Much of the power of genetic algorithms comes from a property called *implicit parallelism*. This exists because the algorithm's operations on a population of strings implicitly processes a much larger number of schemata in parallel. Suppose that the strings are of length l. With the binary alphabet, each string represents 2^l schemata. For example, the string 1101 is of length 4 and therefore represents the following 2^4 (16) schemata:

```
1  1  0  0
1  1  0  *
1  1  *  0
1  1  *  *
1  *  0  0
1  *  0  *
1  *  *  0
1  *  *  *
*  1  0  0
*  1  0  *
*  1  *  0
*  1  *  *
*  *  0  0
*  *  0  *
*  *  *  0
*  *  *  *
```

If there is a population of n strings, the total number of unique schemata represented, N_s is

$$2^l \le N_s \le n2^l \tag{5-1}$$

The actual value of N_s depends upon the diversity of the strings. For example, in a population of ten strings that are all identical, all will represent the same schemata. In this case, the total number of schemata represented by the population would be 2^l, the same as a single string. Other populations having a greater diversity of strings will represent a larger number of schemata, up to the limiting value of $n2^l$.

Since each string can represent many schemata, the effect of each of the operations performed when processing a generation of strings is multiplied manyfold in the schemata population. This explains, in large part, the rapid convergence of the genetic algorithms; this property is called *implicit parallelism*. For this reason much of the theory surrounding genetic algorithms centers on schemata; their characteristics will be the focus of the following sections.

Given a population and using the schema concept we will calculate how many representatives of a given schema will appear in the next breeding population. This number depends upon the operations of reproduction, cross-over, and mutation. The effects of each will be treated separately, then combined to produce a single equation.

Reproduction

Suppose that schema S has $n(S, t)$ representative strings in a population at time t. We have seen that the probability $p(S_i)$ of a representative of S being copied into the next generation, depends upon the ratio of its objective function $f(S_i)$ to the total of all objective functions taken over all strings in the population. Call this total F. Thus,

$$p(S_i) = f(S_i)/F \qquad (5\text{-}2)$$

Extending this idea, it is easy to prove the following

$$n(S, t + 1) = n(S, t)nf(S)/(F)$$

where:

$\quad f(S) =$ the average of the objective functions of schemata S
$\quad\quad n =$ the number of nonoverlapping representative strings
$\quad\quad F =$ the total of all objective functions taken across all strings in
$\quad\quad\quad\quad$ the population

letting $f(P) = F/n$ (the average of the objective functions over all strings in the population).

$$n(S, t + 1) = n(S, t)f(S)/f(P) \qquad (5\text{-}3)$$

This shows that the number of representatives of a schema grows from generation to generation at a rate that depends upon the ratio of their average objective function to the average objective function of the population. Schemas with large objective functions get increasing numbers of representatives, while representation of schemas with small objective functions decreases.

If the representatives of a schema have objective functions that are consistently above the average by a fraction k, then Equation (5-3) may be rewritten as follows, letting $f(S) = f(P) + kf(P)$

$$n(S, t + 1) = n(S, t)[f(P) + kf(P)]/f(P) = n(S, t)(1 + k) \qquad (5\text{-}4)$$

After n additional generations (ignoring all other effects) the number of representatives of S is,

$$n(S, t + n) = n(S, t)(1 + k)^{n+1} \qquad (5\text{-}5)$$

This equation shows a critical fact: The number of representatives of schemata with above average objective functions grows in the population exponentially, while those below average decrease exponentially.

In an important sense, it is the schema itself that grows or shrinks. For this reason it is sometimes convenient to speak of the schema as the entity that undergoes change from generation to generation, this is often found in the literature. While doing so, we must remember that it is the number of strings representing a schema that actually changes in the population.

Crossover

Despite the effectiveness of reproduction in increasing the percentage of superior representatives, the procedure is essentially sterile; it cannot create new and better strings. This function is left to crossover, and, to a lesser but critical extent, to mutation. Crossover operates to define new strings, doing so in a way that interferes little with the process of reproduction.

Assume the population shown in Table 5-4 consists of string A that is a representative of schemata S_1 and S_2, and B which represents neither.

Crossover involves mating random pairs, cutting their strings at a randomly determined position, and interchanging all bits to the right of the cut. Doing so with strings A and B produces the new strings A' and B', where,

$$A' = 0 \ 1 \ 0 \ 0 \ | \ 1 \ 0 \ 0 \ 0$$
$$B' = 1 \ 0 \ 1 \ 0 \ | \ 0 \ 1 \ 0 \ 1$$

Clearly, A' is no longer a representative of either S_1 or S_2, whereas B' has been changed so that it now represents S_2 (but still not S_1). This shows how crossover can reduce the number of representatives of a schema. S_1 started out with a representative and lost it while S_2 still has one representative. What is the difference? The critical factor is the long defining length of S_1. There are five out of seven possible positions where a cut will separate the definite characters of S_1 (those that are not wild cards). Unless A is mated to a string with the same characters in these positions (an unlikely occurrence on long strings), a representative of S_1 will be lost. This loss will occur for 5/7 of the cuts.

For S_2, the situation is more favorable. There is only one position out of

TABLE 5-4 STRINGS AND SCHEMATA

$$
\begin{array}{llllllllll}
S_1 = & * & * & 0 & * & | & * & * & * & 1 \\
S_2 = & * & * & * & * & | & 0 & 1 & * & * \\
A = & 0 & 1 & 0 & 0 & | & 0 & 1 & 0 & 1 \\
B = & 1 & 0 & 1 & 0 & | & 1 & 0 & 0 & 0 \\
\end{array}
$$

seven where a cut will reduce its representation; this is between the two definite characters 0 and 1.

From this it can be seen that the probability P_l of schema S, losing a representative from a randomly chosen cut position, may be expressed as,

$$P_l = \delta(S)/(l - 1) \qquad (5\text{-}6)$$

where:

δ = is the defining length of schema S.
l = is the length of schema S

If we define P_r to be the probability of schema S retaining a representative, then,

$$P_r = 1 - P_l$$

$$= 1 - \delta(S)/(l - 1) \qquad (5\text{-}7)$$

This may be generalized to include the case where a crossover does not occur on every mating. Defining the probability of a crossover on a given mating as P_c,

$$P_r = 1 - P_c\delta(S)/(l - 1) \qquad (5\text{-}8)$$

Combining Equation (5-3) with Equation (5-8) produces the following expression for the number of representatives of schema S in the next generation

$$n(S, t + 1) \geq [n(S, t) f(S)/f(P)][1 - P_c\delta(S)/(l - 1)] \qquad (5\text{-}9)$$

From this it may be seen that the growth of a schema depends upon the value of the objective functions of its representatives, as well as its defining length. Schema with high objective functions and short defining length proliferate at the expense of others less favored.

Mutation

Each bit in a string has a chance of mutating to its opposite binary value. By definition mutation is independent of whether or not mutation occurs at any of the other bit positions in the string. Let P_m be the probability of mutation in any bit position, hence, the probability that a bit does not change is $(1 - P_m)$. If a string currently represents a schema that has $o(S)$ bits that are either 0 or 1, then the probability that all corresponding $o(S)$ bits in the string do not mutate is $(1 - P_m)^{o(S)}$. In other words, the probability that a string remains a representation of a schema after mutation is

$$(1 - P_m)^{o(S)} \tag{5-10}$$

Since P_m is usually small, Equation (5-10) may be approximated by,

$$1 - o(S)P_m \tag{5-11}$$

Schema Theorem

We now have the means to calculate the combined effects of reproduction, crossover, and mutation. Combining Equations (5-9) and (5-10) we obtain the following

$$n(S, t + 1) \geq [n(S, t)f(S)/f(P)]\{1 - P_c[\delta(S)/(l - 1)] - o(S)P_m\} \tag{5-12}$$

where

$$n(S, t) = \text{number of representatives of schema } S \text{ at time } t$$
$$f(S) = \text{the average objective function for schema } S$$
$$f(P) = \text{the average objective function over the population}$$
$$P_c = \text{the probability of a cross-over occurring on a mating}$$
$$\delta(S) = \text{the defining length of schema } S$$
$$l = \text{the string length}$$
$$o(S) = \text{order of } S \text{ (number of 1 or 0 positions)}$$
$$P_m = \text{probability of a mutation at a given bit position}$$

Due to its central position in the theory, this equation is often called the Fundamental Theorem of Genetic Algorithms. It shows that schemata grow exponentially if they have high objective functions, short defining length, and low order. These properties will weigh heavily in our choice of coding schemes.

CODING

Binary Coding

Up to this point we have dealt with a simple coding scheme using a binary alphabet representing binary numbers. How do we know that this is optimal, or even effective? In fact, there is no way to know, other than through simulation. This undesirable characteristic is tempered by the empirical observation that genetic algorithms are robust; they tend to produce good results despite deficiencies in the coding. Nevertheless, it makes good sense to give careful attention to the coding method, as it can have a significant effect on the accuracy and efficiency of the algorithm.

To this end we should look at the characteristics of a code that will lead to good results. For example, we have seen that short defining length, low-order schemata receive favorable treatment by the crossover operation. It makes sense, therefore, to design our coding method so that related symbols are clustered into compact groups. A simple, useful test involves checking the significance of bits in the coding scheme to see that those that are closely related are assigned to nearby positions.

Goldberg (1989) proposes two principles for effective coding, presented here with slightly modified terminology:

1. **The principle of minimal alphabets.**
   "The user should select the smallest alphabet that permits a natural expression of the problem."
2. **The principle of meaningful building blocks.**
   "The user should select a coding so that short defining length, low-order schemata are relevant to the underlying problem and relatively unrelated to schemata over other fixed positions."

Principle #1 is justified because the efficiency provided by implicit parallelism increases with string length. Small alphabets produce long strings. For example, 1011011 in binary is equivalent to 91 in decimal. Goldberg (1989) shows that the binary alphabet yields the maximum number of schemata for a string of a given length, making the binary alphabet the optimal choice in this regard.

Furthermore, the binary alphabet is completely general; anything that can be coded can be represented in binary form. Consider, for example, the case where there are several variables in a problem, as in solving the two equations

$$3x + 4y = 11$$
$$2x + 5y = 12$$

The initial population could be coded as a set of binary strings, each composed of a substring representing a value for x, concatenated with a similar substring for y. In this way a problem with an arbitrary number of variables may be coded. These variables might also represent samples of a process to be optimized, a time series to be processed, or the weights of an artificial neural network to be trained.

Tree Coding

Binary coding is not a requirement; other methods have been used with good effect. Wayner (1990) describes a coding which finds a general solution for two simultaneous equations,

$$ax + by = c$$
$$dx + ey = f$$

An algebraic solution yields

$$x = (ec - bf)/(ae - bd).$$

Assuming, for simplicity, that $ae - bd = 1$, then $ec - bf$ is the desired answer.

Wayner (1990) codes the problem as a set of trees as shown in Figure 5-2, where the leaves represent the parameters and operations are shown as branches. An expression is evaluated from the bottom up. For operations requiring two operands, such as $+ - *$ and $/$, two leaves are selected and combined by the indicated operation, forming a new leaf to replace the old ones and their operators. Unary operations, such as reversing the sign of a number, are similar, except only a single operand is processed. This process is repeated, moving upward through the tree until a result is produced at the top. The objective function may then be evaluated as the square of the difference between the actual and desired result, thereby providing the basis for the reproduction step. Note that entire trees must be reproduced for this coding scheme.

After mating, crossover is accomplished by "pruning" the tree of each mate at a random node, and exchanging subtrees composed of all of the nodes below the pruning point. Wayner reports that he found mutation less effective than simply starting over if the algorithm became trapped with a uniform population of inferior solutions.

Coding for Genetic Control Systems

Genetic algorithms have been used to devise control rules for a variety of dynamic systems. For example, a genetic system successfully solved the

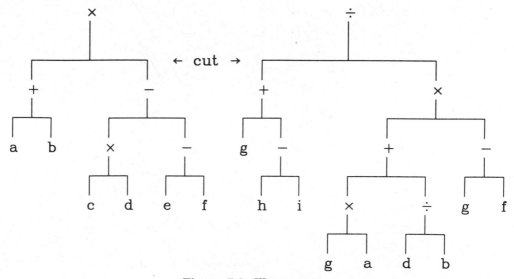

Figure 5-2. Wayner trees.

problem of balancing a vertical pole on a moving cart (Odetayo and McGregor 1989) (Figure 5-3). The system combined a set of 54 rules into a "chromosome." Each rule caused the cart to go either to the right or left depending upon measurements of cart position, cart velocity, pole angle, and time derivative of pole angle. The chromosomes were rated for effectiveness in balancing the pole. Then reproduction, crossover, and mutation were performed. The process was repeated until a satisfactory solution was found. The simulated system performed well relative to other solutions for this problem, including one using artificial neural networks (Barto, Sutton, and Anderson 1983).

A system with quite a different objective but similar means was devised to produce rules that maximized the ability of an airplane to avoid a missile in a simplified environment (Grefenstette 1989). In this application the system started with a population of strategies. Each strategy was composed of a set of rules, where a rule represented a response of the plane, given the distance, bearing, and heading of the missile. The rules were of the familiar if X and Y and . . . and Z then A. Every strategy was tested on several runs, then rated for its ability to evade the missile. Superior strategies were then reproduced, crossover performed on the rules, and mutation allowed to mod-

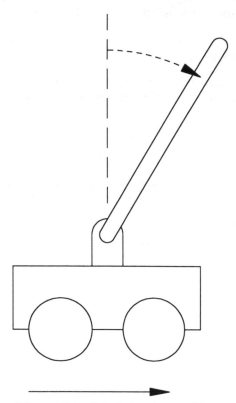

Figure 5-3. Pole-balancing problem.

ify the parameters of the rules. By random maneuvers the plane could evade the missile in about 40% of the trials; the genetic system improved this to over 90%.

Program Coding

The only limit in the coding of genetic algorithms seems to be one's imagination. For example, the U.S. Patent Office has recently granted a patent to John R. Koza of Stanford University (Koza 1990) for his invention of a genetic algorithm which solves symbolic problems. These are coded as a population of Lisp programs. Each program's objective function is determined by its ability to solve a problem, then reproduction takes place as described above. Crossover in this case involves interchange of program segments; mutation varies program segments randomly.

Discussion

These systems have demonstrated the ability of a genetic algorithm to solve difficult problems. Perhaps more importantly, they have shown a beneficial marriage between rule-based systems, programming languages, and genetic algorithms. This demonstrates the generality of these algorithms; both high-level abstractions as well as binary sequences can be encoded and improved through the evolutionary processes of genetics.

EXTENDED GENETIC ALGORITHMS

The simple three operations of reproduction, crossover and mutation have proven to be adequate to solve a wide range of problems. Still, biological genetics research shows that nature's methods are much more diverse. Extending the genetics algorithm to make use of these additional operations shows great promise; problems may become solvable that are difficult or impossible today. Only a few of the myriad of possibilities are presented here. Some have been well explored; others are topics of current research.

Diplody and Dominance

All of the characteristics of an organism are defined by its chromosomes. Copies of the chromosomes are contained in every cell where they serve to define its nature and function. A chromosome consists of a sequence of genes. Complex organisms are equipped with two copies of every chromosome. Each copy contains enough information to fully define the organism. This is called *diplody*. (The sex chromosome is a slightly different story and will be discussed in a later section.) Knowing nature's parsimonious tendencies, it seems unlikely that this diplody is without significance. It has been proposed (Goldberg 1989) that diplody retains a backup copy of a potentially useful gene that might otherwise be destroyed through natural selection. In a changing environment such a long term memory would retain genetic material that was useful in the past, and might become valuable in the future.

Our simple genetic algorithm consists of a set of single strings; in nature this would be called a haploid structure. To include diplody, some means must be devised to select one chromosome over the other when they disagree in a given bit position. Nature solves this by problem by assigning a rank to genes. A high ranking gene in one chromosome is said to dominate its lower ranking counterpart. Thus, if two genes give opposing instructions, the dominating gene controls that aspect of the organism.

There were a number of early efforts to include diplody and dominance in a genetic algorithm (Bagley 1967, Hollstien 1971, Holland 1975). The results of these experiments were inconclusive or negative. Only recently has diplody been tested in an environment where it should be most valuable, on a problem that is time varying (Goldberg and Smith 1987, Smith 1987). In this case the algorithm solved a version of the knapsack problem in which a knapsack is to be filled with objects of identical weight but different values. The goal is to fill the knapsack with objects that maximize the total value of its contents, subject to a maximum weight constraint. Goldberg and Smith complicated the problem by making the weight constraint time varying; i.e., the maximum weight changed periodically between two values. In this time-varying environment the diploid structure showed improved performance over a haploid system; it adapted more rapidly and completely.

Inversion

Despite our best efforts to devise an efficient, effective coding method, there is no way to prove that we have succeeded. Inversion, a method found in natural genetics, allows an algorithm to adapt its coding at the same time that it performs its evolutionary functions. In this respect it mimics the biological system that is continuously adjusting its coding.

Inversion operates by clipping out a section of a string, reversing it, and putting it back. For example, consider the following string

$$1 \ 0 \ 0 \ | \ 1 \ 1 \ 0 \ 1 \ | \ 0 \ 1 \ 0$$

where | marks the two points to cut. After removal and reinsertion the revised string looks as follows

$$1 \ 0 \ 0 \ 1 \ 0 \ 1 \ 1 \ 0 \ 1 \ 0$$

In our simple algorithm such an operation would be ruinous, as the position of the bits determines their weights. This can be solved by modifying our interpretation so that a bit carries its weight along with it when it moves, making a position independent code. If in our original coding we have inadvertently placed related bits far apart, inversion may put them closer. This makes their schema more likely to survive crossover, and more likely to proliferate in succeeding generations, provided that their objective function is high.

Note that inversion is only one way that the strings might be reordered. The literature contains a variety of techniques, some of which show promise in solving problems that are difficult for the simple algorithm (Bagley 1967, Franz 1972, Holland 1975, Bethke 1981, Davis 1985, Goldberg and Lingle 1985, Smith 1985).

Sexual Reproduction

Most higher creatures propagate through sexual reproduction. Humans have 23 pairs of chromosomes, one of which determines sex. Females carry two X sex chromosomes in each ova; males one X and one Y in each sperm. This ensures that 50% of fertilizations will produce males. It is not clear why evolution has found the complexity of sexual reproduction to be superior. There are many plausible theories. For example, it may be that the benefits to the biological organism may come about due to efficiencies achieved through specialization. The different characteristics required for bearing and rearing the young versus hunting and gathering may be so great that it is optimal for the female to be specialized for the former and the male the latter. Sex further refines the natural selection process, whereby males and females select the most healthy (appealing) mates.

The success of sexual reproduction in the biological realm makes it seem likely that genetic algorithms could benefit from its inclusion. Surprisingly, little research has been reported where this was attempted, perhaps because the expected benefits are not clear. One can conceive of a population composed of several classes of strings, each specialized for a particular range of tasks, with rules that restrict their mating.

Uniform Crossover

Recent research (Syswerda 1989) indicates that the crossover scheme described in our simple genetic algorithm can be improved. In our examples only contiguous groups of bits at the right end of the string could be crossed between parents. A bit string called a *crossover mask* is used to generalize the process. A 1 bit in this mask indicates that corresponding bits in the parents are to be interchanged; a 0 bit indicates no bit interchange.

Three types of crossover can be distinguished as defined by the following three bit masks

0	0	0	0	0	1	1	1	Single-Point Crossover
0	0	1	1	1	1	0	0	Two-Point Crossover
0	1	0	0	1	0	1	1	Uniform Crossover

Single-point crossover was used in our example. Its crossover mask has a single group of contiguous 1's located at the right end of the mask. Two-point crossover also requires a similar group of 1's, but they can be located anywhere in the mask. Uniform crossover is perfectly general; 1's can appear at any point in the mask.

For example, given the following bit strings and crossover mask, the indicated children are produced

Parent 1	1	0	1	0	0	1	1	0	
Parent 2	0	1	0	0	1	0	1	1	
Crossover mask:	1	0	0	1	1	0	1	0	
Child 1	0	0	1	0	1	1	1	0	
Child 2	1	1	0	0	0	0	1	1	

Despite the fact that uniform crossover breaks up schema more severely, empirical results on a variety of problems indicate that it produces better populations in fewer trials than either single or two-point crossover. This appears to result from its superior performance with schemata having the long defining lengths commonly encountered.

A procedure called the steady state genetic algorithm (SSGA) was used to evaluate this uniform crossover; this may have influenced the results to some extent. This algorithm is implemented as follows:

1. Produce an initial population.
2. Select the two parents with the highest objective functions.
3. Perform uniform crossover on these, producing two children. Do not delete the parents.
4. Apply mutation to these children.
5. Remove from the population, the two strings having the lowest objective functions.
6. Put the new children into the population.
7. Repeat steps 2–6 until a string with a satisfactory objective function is produced.

SSGA has a number of advantages. Since parents are not automatically deleted or modified, good strings are protected. Also, poor members may be parents, but are soon deleted from the population.

DISCUSSION

Genetic algorithms comprise a young and vital set of techniques for optimization and search. As such, they are capable of innumerable improvements, most of which will disappear as they are replaced by still better techniques. For this reason, this chapter has concentrated on fundamentals that have withstood the test of time, taking only occasional excursions into promising but less proven methods.

The relationships between genetic algorithms, artificial neural networks, fuzzy logic, and expert systems are now being explored by a number of researchers. By themselves each of these techniques has limitations and application problems. It seems reasonable to hope that their synergistic combination will produce new and beneficial systems, perhaps realizing the long sought goal of true Artificial Intelligence.

REFERENCES

Bagley, J. D. 1967. The behavior of adaptive systems which employ genetic and correlation algorithms, Ph.D. dissertation, University of Michigan. *Dissertation Abstracts International* 28(12) 5106B (University Microfilms No. 68-7556).

Bartow, A. G., R. S. Sutton, and C. W. Anderson. 1983. Neuron-like adaptive elements that can solve difficult learning control problems. *IEEE Transactions on Systems, Man, and Cybernetics*, SMC-13(5):834–846.

Belew, R. K. and M. Gherrity. 1989. Backpropagation for the classifier system. *Proceedings of the Third International Conference on Genetic Algorithms*, pp. 275–281. San Mateo: Morgan Kaufmann.

Bethke, A. D. 1981. Genetic algorithms as function optimizers, Ph.D. dissertation, University of Michigan. *Dissertation Abstracts International* 41(9) 3530B (University Microfilms No. 8106101).

Caudell, T. P. and C. P. Dolan. 1989. Parametric connectivity: Training of constrained networks using genetic algorithms. *Proceedings of the Third International Conference on Genetic Algorithms*, pp. 370–374. San Mateo: Morgan Kaufmann.

Davis, L. 1989. Mapping neural networks into classifier systems. *Proceedings of the Third International Conference on Genetic Algorithms*, pp. 375–378. San Mateo: Morgan Kaufmann.

Frantz, D. R. 1972. Nonlinearities in genetic adaptive search, Ph.D. dissertation, University of Michigan. *Dissertation Abstracts International* 33(11) 5240B-5241B (University Microfilms No. 73-11,116).

Goldberg, D. E. and R. E. Smith. 1987. Nonstationary function optimization using genetic algorithms with dominance and diploidy. *Genetic algorithms and their applications: Proceedings of the Second International Conference on Genetic Algorithms*, pp. 59–68.

Goldberg, D. E. 1989. *Genetic Algorithm in Search, Optimization and Machine Learning*. Reading Mass: Addison-Wesley.

Goldberg, D. E. and R. Lingle. 1985. Alleles, loci, and the traveling salesman problem. *Proceedings of an International Conference on Genetic Algorithms and Their Applications*, pp. 154–159.

Grefenstette, J. J. 1989. A system for learning control strategies with genetic algorithms. *Proceedings of the Third International Conference on Genetic Algorithms*, pp. 183–190. San Mateo: Morgan Kaufmann.

Harp, S. A., T. Samad, and A. Guha. 1989. Towards the genetic synthesis of neural networks. *Proceedings of the Third International Conference on Genetic Algorithms*, pp. 360–369. San Mateo: Morgan Kaufmann.

Holland, J. H. 1975. *Adaptation in Natural and Artificial Systems*. Ann Arbor: The University of Michigan Press.

Hollstien, R. B. 1971. Artificial genetic adaptation in computer control systems, Ph.D. dissertation, University of Michigan. *Dissertation Abstracts International* 32(3) 1510B (University Microfilms No. 71-23,773).

Jefferson, D. R. 1990. The Genesys system: Evolution as a theme in artificial life. In *Proceeding of the 2nd Artificial Life Workshop*. C. Langton (ed.), Reading, MA: Addison-Wesley.

Koza, J. R. (1990). Nonlinear genetic algorithms for solving problems. U.S. Patent 4,935,877.

Metropolis, N., A. W. Rosenbluth, M. N. Rosenbluth, A. H. Teller, and E. Teller. 1953. Equations of state calculations by fast computing machines. *Journal of Chemistry and Physics* 21:1087–91.

Miller, G. F., P. M. Todd, and S. U. Hegde. 1989. Designing neural networks using genetic algorithms. *Proceedings of the Third International Conference on Genetic Algorithms*, pp. 379–384. San Mateo: Morgan Kaufmann.

Odetayo, M. O., and D. R. McGregor. 1989. Genetic algorithm for inducing control rules for a dynamic system. *Proceedings of the Third International Conference on Genetic Algorithms*, pp. 177–179. San Mateo: Morgan Kaufmann.

Oosthuizen, G. D. 1989. Machine learning: A mathematical framework for neural network symbolic and genetics-based learning. *Proceedings of the Third International Conference on Genetic Algorithms*, pp. 385–390. San Mateo: Morgan Kaufmann.

Smith, D. 1985. Bin packing with adaptive search. *Proceedings of an International Conference on Genetic Algorithms and Their Applications*, pp. 202–206.

Smith, R. E. 1987. Diploid genetic algorithms for search in time varying environments. *Proceedings of the 25th Annual Southeast Regional Conference of the ACM*, pp. 175–178.

Syswerda, G. 1989. Uniform crossover in genetic algorithms. *Proceedings of the Third International Conference on Genetic Algorithms*, pp. 2–9. San Mateo: Morgan Kaufmann.

Wayner, P. 1990. Genetic algorithms. *Byte*. 15(1):361–368.

Whitley, D. and T. Hanson. 1989. Optimizing neural networks using faster, more accurate genetic search. *Proceedings of the Third International Conference on Genetic Algorithms*, pp. 391–397. San Mateo: Morgan Kaufmann.

6

Backpropagation and Beyond

CHARACTERISTICS OF BACKPROPAGATION

Problems and Advantages

The feed-forward network trained by backpropagation (Werbos 1974; Parker 1982; Rumelhart, Hinton, and Williams 1986) was a key development in the history of artificial neural networks. While gradient descent, its fundamental operating principal, has been known for centuries, this recent work took advantage of the feed-forward network's topology to produce an easily understood, highly effective paradigm. This innovation greatly accelerates the recent growth of activity in the neural network field. For the first time a theoretically sound technique was available to train multilayer, feed-forward networks with nonlinear neurons. The power and generality of such networks was known for many years, but prior to backpropagation there was no efficient, theoretically sound method for training their weights; hence, the hiatus of the 1960's when the limitations of single layer networks became understood (Minsky and Papert 1969).

Due to its priority and ubiquity, the method described by Rumelhart, Hinton, and Williams will be referred to a *standard backpropagation*. This does not declare it to be the most commonly used version of the paradigm (most researchers have their own favorite variation), but rather that it is the source from which the flood of modifications have emanated.

Today, backpropagation (or one of its many variations) is by far the most commonly applied neural network training method. An informal count indicates its use (in one form or another) in more than 85% of published applications. Unfortunately, it is a mixed blessing, exhibiting a number of serious problems while training. For example, the user is required to select three arbitrary coefficients: *training rate, momentum,* and the range of the random weight initialization. There is little theory to guide their determination. An unfortunate choice can cause slow convergence or network *paralysis* where learning virtually stops. Paralysis usually requires a complete retraining, thereby losing all benefit from what may have been days of computation. Also, due to the minimum error seeking nature of the algorithm, the network can become trapped in a local minimum of the error function, arriving at an unacceptable solution when a much better one exists.

While these problems are serious, perhaps backpropagation's most onerous characteristic is its long training time. Training sessions of days, even weeks, are common; this is not merely an inconvenience. While in theory training need only be done once, system development inevitably requires a certain amount of iterative optimization, particularly when developing features from the data set. This means that the backpropagation network must often be trained many times. In most practical applications this imposes long waiting periods in the development process. Given the tight schedules which seem characteristic of today's projects, promising alternatives may go unexplored, parameter optimization may be prematurely terminated, and nonoptimal results are often produced.

With all of these problems, backpropagation remains a highly effective paradigm. In difficult applications where the input/output relationships are nonlinear, and/or involve high-order correlations among the input variables, backpropagation has produced surprisingly accurate results. Furthermore, the disadvantage of its slow training is at least partially offset by its rapid computation in the forward direction. This can provide significant speed advantages in applications over such paradigms as "Probabilistic Neural Networks" (Chapter 3) and "Basis Function Networks" (Chapter 8).

Standard Backpropagation: Principles of Operation
Calculating the Output

This brief introduction is intended to review concepts and establish notation. For a more complete treatment, tutorials on backpropagation are included in the references (Rumelhart, Hinton, and Williams 1986; Wasserman 1989).

In this chapter the following notation is used:

1. Scalar variables are lowercase.
2. Row vector variables are assumed; these are lowercase bold.
3. Matrix variables are uppercase bold.
4. $\mathbf{x}^T$ indicates transposition of the vector $\mathbf{x}$.

Figure 6-1 shows the configuration of a feed-forward network with a single nonlinear hidden layer and a linear output layer. While there are many elaborations, such as adding more layers, or making the output layer nonlinear, this configuration is adequate to approximate any continuous function (Hornik, Stinchcombe, and White 1989).

In operation, a set of inputs, $x_1, x_2, \cdots x_m$ is applied to the network. It is useful to think of these as comprising an *input vector* **x**. The network performs calculations on this vector producing a set of outputs, $out_1, out_2, \cdots out_p$, collectively referred to as the *output vector* **out**.

In the first layer, the input row vector **x** is multiplied by weight matrix $\mathbf{W}^1$, thereby accomplishing the multiplication and summation indicated by Figure 6-1. The product produces a vector called **net**. Each component of **net** is then operated on by nonlinear function $f()$, thereby producing the vector **y**. Thus,

$$\mathbf{y} = f(\mathbf{x}\mathbf{W}^1) \tag{6-1}$$

where **x** and **y** are row vectors; each column of $\mathbf{W}^1$ contains the weights associated with a single hidden layer neuron, and $f()$ operates on the product in a component-by-component fashion. $f()$ is often the sigmoidal *logistic function*

$$y = 1/(1 + e^{-\beta net}) \tag{6-2}$$

Large values of β produce a steep function approaching a step, whereas small values produce a smoother function. Optimizing β is beyond the scope of this discussion; therefore, β will be assumed to be 1.0. The range of the logistic function is 0.0–1.0. Since it bounds the neurons output between these values, it is often called a *squashing function*. Often the function's range is offset by subtracting 0.5, a change that makes training somewhat faster. The

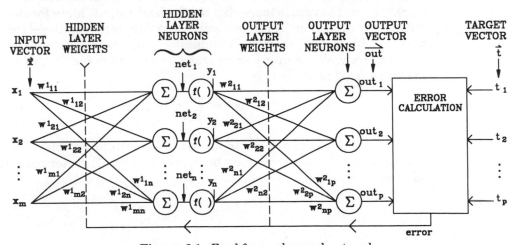

Figure 6-1. Feed-forward neural network.

logistic function has an important computational advantage in that its derivative (which is needed during training) has the simple form

$$f(\text{net})[1 - f(\text{net})]$$

The hyperbolic tangent is another commonly used squashing function.

$$y = \tanh(\text{net}) \tag{6-3}$$

Its range is -1.0–$+1.0$. Both functions are shown in Figure 6-2(a) and (b) where it may be seen that their shapes are similar.

Many other squashing functions have been used; the choice does not seem to be critical as long as the function is nonlinear and bounds the neuron's output.

The output layer then multiplies vector **y** by weight matrix $\mathbf{W}^2$, producing output vector **out**. Hence,

$$\mathbf{out} = f(\mathbf{xW}^1)\mathbf{W}^2 \tag{6-4}$$

Training

Supervised training is used in backpropagation. Therefore, a *training set* is required consisting of vector *training pairs*. Each training pair is composed of an *input vector* **x** and a *target vector* **t**. The target vector represents the set of values desired from the network when the input vector **x** is applied.

Before training, the network weights are initialized to small, random numbers. The optimal range of these numbers is problem dependent, however, it is safest to start with a range around ± 0.1. While larger values can accelerate convergence on some problems, they can also lead to network paralysis.

The object of training is to adjust the weight matrices so that the network's actual output is more like the desired output. More formally, the algorithm minimizes an error measure between the output vector and target vector. This error measure is computed and the weight adjusted for each training pair. While many error measures are possible, in this case the error measure used is

$$\text{sse} = \sum_i [(\mathbf{t}^i - \mathbf{out}^i)^2] \tag{6-5a}$$

where i is the number of components in the output vector.

Alternatively, the error may be averaged over all vector pairs in the training set, in which case the error measure is

$$1/n \sum_n \sum_i [(\mathbf{t}^i - \mathbf{out}^i)^2] \tag{6-5b}$$

where n is the number of training vectors in the training set.

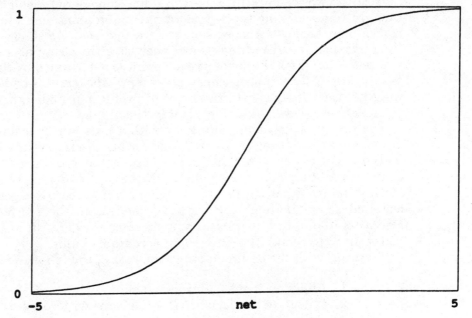

Figure 6-2(a). Logistic function.

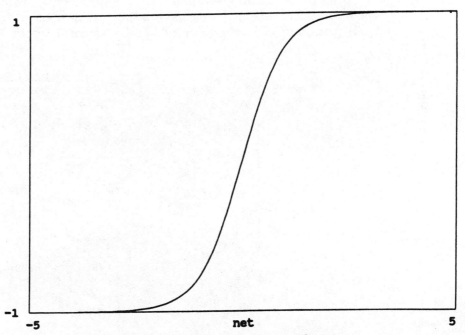

Figure 6-2(b). Hyperbolic tangent function.

If only two weights in a network are considered, their values can be thought of as defining the x–y coordinates of a point on a table top. Visualization breaks down if more weights are involved. As shown in Figure 6-3, the error may be visualized as a rubber sheet hovering above that surface, where the height of the sheet at each point is determined by the error at that x–y position. The rubber sheet represents the *error surface*. With more weights, the rubber sheet image is still useful, but its height at every point on the sheet is now a function of more variables.

The backpropagation training algorithm uses gradient descent, a multidimensional optimization method used for hundreds of years. In essence, the method changes each weight in a direction that minimizes the error. This change may be done at the time each input vector is applied, the *on-line* method using Equation (6-5a), or, changes may be averaged and weights changed after all input vectors have been seen, the *batch* method using Equation (6-5b). In either case, many passes through the training set may be required to reduce the error to an acceptable value.

Training with the on-line method consists of the following steps:

1. Apply an input training vector.
2. Calculate the derivative of the error with respect to each weight.
3. Adjust each weight in the direction of the negative of its derivative.

The batch method is similar except the derivatives are averaged over a pass through the training set, and weight adjustments made at the end. Due to the averaging, the batch method produces a more accurate estimate of the overall gradient; convergence tends to be smoother with fewer erroneous

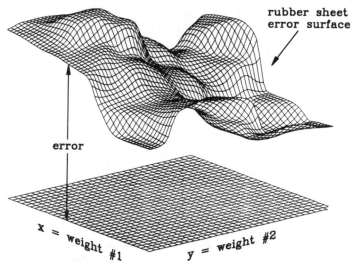

Figure 6-3. Rubber sheet analogy for error.

steps. On the other hand, the on-line method introduces a randomization to the weight steps that may help the network to avoid local minima. There are adherents to each method; no conclusive evidence has been presented for either alternative.

The set of derivatives for all weights with respect to the output error is called the *gradient vector* (∇). Backpropagation is, in essence, a method for calculating the gradient vector. It takes advantage of the unique structure of the feed-forward network to calculate the gradient vector on a layer-by-layer basis using the chain rule for partial derivatives. For weights in the output layer, components of this vector may be evaluated as follows

$$\nabla_{jk} = \partial\text{sse}/\partial w^2_{jk} = (\partial\text{sse}/\partial\text{out}_k)(\partial\text{out}_k/\partial w^2_{jk} \tag{6-6}$$

$$\partial\text{sse}/\partial\text{out}_k = -2(t_k - \text{out}_k) \tag{6-7}$$

$$\partial\text{out}_k/\partial w^2_{jk} = y_j \tag{6-8}$$

defining for later use,

$$\delta\text{out}_k = \partial\text{sse}/\partial\text{out}_k$$

$$\nabla_{jk} = \delta\text{out}_k y_j \tag{6-9}$$

where

  sse = sum of squared error [see Equation (6.5a)]
  ∇_{jk} = the gradient vector component associated with the weight from neuron j in the hidden layer to neuron k in the output layer
  w^2_{jk} = the weight connecting neuron j in the hidden layer to neuron k in the output layer (layer 2 is indicated by the superscript)
  y_j = output of neuron j in the hidden layer
  out$_k$ = output of neuron k in the output layer
  t_k = the target value for neuron k in the output layer

(Note: for simplicity, the training vector index n has been suppressed.)

The weight update rule for the output layer is then

$$w^2_{jk}(n + 1) = w^2_{jk}(n) - \eta\nabla_{jk} \tag{6-10}$$

where:

  $w_{ij}(n)$ = the value of the weight at time n
  η = a learning rate constant, typically <1.0.

Finding the gradient vector components for the hidden layer weights is a little more complicated, as changing one of these weights changes the outputs of all neurons in the output layer. Thus,

$$\nabla_{ij} = \partial sse/\partial w_{ij}^1 = \sum_k (\partial sse/\partial out_k)(\partial out_k/\partial y_j)(\partial y_j/net_j)(\partial net_j/\partial w_{ij}^1) \quad (6\text{-}10)$$

$$\partial sse/\partial out_k = -2(t_k - out_k) = \delta_{out_k} \quad (6\text{-}10a)$$

$$\partial out_k/\partial y_j = w_{jk}^1 \quad (6\text{-}10b)$$

$$\partial y_j/net_j = f'(net_j) \quad (6\text{-}10c)$$

$$\partial net_j/\partial w_{ij}^1 = x_i$$

substituting Equations (6-10a), (6-10b), and (6-10c) into Equation (6-10) and defining

$$\delta h_j = \sum_k \delta out_k \, w_{jk}^1 \, f'(net_j)$$

where $f'(net_j)$ is the derivative of the nonlinear function. Therefore

$$\nabla_{ij} = \delta h_j \, x_i \quad (6\text{-}11)$$

Once the gradient vector component δ_{ij} is found, the form of the weight update rule is the same as for the output layer

$$w_{ij}^1(n + 1) = w_{ij}^1(n) - \eta \nabla_{ij} \quad (6\text{-}12)$$

Note that this method can easily be extended to an arbitrary number of nonlinear hidden layers. At each layer calculate δ_x for each neuron using δs from the previous layer. Then calculate ∇_{xx} for each weight, and adjust weights using Equation (6-12) (with appropriate subscripts).

It is common for each neuron to have a "bias" input. This may be regarded as an additional weight for each neuron connected to +1; it is used and trained like all other weights.

Momentum

Backpropagation training can, on certain problems, cause weights to oscillate rather than converge smoothly to a solution. To alleviate this, some form of smoothing is often used, making the current weight change a function of the previous weight change. Rumelhart, Hinton, and Williams (1986) add momentum to the weight update in the following way

letting $\Delta w_{ij}(n) = -\eta \nabla_{ij}(n)$ (the weight change at step n)

$$w_{ij}(n + 1) = w_{ij}(n) + [\Delta w_{ij}(n) + \alpha(\Delta w_{ij}(n - 1))] \quad (6\text{-}13a)$$

Since the method for adding momentum is the same for all weight layers, the superscript on the weight has been suppressed for clarity.

A slightly different method with similar results amounts to exponential smoothing as described by Sejnowski and Rosenberg (1987). It can be incorporated in the following way

$$w_{ij}(n + 1) = w_{ij}(n) + (1 - \alpha)[\Delta w_{ij}(n)] + \alpha[\Delta w_{ij}(n - 1)] \qquad (6\text{-}13b)$$

where α is, in both cases, the "momentum" term.

As with η, there is little guidance regarding the correct value for α. On some problems, adding momentum does not help and may slow the training process. On others momentum introduced late in the training process will speed convergence.

Standard backpropagation calculates the weight change based solely upon the first derivative of the error with respect to the weight. Presumably, if second derivative information were available, a somewhat better estimate of the optimum step direction could be calculated. Calculating the global second derivatives, the Hessian matrix is a computationally demanding task. Various methods have been developed to use second-order information without the computational burden. Momentum is one such method, in that the weight step depends on the previous as well as the current gradient. This method's effectiveness is problem dependent, and hotly debated. A later section will present methods that are far more effective for calculating and utilizing second-order information.

SPEEDING UP BACKPROPAGATION

Overview

Backpropagation networks are slow to train, often requiring days or even weeks of training time on fast computers. As a result, many researchers have worked to overcome this problem. A number of methods have produced significant improvements, however, results are highly problem dependent. Since the methods are heuristic, there is no way to predict their effectiveness on a given application other than by experiment, a troublesome and time-consuming procedure. Nevertheless, these methods are widely used and should be considered before accepting the glacial training rates of standard backpropagation. There are far too many variations on backpropagation to present them all here. Instead, a few have been selected which are representative of the methods used, all of which have been well tested and proven beneficial in a number of applications. These will be presented in the order they appeared in the literature.

Quickprop

Algorithm

The *quickprop* modification to backpropagation (Fahlman 1988) is an attempt to estimate and utilize second derivative information without calculating the Hessian. While inspired by Newton's method, it is heuristic in nature.

Quickprop requires saving a copy of the previous gradient vector, as well as the previous weight change. The computation of the weight change uses only information associated with the weight being updated

$$\Delta w_{ij} = \nabla w_{ij}(n)/[\nabla w_{ij}(n-1) - \nabla w_{ij}(n)]\Delta w_{ij}(n-1) \qquad \text{(6-13c)}$$

where

$\nabla w_{ij}(n)$ = the gradient vector component associated with weight w_{ij} at step n.

This algorithm makes two highly questionable assumptions:

1. The error surface is parabolic, concave upward around the minimum.
2. The slope change of a weight $\nabla w_{ij}(n)$ is independent of changes in the other weights.

If these two assumptions were true, the algorithm would go the minimum of the error surface in a single step. Because they do not always hold, the training must take four cases into account:

1. The current slope is in the same direction as the previous slope, but smaller. In this case, all is well; we seem to be approaching the bottom of the parabola.
2. The current slope is in the opposite direction as the previous slope, but smaller. This suggests that we have jumped over the minimum to the opposite side of the parabola. This also does not present a problem as the next step will place us closer to the minimum.
3. The current slope is in the same direction as the previous slope, and equal to it. This is a problem, as the formula would require an infinite step.
4. The current slope is in the same direction as the previous slope but greater in magnitude. This also is a problem, as the next step would be in the wrong direction, heading toward a maximum.

Fahlman suggests that a "maximum growth factor," μ, be used to limit the rate of increase of the step size in the following way

$$\text{if } \Delta w_{ij}(n) > \mu \Delta w_{ij}(n-1)$$

$$\text{then } \Delta w_{ij}(n) = \mu \Delta w_{ij}(n-1) \qquad \text{(6-13d)}$$

He suggests an empirically determined value of 1.75 for μ.

Another minor complication is that the step-size calculation requires a previous value that is not available at start-up. This is easily solved by using the standard backpropagation method for the first weight adjustment. In fact, Fahlman indicates that on every step, he adds the gradient descent weight change indicated by Equation (6-12), with a suitably small value for η. The only exception is in case 2 above when the slope is nonzero, in which case adding gradient descent may cause overshoot and oscillation.

An additional problem arises from the fact that the weight values are unbounded; they may become so large that they cause overflow in the computer. One solution is to multiply each calculated slope by a decay factor less than 1.0, thereby indirectly reducing the rate of increase of the weights.

Fahlman observes that a weight connected to a saturated neuron (having its output near its upper or lower bound) cannot be trained because the slope of the squashing function approaches zero, thereby making the weight step approach zero. He counteracts this by adding a small constant (he suggests 0.1) to the calculation of the derivative, $f'(\text{net}_j)$.

Another modification that Fahlman found helpful was to divide the calculated weight change by the fan-in of the destination neuron. This scaling was observed to improve the reliability of convergence.

Finally, Fahlman applied the hyperbolic arctangent function to the output error $(\mathbf{t}^i - \mathbf{out}^i)$ associated with each neuron in the output layer. This function is nearly linear for small errors, but goes to plus infinity for large positive errors and to minus infinity for large negative errors. As a practical matter, it was necessary to limit the values to prevent infinite step sizes.

Quickprop Performance

Fahlman tested Quickprop on a variety of N–M–N encoder problems, where N is the number of inputs and outputs and M is the number of hidden layer neurons. The training set consisted of N input vectors, each with an identical output vector, making this an autoassociative task. Each vector had a single input of 1.0, the rest were 0.0. The object of network training is to reproduce the input vectors at the output. Since M is less than N, the network must perform data compression.

It is arguable if this class of parity problems is a meaningful test. The most important characteristic of neural networks is their ability to generalize; that is, small changes in the input should produce small output changes. The commonly used parity test sets are inappropriate to test this ability as they do just the opposite; small changes (one bit) in the input cause a maximal change in the output.

Quickprop was found to be faster than standard backpropagation by approximately a factor of five on the 10–5–10 encoder problem and a factor of 22 on the exclusive–or problem. While these are encouraging results, the test results are not adequate to make conclusive statements.

Discussion

Quickprop was an attempt to reduce the training time of backpropagation. In the author's experience its performance is highly problem dependent, often requiring several trials before the parameters were set to acceptable values.

Nevertheless, it is a useful technique that sparked interest and much research in accelerating the backpropagation algorithm.

SuperSAB

Algorithm

SuperSAB (Tollenaere 1990) is a modification of self-adapting backpropagation (SAB) (Devos and Orban 1988) that speeds up backpropagation training by making the step size dependent upon the nature of the error surface. It does not, however, make Quickprop's questionable assumption that the error surface is quadratic.

Experimental evidence shows that an optimal step size exists. Small step sizes increase training time and very large steps lead to instability or even network paralysis. Furthermore, the characteristics of the error surface may be quite different when evaluated along the directions associated with the different weights. For this reason, a single step size is generally not optimal for all weights.

SuperSAB uses these observations to produce the following heuristics:

1. Each weight is given its own step size.
2. Step sizes are adjusted during training.
3. If a weight is changed in the same direction as the previous change, that weight's step size should be increased. This is appropriate as when descending down a long slope toward a minimum, larger steps may be taken.
4. When the direction of a weight's change is different from the last change, that weight's step size should be decreased. This indicates that a minimum has been passed; smaller steps should be made when going back to try again.

Others have produced good results with various algorithms using these heuristics (Jacobs 1988, Devos and Orban 1988). SuperSAB builds on those techniques while adding unique methods to further improve performance. In SuperSAB each weight w_{ij} has an associated step size η_{ij} (the layer indication is suppressed for simplicity). In addition there are two constants: $\eta_{up} > 1.0$ is the weight increase factor, and $\eta_{down} < 1.0$ is the weight decrease factor.

The following algorithm is used:

Set all η_{ij} to an initial value η_{start}.

For each training vector (on-line mode) or epoch (batch mode),

Calculate the gradient vector using backpropagation.

If the direction of a calculated weight change is opposite to that of the previous change in that weight,

Then do not make the current weight change and reverse the previous weight change. Also, decrease the step size for that weight, setting

$$\eta_{ij}(n + 1) = \eta_{ij}\eta_{down}$$

Else, make the indicated weight change and increase the step size, setting

$$\eta_{ij}(n + 1) = \eta_{ij}(n)\eta_{up}.$$

This is the author's minor modification of the SuperSAB method as published; the changes in η are multiplicative rather than additive, thereby making the growth rate in step size exponential rather than linear. This has been found to increase convergence rates. However, it was necessary to limit the maximum value of η to avoid instability. While the values for the constants are problem dependent, $\eta_{up} = 1.05$ and $\eta_{down} = 0.2$, respectively, are conservative values that have performed well if the maximum value for η_{ij} is limited to 10.

Performance

SuperSAB is often 10–100 times faster than backpropagation training; however, it is difficult to make general comparisons to Quickprop or other methods, as no generally accepted set of test problems is available.

Discussion

SuperSAB requires storage for each weight of η_{ij} as well as the previous weight change. There is a small increase in computational load, but the speed increase makes this negligible. SuperSAB has two more parameters than backpropagation, but their values are not critical. The author has found SuperSAB, if not the fastest, to be a reliable, stable algorithm for accelerating gradient descent.

SECOND-ORDER METHODS

Overview

Backpropagation's convergence path follows the error function's direction of steepest descent. While plausible, in many cases this is not the direct route to a minimum. Backpropagation is blind to certain opportunities, as it uses only the first derivatives (the slope) of the error surface. By making use of the second derivatives as well (the rate of change of slope), training times have been reduced by up to a factor of 100. There are a variety of these *second-order* methods in use, most with long histories in the field of numerical analysis. The following treatment will describe some of the more promising techniques, providing algorithms so that programs can be written to implement them.

Unlike many of the speedup methods for backpropagation, the conjugate gradient methods (Johansson, Dowla, and Goodman 1992; Moller 1990; Battiti 1992; Press *et al.* 1988) have a sound theoretical foundation. These methods are well known among numerical analysts, and offer, at least in theory, convergence in fewer passes through the training set—at a cost of increased computation per pass. While actual speedup is highly problem dependent, some applications have reported an overall speed increase exceeding a factor of 10, despite the increased computation.

Conjugate Gradient Descent

Conjugate gradient descent is a general purpose second-order technique that minimizes a function of several variables. In the case of a feed-forward neural network, these variables are the network weights and biases. Used in the batch mode, the minimized function is the output error, summed over all outputs and averaged over all vectors in the training set. This is expressed by Equation (6-5b), and repeated here for reference.

$$1/j \sum_n \sum_i [(\mathbf{t^i} - \mathbf{out^i})^2] \qquad (6\text{-}5b)$$

Figure 6-4 graphs error as a function of two weights in a network, one representing the x axis, the other the y axis. The lines mark contours of constant error, with the outer lines being the highest error, the inner lines the lowest. The resulting "error surface" may be thought of as a valley with the error lines indicating height above the valley floor. Backpropagation's steepest descent method always adjusts weights so as to decrease error most rapidly. This direction is the negation of the *gradient vector* found by differ-

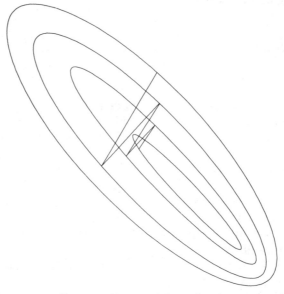

Figure 6-4. Contour diagram of quadratic error surface.

entiating the function. While superficially plausible, this "greedy" approach results in many false steps, as it does not always take the most direct path. For example, on the constant error lines the gradient is perpendicular to the line; it does not always indicate the direction to the minimum error point. This can result in a long series of zigzag steps, each largely undoing the work of those that preceded it.

Conjugate gradient descent proceeds not down the gradient, but instead in a direction which is *conjugate* to the direction of the previous step (and preferably to all previous steps). The gradient on the current step stays perpendicular to the previous step direction. Therefore, the change in the gradient must be perpendicular to the direction of the previous step. Such a series of steps is noninterfering, in that the minimization performed in one step is not partially undone by the next.

Conjugate gradient methods approximate this conjugate direction by taking into account second derivative information that is not used by backpropagation. A *quadratic* error surface is assumed, that is, a function expressible by a Taylor expansion with only first and second derivatives (backpropagation uses only first derivatives). Doing this exactly involves computing the matrix of second derivatives (the Hessian), a computationally expensive procedure with $O(N^3)$ operations. Furthermore, a solution must be found to n-linear equations in n unknowns (where n is the number of weights), a major task for a network with thousands of weights. Instead, a number of clever methods have been devised to approximate a series of conjugate steps. If the error surface is quadratic, convergence occurs in n steps. Close to the minimum, the error surface is usually approximately quadratic, therefore the methods perform well in this region. In regions far from the error minimum the results are much less predictable.

There are a number of methods that use second-order information in this way, only a few of which will be presented here. The methods discussed have all provided major convergence speed improvements. However, there has been no adequate test of their relative advantages. Problems that may crop up with each approach will be discussed later.

The Quadratic Error Function

The error as a function of the network's weights can always be expressed as a multidimensional Taylor series

$$f(\mathbf{w}) = f(\mathbf{w}_0) + \sum_i \frac{\partial f}{\partial w_i} w_i + \frac{1}{2} \sum_i \sum_j \frac{\partial_f^2}{\partial w_i \partial w_j} w_i w_j + \cdots \qquad (6\text{-}13)$$

where $\mathbf{w}_0$ = origin row vector in weight space. This may be approximated by ignoring higher-order terms as

$$f(\mathbf{w}) = c - \mathbf{b}\mathbf{w}^T + \tfrac{1}{2}\mathbf{w}\mathbf{H}\mathbf{w}^T \qquad (6\text{-}14)$$

where

> $\mathbf{w}$ = the weight row vector composed of all weights in the network
> $c = f(\mathbf{w_0})$, the function value at the origin
> $\mathbf{b} = -\nabla f |\mathbf{w}_0$, the gradient row vector at the origin
> $\mathbf{H} = \partial^2 f / \partial w_i w_j$, the *Hessian* matrix of partial second derivatives at the origin

Given a quadratic function, the error is minimum where the gradient is zero. Therefore, by differentiating Equation (6-14) and rearranging, we find that

$$\mathbf{H}\mathbf{w}^T = \mathbf{b}^T \qquad (6\text{-}15\text{a})$$

is a linear equation that may, in principle, be solved for the weight vector if $\mathbf{H}$ is invertible. Any optimism this inspires is quickly dispelled when it is realized that calculating $\mathbf{H}$ requires $O(n^3)$ operations, and there are n equations in n unknowns to be solved, where n is the number of weights.

A better way to find the weight vector uses the concept of *conjugate directions*. In general, direction vectors $d_i, d_2, \cdots, d_n$ are *H conjugate* if

$$\mathbf{d}_i \mathbf{H} \mathbf{d}_j^T = 0 \text{ for all } i \neq j. \qquad (6\text{-}15\text{b})$$

It can be shown that $\mathbf{d}_0, \mathbf{d}_1 \cdots \mathbf{d}_k$ are linearly independent and form a basis for the vector space of $\mathbf{x}$.

Given this set of vectors and starting at point $\mathbf{w}_0$, the objective is to move to the point of minimum error, $\mathbf{w}^*$. Using our basis, this may be expressed as

$$\mathbf{w}^* - \mathbf{w}_0 = \sum_{i=0}^{n-1} \alpha_i \mathbf{d}_i \qquad (6\text{-}16)$$

where the α's are scalars to be determined later. Multiplying by $\mathbf{d}_j \mathbf{H}$ and substituting $\mathbf{b}^T$ for $\mathbf{H}\mathbf{w}^*$

$$\mathbf{d}_j (\mathbf{b}^T - \mathbf{H}\mathbf{w}_0^T) = \sum_{i=0}^{n-1} \alpha_i \mathbf{d}_j \mathbf{H} \mathbf{d}_i^T \qquad (6\text{-}17)$$

At this point the advantages of our *H*-conjugate basis becomes clear.

If the $\mathbf{d_i}$ were not *H* conjugate, solving this equation for the weights would require the solution of n equations in n unknowns. Instead, for each j, all terms under the summation are zero except for the one where $i = j$, therefore, we can find the scalars as

$$\alpha_j = \mathbf{d}_j (\mathbf{b}^T - \mathbf{H}\mathbf{w}_0^T) / (\mathbf{d}_j \mathbf{H} \mathbf{d}_j^T) \qquad (6\text{-}18)$$

Defining,

$$\mathbf{w}_k = \mathbf{w}_0 + \sum_{j=0}^{k-1} \alpha_j \mathbf{d}_j \qquad (6\text{-}19)$$

the position at any step may be calculated using Equation (6-16) as

$$\mathbf{w}_k = \mathbf{w}_0 \sum_{j=0}^{k=1} \alpha_j \mathbf{d}_j \qquad (6\text{-}20)$$

It is possible to find the position at any step, given the position at the previous step as

$$\mathbf{w}_{k+1} = \mathbf{w}_k + \alpha_k \mathbf{d}_k \qquad (6\text{-}21)$$

where after n such steps $\mathbf{w}_n = \mathbf{w}^*$, the desired point of minimum error.

From Equations (6-15b) and (6-19) it can be shown that $\mathbf{d}_k \mathbf{H} \mathbf{w}_k^T = \mathbf{d}_k \mathbf{H} \mathbf{w}_0^T$. Using the notation $\mathbf{g}_k^T = \nabla f(\mathbf{w}_k^T) = \mathbf{H} \mathbf{w}_k^T - \mathbf{b}^T$, produces

$$\alpha_k = -(\mathbf{d}_k \mathbf{g}_k^T)/(\mathbf{d}_k \mathbf{H} \mathbf{d}_k^T) \qquad (6\text{-}22)$$

Armed with Equations (6-21) and (6-22) we are ready to define a set of steps that will minimize the error—provided that we can find the set of conjugate direction vectors. To do so, set the first direction vector to the negative gradient at the starting point,

$$\mathbf{d}_0 = -\mathbf{g}_0 \qquad (6\text{-}23\text{a})$$

Now find each new direction vector from the previous one by

$$\mathbf{d}_{k+1} = -\mathbf{g}_{k+1} + \beta_k \mathbf{d}_k \qquad (6\text{-}23\text{b})$$

Since each direction must be conjugate to the previous one,

$$\mathbf{d}_{k+1} H \mathbf{d}_{kT}^T = (-\mathbf{g}_{k+1} + \beta_k \mathbf{d}_k) H \mathbf{d}_k^T = 0 \qquad (6\text{-}24)$$

hence,

$$\beta_k = \mathbf{g}_{k+1} H \mathbf{d}_{kT}^T / (\mathbf{d}_k H \mathbf{d}_k^T) \qquad (6\text{-}25)$$

Of course, we are still in trouble because we do not know the Hessian matrix and finding it takes a prohibitive amount of computation. Fortunately, it is possible to do without it by observing that α is used as a step size in Equation (6-21) telling how far to go in direction $\mathbf{d}_k$ to minimize the error function. The value of α can be found by a line search to find the minimum in that direction. Given α we eliminate $\mathbf{H}$. First, from Equation (6-21) it can be shown that

$$(\mathbf{g}_{k+1} - \mathbf{g}_k)^T = \mathbf{H}(\mathbf{w}_{k+1} - \mathbf{w}_k)^T = \alpha_k \mathbf{H} \mathbf{d}_k^T \qquad (6\text{-}26)$$

therefore,

$$\mathbf{H}\mathbf{d}_k^T = (\mathbf{g}_{k+1} - \mathbf{g}_k)_T^T / \alpha_k \qquad (6\text{-}27)$$

Substituting Equation (6-27) into Equation (6-25)

$$\beta_k = \mathbf{g}_{k+1}(\mathbf{g}_{k+1} - \mathbf{g}_k)^T / [\mathbf{d}_k(\mathbf{d}_k^T - \mathbf{g}_k^T)] \qquad (6\text{-}28)$$

This is called the Hestenes–Stiefel formula for β_k.

Conjugate Gradient Descent Algorithm

At last we are able to write the algorithm (suppressing unnecessary subscripts):

> Set $k = 0$; select a starting point for the weights, $\mathbf{w}$.
> **1.** Use backpropagation to calculate the gradient vector g.
> $\mathbf{g} = \nabla f(\mathbf{w})$
>   if $\mathbf{g} = 0$
>   stop
>   else
> $\mathbf{d} = -\mathbf{g}$
>   endif
> **2.** Do line search for step size; update weights
> $\alpha = \text{argmin}_\alpha [f(\mathbf{w} + \alpha \mathbf{d})]$
> $\mathbf{w} = \mathbf{w} + \alpha \mathbf{d}$
>   ;find new gradient vector by backpropagation
> $\mathbf{g}_p = \nabla f(\mathbf{w})$
>   if $\mathbf{g}_p = 0$
>   stop
>   endif
> $\beta = \mathbf{g}_p(\mathbf{g}_p - \mathbf{g})^T / [\mathbf{d}(\mathbf{d} - \mathbf{g})^T]$
> $\mathbf{d} = -\mathbf{g}_p + \beta \mathbf{d}$
>   if $k = n - 1$
>   goto 3 ; n is the number of weights, restart
>   else
> $k = k + 1$
> $g = g_p$
>   goto 2
>   endif
> **3.** Set $k = 0$
>   goto 1   ;start

There are two other common formulas to calculate β

1. Fletcher–Reeves (1964)

$$\beta = (\mathbf{g}_p \mathbf{g}_p^T)/(\mathbf{g}\mathbf{g}_T)$$

2. Polak–Ribière (1969)

$$\beta = \mathbf{g}_p(\mathbf{g}_p - \mathbf{g})^T/(\mathbf{g}\mathbf{g}^T)$$

There is evidence that the Polak–Ribière formula improves performance somewhat, although this is quite problem dependent.

All three methods require a line minimization for each iteration. Any standard multidimensional algorithm will do—for example, the procedure *dlinmin* (Press *et al.* 1988). Since each iteration of the line search routine requires the calculation of the error and often the gradient vector, it can be quite time consuming. In spite of this, overall speed is often faster than back-propagation. It has been shown to be faster by more than a factor of 10 on parity problems of various sizes (Johansson, Dowla, and Goodman 1992).

Scaled Conjugate Gradient Descent Algorithm

The conjugate gradient descent algorithm converges well on functions whose Hessian matrix is positive definite, however, this condition is not always met, especially in regions far removed from error minimum. Another method has been developed (Moller 1990) that solves this problem by determining when the Hessian is not positive definite, and adjusting a parameter to make it so. It also avoids the time-consuming line search procedure (Moller 1990) by using a Levenberg–Marquardt approach to determine the step size. Due to the length of its derivation, only the algorithmic form is presented here (slightly modified from the original).

Choose a starting weight vector **w** and find its gradient;
$$\mathbf{p} = \mathbf{r} = -\nabla(\mathbf{w})$$
1. Initialize the following scalars:
$0 < \sigma < 10^{-4}$; a small number, its value is not critical
$0 < \lambda < 10^{-6}$
$\overline{\lambda} = 0$
Success = true
2. If Success = true then calculate second-order information
$\sigma = \sigma/\|\mathbf{p}\|$
$\mathbf{s} = [\nabla(\mathbf{w} + \sigma\mathbf{p}) - \nabla(\mathbf{w})]/\sigma$
$\delta = \mathbf{p}\mathbf{s}^T$
endif
$\delta = \delta + (\lambda - \overline{\lambda})\|\mathbf{p}\|^2$;scale δ
if $\delta < 0$;make the Hessian matrix positive definite
$\overline{\lambda} = 2(\lambda - \delta/\|\mathbf{p}\|^2)$
$\delta = -\delta + \lambda\|\mathbf{p}\|^2$
$\lambda = \overline{\lambda}$
endif
$\mu = \mathbf{p}\mathbf{r}^T$;calculate step size.

$\alpha = \mu/\delta$

$\Delta = 2\delta[\text{error}(\mathbf{w}) - \text{error}(\mathbf{w} + \alpha\mathbf{p})]/\mu^2$;calculate the comparison parameter

if $\Delta \geq 0$ then the error can be reduced:

$\mathbf{w} = \mathbf{w} + \alpha\mathbf{p}$; update weights

$\mathbf{r}_p = -\nabla(\mathbf{w})$

$\lambda = 0$

Success = true

if the number of epochs is greater than the number of weights, restart the algorithm

$\mathbf{p} = \mathbf{p}_p$

$\mathbf{r} = \mathbf{r}_p$

goto 1

else

$\beta \quad = (\|\mathbf{r}_p\|^2 - \mathbf{r}_p\mathbf{r}^T)/\mu$

$\mathbf{p}_p = \mathbf{r}_p + \beta\mathbf{p}$

endif

if $\Delta < 0.75$ then reduce the scale parameter

$\lambda = \lambda/4$

else a reduction in error is not possible

$\bar{\lambda} = \lambda$

Success = false

endif

endif

if $\Delta < 0.25$ then increase the scale parameter

$\lambda = \lambda + [\delta(1 - \Delta)]/|\mathbf{p}|^2$

endif

if the norm of the steepest descent direction vector $\mathbf{r}$ is less than TARGET_NORM, or the error is <TARGET_ERROR then exit,

returning $\mathbf{w}$ as the desired weight vector.

else

$\mathbf{p} = \mathbf{p}_p$

$\mathbf{r} = \mathbf{r}_p$

goto 2

endif

end

DISCUSSION

Backpropagation, its host of improved versions, and the more complex second-order methods all suffer from the unpredictability of their training process. While some are faster than others, the best can require days of training on a large problem. Furthermore, all of these methods are subject to entrapment in local minima; there is no way to tell if a solution is the best possible. If the network trains to an unacceptable result, the only alternative is to repeat the training process until a suitable result is achieved.

A more subtle problem is encountered when a vector is input that is unlike any in the training set. Under these circumstances, the network will produce an output that may be totally incorrect, with no indication that it has done so. For example, a control system based upon a backpropagation network can malfunction badly when a novel input is applied. This can have unacceptable consequences if expensive machines, the environment, or human lives are at stake.

Despite these problems, the techniques presented in this chapter constitute the methods behind most successful neural network applications. While we eagerly await faster, more reliable methods, neural network engineers will continue to use these techniques because they solve real-world problems, and there is nothing better at hand.

REFERENCES

Battiti, Roberto. 1992. First- and second-order methods for learning: Between steepest descent and Newton's method. *Neural Computing* 4:141–166.

Devos, M. R. and G. A. Orban. 1988. Self-adaptive backpropagation. *Proceedings, NeuroNimes*. Nanterre, France.

Fahlman, S. E. 1988. Faster-learning variations on backpropagation: An empirical study. In *Proceedings of the Connectionist Models Summer School*, eds. D. Touretzky, G. Hinton, and T. Sejnowski. San Mateo, CA: Morgan Kaufmann.

Fletcher, R. and C. M. Reeves. 1964. Function minimization by conjugate gradients. *Computer Journal* 7:149–154.

Fletcher, R. 1975. *Practical Methods of Optimization*. New York: Academic Press.

Hornik, K. M., M. Stinchcombe, and H. White. 1989. Multilayer feedforward networks are universal approximators. *Neural Networks* 2:359–366.

Hestenes, M. R. and E. L. Stiefel. 1952. Methods of conjugate gradients for solving linear systems. *Journal of Research of the National Bureau of Standards* 49(6):409–436.

Jacobs, R. A. 1988. Increased rates of convergence through learning rate adaption. *Neural Networks* 1(4):295–307.

Johansson, E. M., F. U. Dowla, and D. M. Goodman. 1992. Backpropagation Learning for MultiLayer Feed-Forward Neural Networks Using the Conjugate Gradient Method. Lawrence Livermore National Laboratory, UCRL-JC-104850 Rev. 1.

Minsky, M. L. and S. Papert. 1969. *Perceptrons*. Cambridge, MA: MIT Press.

Moller, Martin F. 1990. A Scaled Conjugate Gradient Algorithm for Fast Supervised Learning. Computer Science Department, University of Aarhus, Denmark.

Parker, D. B. 1982. *Learning Logic*. Invention Report S81-64, File 1, Office of Technology Licensing, Stanford University, Stanford, CA.

Polak, E. and Ribière, "Note sue la Convergence de Methods de Directions Conjures. *Revue Francaise* Information Recherche Operationnelle, vol. 16, pp. 35–43, 1969.

Press, W. H., B. P. Flannery, S. A. Teukolsky, and W. T. Vetterling. 1988. *Numerical Recipes in C.* New York: Cambridge.

Rumelhart, D. E., G. E. Hinton, and R. J. Williams. 1986. Learning internal representations by error propagation. In *Parallel Distributed Processing*, vol. 1, pp. 318–62. Cambridge, MA: MIT Press.

Sejnowski, T. J., and C. R. Rosenberg. 1987. Parallel networks that learn to pronounce English text. *Complex Systems* 1:145–68.

Tollenaere, T. 1990. SuperSAB: Fast adaptive backpropagation with good scaling properties. *Neural Networks* 3:561–573.

Wasserman, P. D. 1989. *Neural Computing, Theory, and Practice.* New York: Van Nostrand Reinhold.

Werbos, P. 1974. *Beyond regression: New tools for prediction and analysis in the behavioral sciences*, Ph.D. dissertation, Harvard University.

7

Neural Control

INTRODUCTION

Automatic control, once regarded as exotic technology, has become commonplace. In consumer products automatic controllers regulate the temperature and humidity in our homes, the speed of our automobiles, the chlorine in our swimming pools, even the cooking of our food. Modern industry uses these systems in a myriad of applications. Without them large segments of the petrochemical, pharmaceutical, semiconductor, machine tool, and many other industries could not exist in their present form. Lacking automatic control we could not have gone to the moon, nor could we have produced most of our modern weapons systems. Most of these applications have developed within the past 50 years; prior to World War II automatic control was poorly understood and little used. Now, armed with better theory and growing demand, the number of systems is increasing exponentially, fueled by an inexorable drive toward automation.

Neural network control systems allow the optimal control of nonlinear systems. Mathematical systems theory, despite its success with linear systems, is of little help with nonlinear systems; its results are sparse and system specific. Hence, for the sake of mathematical tractability, nonlinear systems are usually analyzed by making linear approximations of their performance. While useful, this method never truly represents a real-world system. If for no other reason, physical systems are nonlinear due to their bounded outputs; they are unable to produce an output beyond some limit. This and more subtle deviations from linearity may make a linear system solution nonoptimal, thereby producing unexpected performance degradation, instability, and even outright failure in practical applications.

In this area of nonlinear control, neural networks show great potential. They eliminate the need to set up and solve difficult nonlinear mathematical models; instead, the network learns from example to optimize performance regardless of the system's nonlinearity. Furthermore, they can be trained on-line to optimize continuously the system's operation despite a changing environment.

The range of neural network techniques for adaptive control is so large that it cannot be covered adequately in this chapter; therefore, some strategy was required to limit the chapter's size while maximizing its utility. Rather than provide a "broad brush" treatment of a large number of methods, a few workable methods are presented in enough detail to allow their use. Also, references are provided to review papers (Werbos 1989a, Franklin 1989) where a broad range of methods is presented, as well as additional references to more specialized papers that describe theory and applications in greater depth. Certain writings have been found especially valuable, and are the source of much that follows (Miller 1990; Narendra 1989; Narendra and Parthasarathy 1990; Nguyen and Widrow 1989; Scott, Shavlik, and Ray 1992; Hosogi 1990; Kumar and Guez 1990; Jordon and Jacobs 1990; Werbos 1989).

Werbos (1989) divides neural control into five basic types:

1. supervised control systems
2. direct inverse control
3. neural adaptive control
4. backpropagation through time
5. adaptive critic methods

The field is so diverse that this division is controversial; even the names are far from universally accepted; therefore, no claim is made regarding the suitability of either beyond this chapter. While the depth of presentation varies greatly, an attempt has been made to convey an understanding of the basic principles governing each, as well as some idea of their areas of applicability and potential limitations.

FUNDAMENTALS OF AUTOMATIC CONTROL

The basic concept of automatic control is illustrated in Figure 7-1. This configuration, while highly simplified, embodies the essential elements of the most common systems. Here an automatic control system maintains a tank of liquid, called the *plant*, at a constant temperature. An input x, determining the desired temperature at the output of the reference model is applied to the controller along with a feedback signal from the plant indicating the current temperature. The controller subtracts these inputs, producing a control signal c that causes a proportional change in the heater power. The direction of the change is such that, in time, the temperature of the liquid

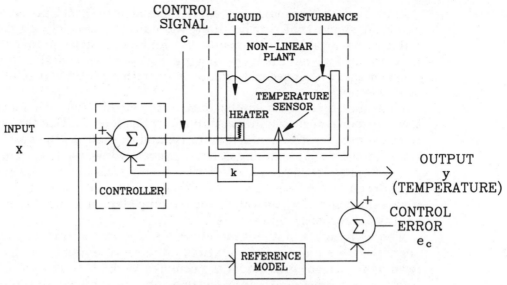

Figure 7-1. Control system.

will approach the desired temperature indicated by the reference model output. If a disturbance occurs (such as a change in ambient temperature), the system compensates, automatically adjusting the heater power to maintain a more nearly constant temperature. This is an example of *negative feedback*, one of the major scientific achievements of modern times.

The *reference model* represents the input–output relationship desired from the system. In this case it is not a physical component, but rather the designer's intention of how the system should respond to a change in the input, *x*. The difference between the output of the reference model and the system, the *control error* e_c, is a measure of the degree to which the system's performance deviates from the designer's intent; ideally it would be zero. This method is called *model reference adaptive control* (MRAC). It assumes that the designer knows the system well enough to be able to define the desired output for every input, usually in mathematical form.

The static performance of the system is expressed by a simple algebraic expression. First, lumping the controller with the heater and sensor, define an open loop gain as

$$A = y/(x - ky)$$

a little algebraic manipulation produces the following expression

$$y/x = \frac{A}{1 - Ak} \qquad (7.1)$$

where y/x is the closed loop gain.

Note that as A becomes large, y/x approaches $-1/k$. This is an important result. It shows that, in the limit, the output y is solely a function of the input x and constant k; the value of A and its linearity properties are insignificant—as long as A is large enough. This allows the design of highly accurate systems with inaccurate components, either in the controller, the heater, or the sensor.

Note that this result applies only to the steady state. Generally, the system's response to a step increase in x is not a step in y. Due to response times in the controller, the heater, the tank, and the sensor, the system can overshoot before stabilizing, undershoot, or even worse, oscillate continuously. If the system's response characteristics are not satisfactory, the controller can be tailored to minimize the error. This is done by adjusting the gain A (set inside the controller), as well as introducing elements into the controller that modify its response characteristics.

The dynamic input–output characteristics of a linear system can be described by a differential equation, often represented by its Laplace transform as a rational function of the complex variable s. This is called the system *transfer function*. In discrete time systems a difference equation is used, often represented by its z transform; therefore, the transfer function is a rational polynomial in z. These methods are beyond the scope of this discussion, however, the reader should realize that producing a desirable time response is a complicated problem. If the system is linear, powerful and general mathematical methods exist for its solution, but, no such general solutions are available for nonlinear systems. One of the motivations for using neural networks is the hope that stable solutions for nonlinear control systems can be discovered through training, without the need for a comprehensive theory. This premise will be examined in the following sections.

SUPERVISED CONTROL SYSTEMS

In many cases it is possible to perform a needed automatic control function by simply teaching a neural network to mimic the behavior of a human doing the same task. This technique assumes the availability of a human who performs adequately, and some motivation for producing a machine replacement, such as cost, speed, consistency, or safety.

Figure 7-2(a) shows how the neural network is trained. The network receives the same inputs as the human—the input x, and the state vector (the actual system output in this case). The output of the network is compared with that of the human and the difference is fed back to modify the network's weights in a direction that reduces the error. Backpropagation is commonly used for this purpose, although any supervised training method is a candidate.

When the network has been adequately trained, that is, when it responds sufficiently like the human, training is terminated, the human is removed

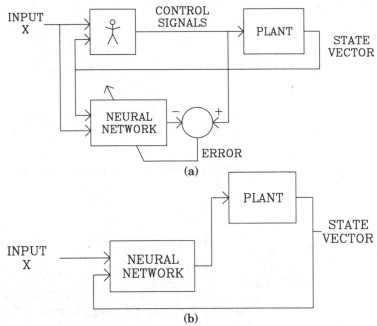

Figure 7-2. Supervised control. (a) Network training phase. (b) Automatic operation.

from the loop, and control is turned over to the neural network as shown in Figure 7-2(b).

Supervised control is conceptually simple and easy to implement. However, it cannot improve upon the performance of the human who may operate in an unacceptably nonoptimal manner. Nevertheless, humans routinely perform complex, nonlinear control tasks that, in many cases, we have been unable to duplicate with automatic systems. Simply walking across the room involves a control task of such tremendous complexity and subtlety that our most sophisticated automatic systems are trivial by comparison. While less than satisfying from a theoretical standpoint, supervised control with neural networks will allow access to some of these human abilities that have been optimized over millions of years of evolution.

DIRECT INVERSE CONTROL

If the plant can be represented by an invertible function, a simple method of automatic control is possible. Figure 7-3(a) shows the training phase where the network learns this inverse function. The network receives the plant state vector as input. The difference between the network output and the control input to the plant constitutes an error signal used to adjust network weights by backpropagation or other supervised training means.

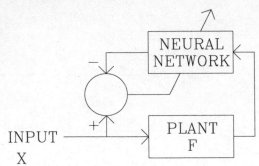

Figure 7-3(a). Learning the inverse function.

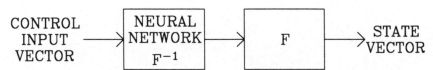

Figure 7-3(b). Control using the inverse function.

Once trained, the arrangement of Figure 7-3(b) is used to control the system. Since the composition of $F(F^{-1}) = 1$, the state vector equals the control input; therefore, to achieve a desired system output it is only necessary to provide it as input.

In some cases this method has a serious problem: The plant function may not be invertible. For example, considering only the static problem, the plant may produce the same output for more than one input. Training to produce the inverse function would require the network to produce different outputs for the same input; an unachievable condition. If the system is considered dynamically the situation is still more complicated. The frequency response of the plant may go to zero at some input frequency. Since this would require an infinite response from the neural network at this frequency, the inverse is again not physically realizable.

With these caveats, the method of direct inverse control is still worthy of consideration if the characteristics of the plant are well understood, and its transfer function is known to be invertible.

NEURAL ADAPTIVE CONTROL

Adaptive Control: Linear and Nonlinear

In designing nonlinear neural control systems, it seems reasonable to start with the successful models developed for linear systems, suitably modified to include neural networks. This is the approach taken by Narendra (1989) who has shown a set of powerful and general methods for achieving stable adaptive control of linear time-invariant systems. He and others have extended this work to nonlinear neural network applications with considerable success (Narendra 1990), using structures similar to those developed for linear adaptive control systems, with nonlinear neural networks substituted for the linear processing elements.

Adaptive control produces a system capable of maintaining optimal performance despite variations in its environment. In the nonadaptive system shown in Figure 7-1 the controller's characteristics can be designed to optimize the system's response with a given plant. If, however, the characteristics of the plant change over time, there is no provision to maintain optimality. Often, plant characteristics will vary substantially during operation. For example, the response time of the tank in Figure 7-1 will depend heavily upon the liquid level; a full tank will heat more slowly than one that is nearly empty. The result may be a system that is operating with highly nonoptimal characteristics, even to the point of continuous oscillation.

Figure 7-4 shows an adaptive control configuration intended to solve this problem. Here, the control error e_c (the difference between the actual and desired system output) is minimized by feeding it back to the controller, where it is used to modify the controller's characteristics in such a way as to reduce this error. The mechanism by which this modification is achieved constitutes a large part of the highly developed science of adaptive control theory (Narandra and Annaswamy 1989). Again, linear systems have

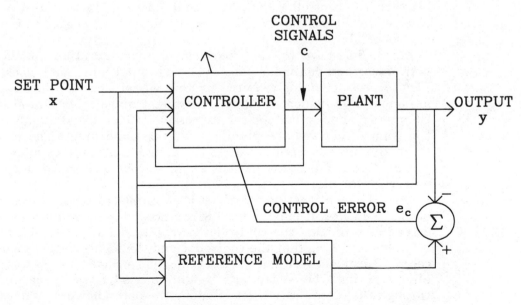

Figure 7-4. Direct adaptive control.

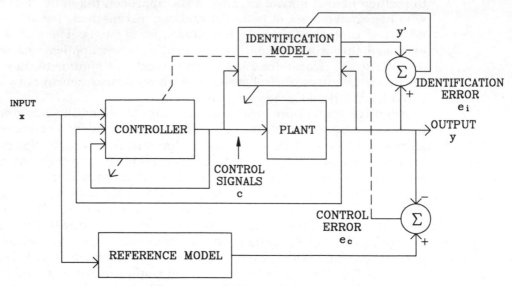

Figure 7-5. Indirect adaptive control.

received most of the attention; the theoretical results for nonlinear systems are sparse and specialized.

The configuration shown in Figure 7-4 is called the *direct method*. Unfortunately there is no known way to use it with nonlinear plants. The problem lies in the location of the unknown nonlinear plant. Lying as it does between the controller and the output, there is no way to determine the changes in the controller's response characteristics needed to minimize the control error.

Figure 7-5 shows the *indirect method*, a configuration that is useful for both linear and nonlinear plants. An additional functional block called the *identification model* is required. In this section the identification model is assumed to be implemented by a network trained by backpropagation (see Chapters 6 and 8; other choices are possible). During training, both the identification model and the plant receive the same input. The identification error, the model's deviation from the actual plant output, is used by backpropagation to adjust the model's weights. Once trained, the model's output will track the plant's output.

Once the identification model has been trained to mimic the plant's input–output behavior, it may be used in a procedure that minimizes the control error by optimizing the controller's weights. This process is easily understood by assuming that the controller and the identification model are cascaded neural networks. If the identification model's weights are "frozen" after training, the controller's weights are adjusted by backpropagation through the identification model along the path shown as a dashed line in Figure 7-5.

System Identification

As we have seen, the indirect method of adaptive control requires a trained identification model that mimics the input-output characteristics of the plant. To simplify the discussion it will be assumed that the plant and the identification model each have a single input and a single output (SISO), however, the principles can be extended easily to multiple-input, and/or multiple-output systems. Furthermore, it will be assumed that the plant is bounded-input bounded-output stable (BIBO) for the class of inputs to be considered. This means that no finite input will cause the output to go toward infinity (stopping only at its physical limit) or to oscillate continuously.

The first step in developing an identification model is to establish a suitable architecture. In feed-forward neural network terms this means determining the number of layers and neurons per layer. In addition, the network may be nonrecurrent (without feedback loops) as in Figure 7-6, or recurrent as in Figure 7-7 where suitably delayed network outputs are fed back as inputs. Note that Z^{-1} indicates a delay of one time unit. This delay may be implemented either digitally, or as a delay line in a discrete time analog system. In this chapter the sequence of delays will be referred to as a tapped delay line. Recurrent systems have been studied extensively (Pineda 1989, Williams and Zipser 1989, Narendra and Parthasarathy 1991) and algorithms developed for their training that are computationally expensive, but have good convergence properties.

For maximum accuracy with minimum complexity, the architecture of the network should match whatever is known about the characteristics of the plant. Plants may be *static* or *dynamic*. The output of a static plant is solely a function of its current and previous inputs. Therefore, it may be modeled by the nonrecurrent network of Figure 7-6 where the network operates on current and previous values of the input. A dynamic plant's current output depends upon its previous outputs; if independent of previous inputs it is best modeled by the recurrent network of Figure 7-7. If the plant's output is a

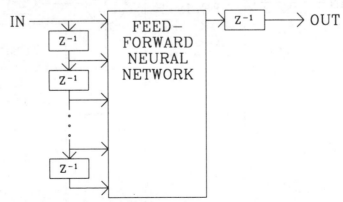

Figure 7-6. Nonrecurrent neural network model.

function of both previous inputs and previous outputs, the configuration of Figure 7-8 should be used—if these effects are separable; if not, the more general configuration of Figure 7-9 should be used.

The number of delay line stages required in both the forward and feedback paths depends upon the characteristics of the plant; ideally they should be selected to match the plant as closely as possible. If the plant's transfer function is sufficiently well known to describe it with the Z transform of a difference equation, the number of delays in the model should equal those of the plant. Often, this information is unavailable. The engineer is then obliged to rely on prior knowledge, experimentation, or an understanding of the underlying physics to estimate the number of delays.

Note that nonrecurrent models are unconditionally stable—they cannot

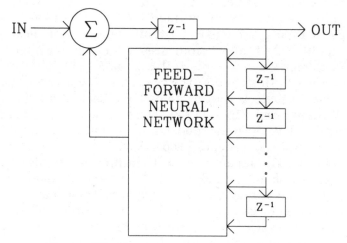

Figure 7-7. Recurrent neural network model.

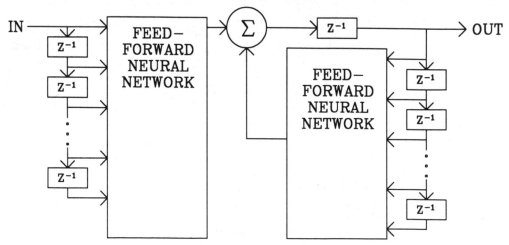

Figure 7-8. Nonrecurrent and recurrent model.

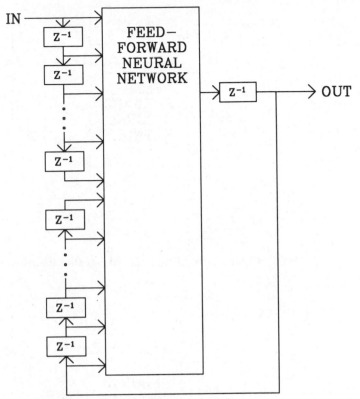

Figure 7-9. General neural network model.

oscillate regardless of the values assigned to their weights. Recurrent models have feedback, therefore, they may be unstable over some ranges of their weights. If the plant is stable, and if the neural network training algorithm is guaranteed to converge to a stable solution, no stability problem exists.

Another stability issue becomes important when one is selecting an identification model. Figure 7-10 shows a *parallel* identification model implemented with a nonrecurrent neural network; this can be trained without difficulty. Figure 7-11 shows the same configuration with a recurrent network. The recurrent parallel identification model has a serious problem in that there is no guarantee that the neural network will converge to a stable solution when modeling the system. In fact, despite many years of research this remains an unsolved problem even when the neural network is replaced by a linear system.

A variation called the *series-parallel* model solves this problem nicely. Figure 7-12 shows a series-parallel configuration with a recurrent network. Figure 7-13 adds a tapped delay line to the input to produce a highly general recurrent model. In these configurations convergence to a stable solution is guaranteed as there is no feedback path between the neural network output and input; the output of the plant, rather than the model, is fed back to the

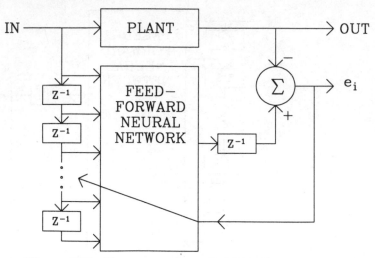

Figure 7-10. Nonrecurrent parallel identification model.

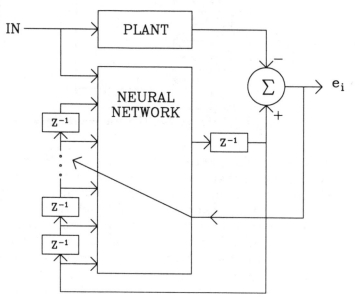

Figure 7-11. Parallel identification model.

tapped delay line. Also, the lack of feedback allows the network to be trained using standard backpropagation techniques rather than the computationally expensive recursive backpropagation training algorithms. In addition, the trained network may, after freezing its weights, be substituted into a parallel model used for training the controller. Because of these superior properties the series-parallel model is by far the most widely used configuration.

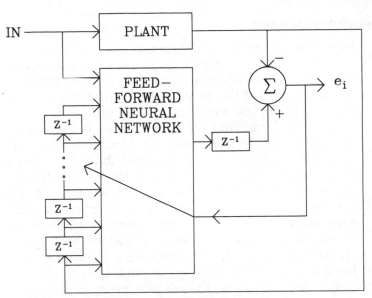

Figure 7-12. Recurrent series-parallel identification model.

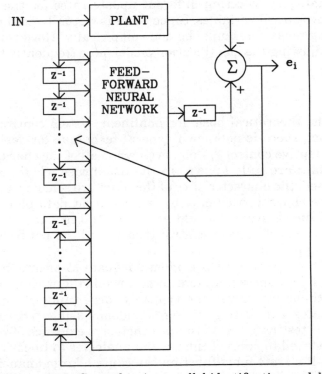

Figure 7-13. General series-parallel identification model.

Combining Identification and Control

In the preceding discussion it was assumed that the weights of the identification model, once set by training, are fixed. This is seldom the case. In general, the identification model must be updated periodically as the characteristics of the plant change with time and operating conditions; this is the major purpose of adaptive control.

Another factor that forces retraining is the limited nature of most training sets. The ideal training set would constitute a complete, statistically accurate representation of the input data. This may not be possible in practice. Acquisition of such a set may be technically or economically infeasible, or it may be impossible to anticipate how the input data statistics will change over time. As a result, the identification model, as initially trained, may only accurately represent the actual plant's characteristics over a limited range of inputs. For example, an identification model trained when the input is sinusoidal may track the plant with high accuracy for this input, but produce large deviations if a triangular input is applied.

For these reasons, the identification model must be retrained, usually without disrupting normal control operation. This on-line retraining is highly desirable but complicated. Updating the identification model may produce complex interactions with the control loop, thereby interfering with correct operation of the overall control system. This problem may be alleviated by selecting different update rates for the identification model and the control variables. Since there is virtually no theoretical guidance, selecting these rates must be done empirically. However, most researchers report adjusting the identification model more frequently than the control variables.

Discussion

The theoretical basis for nonlinear system control is far from complete. In fact, there is no known general technique for designing a stable nonlinear adaptive control system, even when all of the characteristics of the nonlinear plant are fully known. In the usual case where neural networks are to be used, the characteristics of the plant are seldom well known; frequently, they are characterized only by input–output data pairs. Therefore, the designer of such a system should proceed with great caution, understanding the limitations of current control theory, and the nature of the instabilities which might occur.

System testing is seldom adequate to ensure correct operation. While a test can show a system to be unreliable, it cannot prove reliability unless exhaustive. Given the typically large range of inputs and internal system states, exhaustive testing is seldom feasible. Therefore, with neither theory nor testing able to provide conclusive evidence of reliability, the designer is reduced to rules of thumb and analogies to linear systems.

If a system malfunction can cause a large financial loss, endanger human life, create environmental hazards, or cause other serious consequences, the use of these techniques should be approached with great caution (or possibly avoided altogether), unless additional measures can be taken to ensure system safety. For example, it may be possible to incorporate independent safeguards that limit the system's operating range to safe regions.

BACKPROPAGATION THROUGH TIME

Often we can tell better what to do next if we remember what has happened in the past. Similarly, a control system may perform more accurately if it has access to the values of its variables at previous times; this fundamental assumption has motivated the development of a set of techniques called backpropagation through time (Werbos 1990a).

The Truck Backer-Upper

A striking application of a backpropagation through time controller was presented by Nguyen and Widrow (1989) in their paper on the "Truck Backer-Upper." Since it exemplifies many of the ideas common to these techniques, it will be discussed in some detail.

This application trained a controller to back a trailer truck up to a loading dock, starting from an arbitrary position. This is a nonlinear control problem whose solution often defies novice human drivers. A great deal of practice is usually required before one can make the necessary, somewhat counter-intuitive, series of maneuvers. When this article was written there was no other known method for designing an automatic control system to perform this task.

Figure 7-14 shows the problem's geometry. The six independent state variables are:

1, 2. The position of the rear center of the trailer ($x_{trailer}$, $y_{trailer}$) relative to the center of the dock.
3, 4. The position of the yoke (x_{cab}, y_{cab}).
5. The cab angle (θ_{cab}).
6. The trailer angle ($\theta_{trailer}$).

Collectively these will be referred to as the state vector. In the simulation, the truck backs up in steps until it hits the loading dock. The controller (a feed-forward neural network) is trained to produce a series of steps that place the center of the trailer at the center of the dock, with the trailer perpendicular to the dock, ($\theta_{trailer} = 0$).

As with neural adaptive control (discussed above), training is performed in two phases. In phase 1 an emulator (a feed-forward neural network) is trained to mimic the truck-trailer system (the plant). The block diagram for phase 1 is shown in Figure 7-15. During training, a random sequence of steering signals is applied to the truck and neural network emulator. The

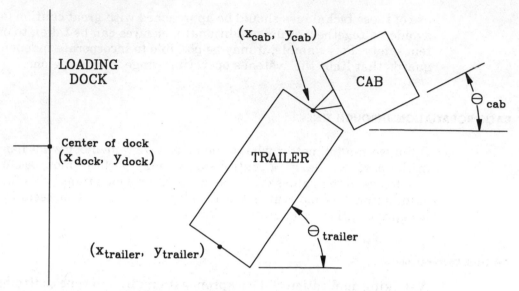

Figure 7-14. Cab, trailer, and loading dock.

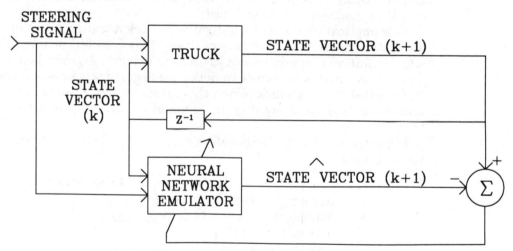

Figure 7-15. Training the emulator.

emulator is trained by backpropagation until the mean squared error between its estimated state vector and that of the truck is acceptably low.

Throughout phase 2 the emulator's weights are fixed. At the start of phase 2 the controller weights are initialized to small random numbers. Phase 2 is divided into two stages:

1. The truck motion stage during which the truck backs up in steps until it hits the loading dock. Both emulator and controller weights are frozen during this stage.

2. The controller weight adjustment stage; controller weights are adjusted using backpropagation.

Figure 7-16 shows the state diagram for the truck motion stage. At the starting position the controller inputs state vector zero ($SV(0)$), and produces steering signal $u(0)$. The emulator then produces $SV(1)$ indicating the new position of the truck. This is repeated through a sequence of controller-emulator pairs until the truck hits the wall at step K, producing $SV(K)$.

During stage 2 the output position is compared with the desired position (see Figure 7-17), and the resulting error is propagated backward through the entire sequence of emulator-controller pairs, adjusting controller weights along the way.

It is important to note that there is, in fact, only one set of controller weights and one set of emulator weights; they are always identical in every step in Figures 7-16 and 7-17. Backpropagation, however, requires the availability of the output signal from each neuron in both the controller and emulator; these *will be different* for each controller-emulator pair. They are calculated during stage 1 and stored for use during stage 2.

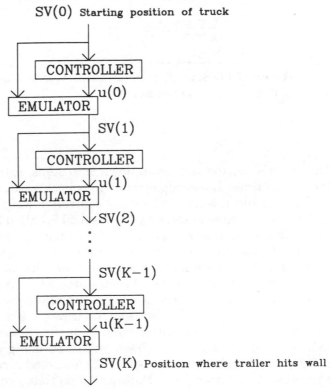

Figure 7-16. State diagram: Phase 2, stage 1. Truck motion stage. $SV(n)$ = state vector at step N.

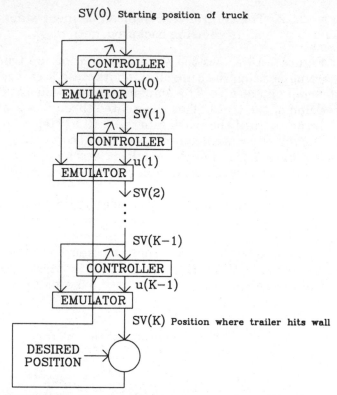

Figure 7-17. State diagram: Phase 2, stage 2. Controller training stage. $SV(n)$ = state vector at step N.

Discussion

The truck's motion is broken down into steps, each of which represents an instant in time. Backpropagation goes backward, from the ending position to the starting position, adjusting controller weights at each such instant. From this it is easy to see why the method is called backpropagation through time. There are many variations of this method and a wide range of applications. The technique is useful wherever a sequence of actions leads from a starting state toward a desired conclusion. The method suffers from a great sensitivity to the accuracy of the emulator. Since it is used a number of times errors are cumulative and can degrade training accuracy.

At the time when Nguyen and Widrow's (1989) original paper was presented there was no known solution to the truck backer-upper problem. Since then several solutions have been published using other methods, including a fuzzy logic technique (Kosko 1992) and model reference method (Kuntanapreeda, Gunderson, and Fullmer 1992) that avoids the sensitivity to the emulator accuracy. A very simple solution was found (Jenkins and Yuhas 1992) that requires only three neurons, five weights, and no backpropagation through time. This solution was produced by "intuitively decomposing the problem," demonstrating the power of using the human intellect to simplify the neural network's task.

ADAPTIVE CRITIC

Often a sequence of decisions must be made without an immediate indication of their effectiveness. For example, when playing chess there is no conclusive indication of performance until the last move has been made. Despite this lack of intermediate information, the skillful player has learned to make "good" moves at every step of the game. This points up the difficult training problem of *credit assignment*, that is, determining which series of actions should be reinforced when only the final result is known.

The truck backer-upper problem described above is typical of a wide range of control problems of this sort. A complex sequence of actions is required with no indication of performance until the truck hits the wall. Backpropagation through time solves the problem, but as we have seen, it has its own complications and performance difficulties.

Foundations of the Method

The *adaptive critic* approach (Barto, Sutten, and Anderson 1983) is an alternative, and in some ways, a superior method. It does not require storage of intermediate neuron activations and does not suffer from the problems of emulator accuracy.

The method is an outgrowth of earlier work on a system called "boxes" (Michie and Chambers 1968); therefore, it will be worthwhile to consider its construction and performance. The well-known pole balancing problem (Widrow and Smith 1964) was simulated, both for boxes and the adaptive critic, and served to evaluate their performance. Since it shows the system operation in concrete form, it will be described in some detail.

The Box Method

As shown in Figure 7-18, a cart with a vertical pole attached is placed on a short track. The pole is free to pivot both left and right, but not forward or backward. The controller's task is to balance the pole as long as possible by moving the cart to the left or right with impulsive "pushes," without causing it to run off the end of the track.

The system has four state variables:

1. x position of the cart.
2. θ angle of the pole with the vertical.
3. dx/dt cart velocity.
4. $d\theta/dt$ rate of change of angle.

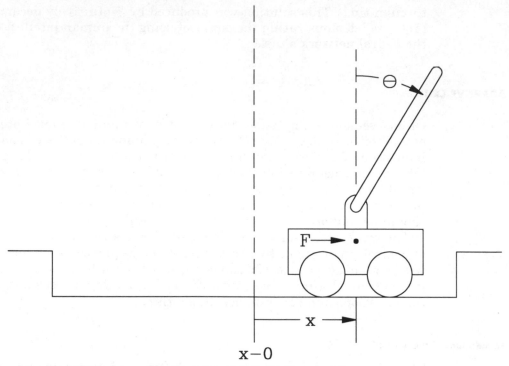

Figure 7-18. Pole-balancing problem.

These variables, taken together, constitute a *state vector* that uniquely describes the condition of the system at each step of the simulation.

The dynamics of the system are determined by the following parameters:

1. pole length
2. pole mass
3. cart mass
4. friction between cart and track
5. friction in the pole-cart hinge
6. impulsive force magnitude
7. force of gravity
8. simulation time step

Remarkably, there is no need for the controller to know the system parameters. (Contrast this with the emulator required for backpropagation through time.) Furthermore, while it inputs the value of the state vector at each step of the simulation, it receives no feedback on performance until the pole falls, or the cart hits the end of the track.

For example, the domain of each state variable may be divided into the following regions.

1. Position x (in meters)
   $$-2.4 \leq x < -0.8$$

$$-0.8 \leq x < \quad 0.8$$
$$0.8 \leq x \leq \quad 2.4 \text{ meters}$$

2. Angle θ (in degrees)

$$-12.0 \leq \theta < -\ 6.0$$
$$-6.0 \leq \theta < -\ 1.0$$
$$-1.0 \leq \theta < \quad 0.0$$
$$0.0 < \theta < \quad 1.0$$
$$1.0 \leq \theta < \quad 6.0$$
$$6.0 \leq \theta \leq \quad 12.0$$

3. Velocity dx/dt (in meters/second)

$$dx/dt < -0.5$$
$$-0.5 \leq dx/dt < \quad 0.5$$
$$0.5 \leq dx/dt$$

4. Rate of change of angle $d\theta/dt$ (in degrees/second)

$$d\theta/dt < -50.0$$
$$-50.0 \leq d\theta/dt < \quad 50.0$$
$$50.0 \leq d\theta/dt$$

Each region represents one side of a hypercube, a "box," in four-dimensional space (one dimension for each variable). Each box defines an operating region for the system. Given the number of subdivisions of each dimension, the total number of boxes is $3 \times 6 \times 3 \times 3 = 162$. Thus, we consider the system to have 162 operating regions, each with its own characteristics. This "divide and conquer" strategy breaks a complicated problem into small subproblems, each of which may be treated in a way appropriate to its requirements.

Each box contains a simple control rule. When the system state enters a box, the cart is given an impulse (push) either to the left or to the right. The magnitude of the push is the same for all boxes; only the direction differs.

Each box has two timers; one starts when a left push is issued, the other on a right push. When a failure occurs (the pole falls or the cart runs off the track end) all boxes are notified, and all timers are stopped.

Also, each box maintains two averages. One indicates the average time to failure following left pushes; the other, the average time for right pushes. These are running averages, calculated over all previous pushes. When the system state enters a box it issues a push in the direction associated with the greater of these two averages. When a failure occurs the averages are updated and the counters reset.

Figure 7-19(a) shows two dimensions of the box structure. Each of the 162 boxes has a controller which performs the tasks shown in Figure 7-19(b).

In operation the system is repeatedly run until a failure occurs. The averages are saved from run to run; each represents the information learned regarding the relative effectiveness of a left or right push when the system enters that state box.

This system has been simulated using realistic parameters for the system dynamics. While performance varied among the runs, in one case it balanced

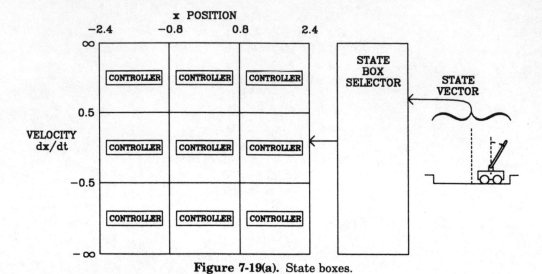

Figure 7-19(a). State boxes.

Figure 7-19(b). Controllers.

the pole for the equivalent of approximately one hour of real time. Thus, the system learned to solve a difficult, nonlinear control problem with no knowledge of the dynamics of the cart, and with reinforcement only on system failure.

Adaptive Critic System

Based upon the boxes system, the adaptive critic produces superior results with somewhat higher complexity. As with the "boxes" system, the adaptive critic divides the state space into boxes, each of which has a controller. The controller is composed of two neuron-like elements, the adaptive search element (ASE) and the adaptive critic element (ACE).

Adaptive Search Element

The ASE, shown in Figure 7-20, inputs the state vector from the cart–pole system. The state box indicator then determines which box the vector is in, and sets the appropriate box_i output to 1.0; all others are set to 0.0. This is multiplied by the weight w_i and summed with a random input labeled "noise." A nonlinear function $f(.)$ is then applied (a linear threshold function is often used), where

$$y = \quad 1.0 \quad \text{if } x \geq 0.0$$
$$y = -1.0 \quad \text{if } x < 0.0$$

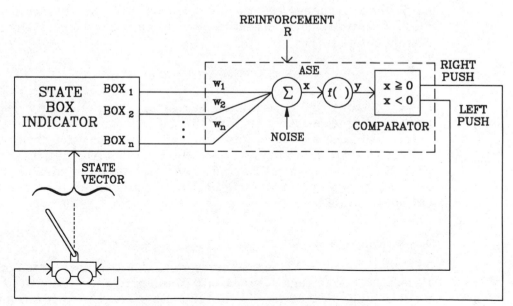

Figure 7-20. Adaptive search element.

The neuron output y is compared with zero, and one of the two comparator outputs is activated, thereby giving the cart a left or right push. This configuration, except for the noise, is like the familiar artificial neuron used in perceptron neural networks.

Due to the noise, the actual output is stochastic; the weight biases the probability of the push direction rather than controlling it deterministically as in the boxes system.

The weights of the ASE are updated according to the following rule

$$w_i(n + 1) = w_i + \alpha r(t) e_i(t)$$

where

α = learning rate constant
$r(t)$ = *reinforcement* at time t
$e_i(t)$ = *eligibility* at time t

Reinforcement, $r(t)$ indicates the change in a performance measure. In the cart-pole problem, it is zero while the pole is being balanced, going to -1.0 on failure, i.e., when the pole falls or the cart comes to the end of the track. Therefore, learning occurs only on failure.

Since the last control action resulted in failure, in the future that action should become less likely for the box. The learning rule accomplishes this by modifying the box's weight so that if the same box is entered in the future, the undesired control action is less probable.

Eligibility is a more complicated matter, but quite logical. An exponentially decaying eligibility value is maintained for each box. Conceptually, eligibility determines the size and direction of the weight modification. It is an exponentially smoothed estimate of the output, y, which results when the system enters its box.

$$e_i(t + 1) = \delta e_i(t) + (1 - \delta) y(t) x_i(t)$$

δ is a constant that determines the rate at which eligibility decays if not reinforced, thus, a change in eligibility persists for a period after the system enters its box. Note that eligibility may be either positive or negative.

This rule for eligibility is consistent with modern theories of long-term potentiation in biological learning systems, where the pairing of a presynaptic excitation and a postsynaptic depolarization leads to a time-dependent enhancement of learning.

Adaptive Critic Element

The adaptive critic element extends and enhances the function of the ASE. It uses the reinforcement signal $r(t)$ to compute a new, improved reinforcement signal $r'(t)$ that goes to the ASE. Its job is to predict a reinforcement signal appropriate for the current box at every time t, rather than only when a failure occurs. This greatly enhances the performance of the ASE as it has much more information to use in adapting its weights.

Figure 7-21 shows the combined ASE–ACE system. Like the ACE system a weight, v_i, is associated with each box. It is used as follows to calculate a prediction of the eventual reinforcement

$$p(t) = \sum_i v_i x_i$$

The weights are updated according to the following rule

$$v_i(t + 1) = \beta[r(t) + \gamma p(t) - p(t - 1)]x_i^{\text{avr}}(t)$$

where

$$\beta = \text{positive learning rate constant}$$
$$\gamma = \text{prediction decay factor. It causes eventual extinction of predictions if they are not reinforced}$$
$$x_i^{\text{avr}} = \text{exponentially averaged value of } x_i$$
$$r(t) = \text{external reinforcement signal at time } t$$

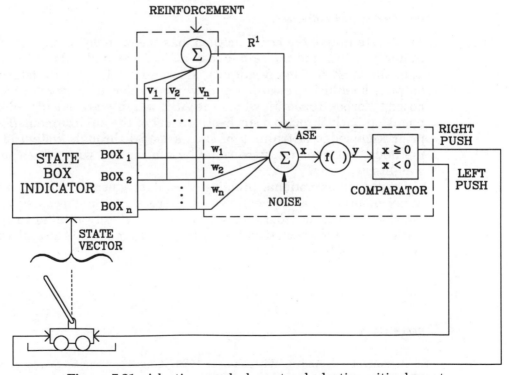

Figure 7-21. Adaptive search element and adaptive critic element.

The derivation of this learning rule is complex and fully described elsewhere (Barto and Sutten 1981, Sutten and Barto 1981). It is beyond the scope of this chapter and will not be treated in detail here. In outline, each box contains a variable $x_i^{\text{avr}}(t)$, calculated as:

$$x_i^{\text{avr}}(t + 1) = \lambda x_i^{\text{avr}}(t) + (1 - \lambda)x_i(t)$$

where λ is a decay rate coefficient.

A weight, v_i, changes whenever the current reinforcement $r(t)$, plus the weighted prediction $\gamma P(t)$, does not equal the previous prediction of the sum $p(t - 1)$. This rule attempts to find weights such that the neuron output correctly predicts the sum of the current reinforcement plus the next prediction.

The ACE's output $r'(t)$, used as the reinforcing signal to the ASE, is calculated as follows

$$r'(t) = r(t) + \gamma p(t) - p(t - 1)$$

This system was simulated (Barto and Sutten 1983) and found to converge more rapidly than the boxes method, and balanced the pole for substantially longer periods.

Modifications and Refinements

This system, like the boxes method, has the problem of having only a single number to indicate the reinforcement. If instead of only left and right outputs the ASE has many outputs, it would be difficult to determine which outputs should be rewarded and which punished. A system has been proposed (Werbos 1990a) in which the ASE weights are calculated by backpropagation back through a stochastic model of the environment. This requires prior knowledge or training of such a model through system identification methods, but supplies more reliable information with which to adjust the weights.

Due to its exceptional promise, the adaptive critic concept has produced many modifications and extensions. Werbos (1989b) discusses variations on heuristic dynamic programming, a method closely related to the adaptive critic technique. For other interesting and potentially useful variants, see Werbos (1990b).

REFERENCES

Astrom, K. J. and B. Wittenmark. 1989. *Adaptive Control*. Reading, MA: Addison-Wesley.

Barto, A. G. and R. S. Sutten. 1981. Simulation of anticipatory responses in classical conditioning by a neuron-like adaptive element. *Behavioral Brain Research* 42:1–8.

Barto, A. G., R. S. Sutten, and C. W. Anderson. 1983. Neuronlike adaptive elements that can solve difficult learning control problems. *IEEE Transactions on Systems, Man, and Cybernetics* SMC-13:834–846.

Cohen, M. and S. Grossberg. 1983. Absolute stability of global pattern formation and parallel memory storage by competitive neural networks. *IEEE Transactions on Systems, Man, and Cybernetics* SMC-13:815–926.

Franklin, J. A. 1989. Historical perspective and state of the art in connectionist learning control. *Proceedings of the 28th Conference on Decision and Control*. Tampa, Florida.

Guez, A., V. Protpopsecu, and J. Barhen. 1988. On the stability, storage capacity, and design of nonlinear continuous neural networks. *IEEE Transactions on Systems, Man, and Cybernetics* SMC-18:80–87.

Hosogi, S. 1990. Manipulator control using layered neural network model with self-organizing mechanism. *Proceedings of the International Joint Conference on Neural Networks*, vol. II, pp. 217–220. New York: IEEE Press.

Jenkins, R. E. and B. P. Yuhas. A simplified neural-network solution through problem decomposition: The case of the truck backer-upper. *Neural Computation* 4(5):647–649.

Jordan, M. I. and R. A. Jacobs. 1990. Learning to control an unstable system with forward modeling. In *Advances in Neural Information Processing Systems 2*. ed. D. S. Touretzky. pp. 324–331. San Mateo, CA: Morgan Kaufmann.

Kumar, S. S. and A. Guez. 1990. Adaptive pole placement for neurocontrol. *Proceedings of the International Joint Conference on Neural Networks*, vol. II, pp. 397–400. New York: IEEE Press.

Kosko, B. 1992. Comparison of fuzzy and neural truck backer-upper control systems. *Neural Networks and Fuzzy Systems*, pp. 339–361. New Jersey: Prentice Hall.

Kuntanapreeda, S., R. W. Gundersen, and R. R. Fullmer. 1992. Neural network model reference control of nonlinear systems. *Proceedings of the IJCNN, Baltimore 1992*.

Miller, T. W., R. S. Sutten, and P. J. Werbos. 1990. *Neural Networks for Control*. Cambridge MA: MIT Press.

Michie, D. and R. A. Chambers. 1968. "Boxes" as a model of pattern formation. In *Towards a Theoretical Biology*, ed. C. H. Waddington, pp. 206–215. Edinburgh: Edinburgh Univ. Press.

Narendra, K. S. and A. M. Annaswamy. 1989. *Stable Adaptive Systems*. Englewood Cliffs, NJ: Prentice Hall.

Narendra, K. S. and K. Parthasarathy. 1990. Identification and control of dynamical systems using neural networks. *IEEE Transactions on Neural Networks* 1(1):4–27.

Narendra, K. S. and K. Partheasarathy. 1991. Gradient methods for the optimization of dynamical systems containing neural networks. *IEEE Transactions on Neural Networks* 2(2):252–62.

Nguyen, D. and B. Widrow. 1989. The truck backer-upper: An example of self-learning in neural networks. *Proceedings of the International Joint Conference on Neural Networks*, Vol. II, pp. 357–361. New York: IEEE Press.

Pineda, J. F. 1989. Recurrent backpropagation and the dynamical approach to adaptive neural computation. *Neural Computation* 1(2):161–172.

Scott, G. M., J. W. Shavlik, and W. H. Ray. 1992. Refining PID controllers using neural networks. *Neural Computation* 4(5):746–757.

Sutten, R. S. and A. G. Barto. 1981. Toward a modern theory of adaptive networks: Expectation and prediction. *Psychol. Rev.* 88:135–171.

Werbos, P. J. 1989. Neural networks for control and system identification. *Proceedings of the 28th Conference on Decision and Control*. Tampa, FL.

Werbos, P. J. 1990a. Backpropagation through time: What it does and how to do it. *Proceedings of the IEEE* 78(30):1550–1560.

Werbos, P. J. 1990b. A menu of designs for reinforcement learning over time. In W. T. Miller, R. S. Sutten, and P. J. Werbos (eds.), *Neural Networks for Control*. Cambridge, MA: MIT Press

Widrow, B. and F. W. Smith. 1964. Pattern-recognizing control systems. In *Computer and Information Sciences*, eds. J. T. Tow and R. H. Wilcox, pp. 288–317. New York: Clever Hume Press.

Williams, R. J. and D. Zipser. 1989. A learning algorithm for continually running fully recurrent neural networks. *Neural Computation* 1(2):270–281.

8

Radial Basis-Function Networks

INTRODUCTION

Radial basis-function networks are attracting a great deal of interest due to their rapid training, generality, and simplicity. It has become clear that they are members of a broader class of techniques including the PNN classifier (see Chapter 3). This class also includes a host of similar paradigms directed toward function approximation rather than classification, thereby increasing their range of applicability. Although closely related, these paradigms have been given such diverse names as "Gaussian potential functions" (Lee and Rhee 1991), "localized receptive fields" (Moody and Darken 1988), "regularization networks" (Poggio and Girosi 1990), and "locally tuned processing units" (Moody and Darken 1989). For the purposes of this chapter they will be referred to collectively as *basis-function* techniques.

Basis-function methods are often compared with the backpropagation trained, feed-forward network, the most widely-used neural network paradigm. Despite its ubiquity, backpropagation has serious training problems; basis-function networks overcome many of these. Basis-function networks train rapidly (usually orders of magnitude faster than backpropagation) while exhibiting none of backpropagation's training pathologies such as paralysis or local minima problems. In some paradigms such as PNN and GRNN (to be described later), no training at all is required. Basis-function networks have one major disadvantage: After training, they are generally slower to use, requiring more computation to perform a classification or function approximation.

These training advantages do not come at the expense of generality. It has been proven (Girosi and Poggio 1990, Hartman and Keeler 1990) that they are universal approximators, that is, given a network with enough hidden layer neurons, they can approximate any continuous function with arbitrary accuracy. This is a property they share with other feedforward networks having one hidden layer of nonlinear neurons. Stinchcombe and White (1989) have shown that the nonlinearity need not be sigmoidal—it can be any of a wide range of functions. Therefore, the generality of basis-function methods is not surprising.

The basis-function network shown in Figure 8-1 looks much like the common feed-forward topology used with backpropagation training; however, its operation is fundamentally different. Rather than starting with random values, the weights of each hidden layer neuron are set to values that produce the desired response: A maximum output for an input identical to its weights, with a lesser output for dissimilar inputs.

Considering the input vector and weight vector each to define a point in N-dimensional space, the neuron's response function $h(.)$ diminishes rapidly as the two points are separated. This response is often determined by a Gaussian exponential function in the neuron, thereby giving each neuron a localized "Gaussian bump" response. The set of hidden layer neurons is designed so that their responses cover all significant regions of the input vector space. Since the Gaussian is radially symmetrical, such neurons produce the well-known radial basis-function network. As we shall see, this is only one of many possible shapes for the response function.

In the simplest case, both the hidden layer, h_{xx}, and output layer weights, w_{xx}, remain fixed (see PNN, Chapter 3 and GRNN below); there is no training at all. In other paradigms, only the output layer weights are trained,

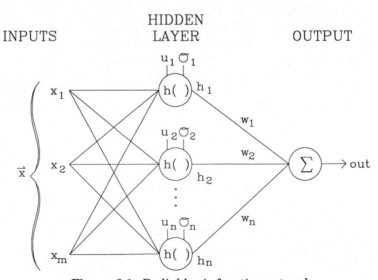

Figure 8-1. Radial basis function network.

reducing the process to the rapid, reliable training of a single layer linear network. There are, however, many variations on this theme; in some paradigms, both hidden and output layer weights are trained, as are the location and shape of the hidden neuron's response curve. These diverse techniques will be discussed in the following sections in order of increasing complexity—roughly the order in which they became well known to the neural network community. It should be recognized that the roots of these methods lie in approximation theory, a science with a long history and a huge literature. Early applications of radial basis functions for classification using a trained output layer were published by Baskirov and Aizerman (1964) and Braverman and Roozoneer (1964). The first use of Parzen window methods to find the weights of a network in one pass, through the data, was published by Specht (1968). Both approaches continued to be used. There has been no consistent attempt to establish priority of ideas, only to present them in a coherent fashion.

RADIAL BASIS FUNCTIONS

The radial basis-function paradigm is the best known and most commonly applied of these methods. It typically uses hidden layer neurons with Gaussian response functions.

Network Structure

Figure 8-1 shows the topology of this network. Here, inputs $x_1, x_2 \cdots x_m$, comprising an input vector $\mathbf{x}$, are applied to all neurons in the hidden layer. Each hidden layer neuron computes the following exponential function:

$$h_i = \exp\left[-D_i^2/(2\sigma^2)\right] \tag{8-1}$$

where

> $\mathbf{x}$ = an input vector
> $\mathbf{u}_i$ = weight vector of hidden layer neuron i. (Note that this equals an input training vector. There must be one hidden layer neuron for each such training vector.)
> $D_i^2 = (\mathbf{x} - \mathbf{u}_i)^T(\mathbf{x} - \mathbf{u}_i)$
> $\mathbf{x}$ and $\mathbf{u}$ = column vectors
> T = indicates the vector transpose

Note that the weights of each hidden layer neuron are assigned the values of an input training vector.

The output neuron produces the linear weighted summation of these

$$y = \sum_i h_i w_i \qquad (8\text{-}2)$$

where w_i = a weight in the output layer.

The operation of the network may be seen more clearly by referring to Figure 8-2(a) which shows the simplified single neuron case. Here a hidden layer neuron has only a single input, x. The exponential function is applied to this input

$$h = \exp\,[(\mathbf{x} - \mathbf{u})^2/2\sigma^2] \qquad (8\text{-}3)$$

Figure 8-2(b) shows how this output, $h(x)$, varies with x. When $x = u$, the function is 1.0. Thus **u** determines the value of **x** which produces the maximum output from the neuron; the response at other values of **x** drops quickly as **x** deviates from **u**, becoming negligible in value when **x** is far from **u**. From this it may be seen that the output has a significant response to the

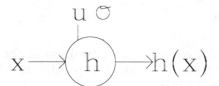

Figure 8-2(a). One-dimensional basis function.

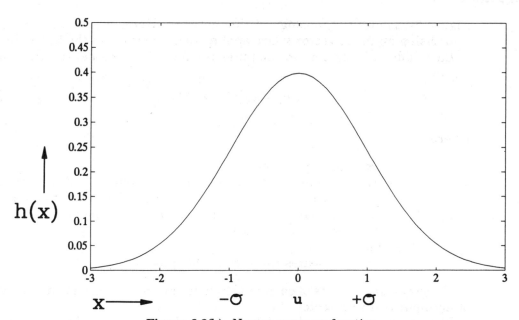

Figure 8-2(b). Neuron response function.

input **x** only over a range of values of **x** called the *receptive field* of the neuron, the size of which is determined by the value of σ. By analogy to the normal distribution of statistics which has the same shape, **u** may be called the *mean* and σ the *standard deviation* of the response curve of the neuron.

Figure 8-3(a) generalizes this idea to two inputs, x_1 and x_2. Now, the radial basis-function $f(\cdot)$ is two dimensional as is shown in Figure 8-3(b). Note also that **u** which defines the point of maximum response is now a vector with two components, as it must define a point in two-dimensional space. The source of the name, radial basis-function, is now obvious; the function is radially symmetric around the mean **u**.

As shown in Equation (8-1) and Figure 8-1, the radial basis-function concept can be extended to any number of inputs, although visualization becomes impossible beyond our familiar three dimensions. Multiple outputs may also be added to the network as shown in Figure 8-4. Also shown in this figure is an optional normalization function, that divides the output of each neuron in the output layer by the sum of all hidden layer outputs. This produces the following output function

$$\text{out}_i = \sum_i h_i w_{ij} \Big/ \sum_i h_i \qquad (8\text{-}4)$$

The network of Figure 8-4 will be shown to be a general form that, with suitable values for the weights, represents GRNN, which subsumes all other

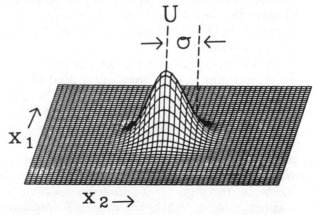

Figure 8-3(a). Simplified single neuron.

Figure 8-3(b). Two-dimensional radial basis function.

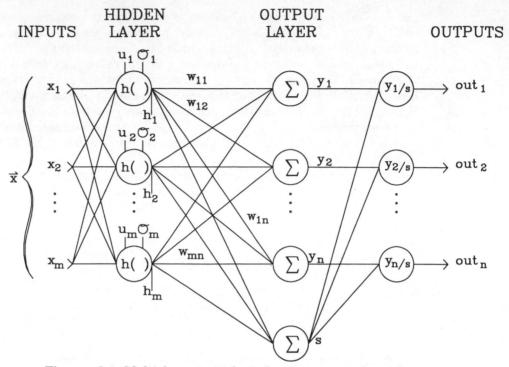

Figure 8-4. Multiple output basis-function network with output normalization.

basis-function methods. The proof of this assertion will be presented in later sections.

It is important to understand clearly the concept of the neuron's receptive field. Figure 8-1 shows that the hidden layer is fully connected to the input; the receptive field is not determined by the interconnection pattern. Rather, it is controlled by the center, **u**, and the standard deviation σ of the neuron. Considering the input vector **x** as defining a point in **n**-dimensional space, the receptive field is that region of the space over which the neuron has appreciable response.

Weighting functions other than the exponential may also be used. The major requirement is that they must tend to zero quite rapidly as the distance increases between an input vector **x** and the mean vector **u**. This ensures that the receptive field is restricted to a small region of the input space. A reason for choosing the exponential function is a proof (Girosi and Poggio 1990) showing that it is in a class of functions possessing the "best approximation property." This ensures that there exists a set of weights that approximates the desired function better than any other set, an attribute not shared by the sigmoidal functions commonly used in networks trained by backpropagation. While the practical implications of this property have not been established, it is at least a suggestion that the exponential function may have fundamental advantages.

It should be noted that the receptive field of a basis-function neuron differs from that of a neuron in the visual cortex (and other areas) of the human brain, where the receptive field is determined by the connectivity of the neuron, that is, the extent over which the dendrites of a neuron connect to adjacent neurons. In contrast, the basis-function network's receptive field range is controlled by the shape of the exponential weighting function.

Network Operation

The network has two operating modes, named, for the purposes of this chapter, *training* and *reference*. During training the adjustable parameters of the network ($\mathbf{u}_i$, σ_i, and the output layer weight matrix $\mathbf{W}$) are set so as to minimize the average error between the actual network output and the desired output over the vectors in a training set. In the reference phase, (where the network is used), input vectors are applied and output vectors are produced by the network.

Training itself has two stages. First the center $\mathbf{u}_i$ and σ_i of each hidden layer neuron must be assigned values, next, the weight matrix $\mathbf{W}$ must be trained. These weights are adjusted by a supervised training method, therefore a training set is required. This set is composed of input vector, target-vector pairs, where the input vector will be referred to as $\mathbf{x}$ and the target vector as $\mathbf{t}$.

The most fundamental form of the radial basis-function network will be described first, more powerful and complicated variations will follow. Their principles will be easier to understand after establishing this background. In this version, the means $\mathbf{u}_i$ and standard deviations σ are fixed; only the weight matrix $\mathbf{W}$ is adjusted during the second phase of the training process. Training is greatly simplified and accelerated compared to the backpropagation paradigm, as only the single output layer is trained, and its neurons have linear transfer functions.

Locations of the Centers u

The location of the centers of the receptive fields is a critical issue and there are many alternatives for their determination. For example, a center and corresponding hidden layer neuron could be located at each input vector in the training set. Because training vectors tend to occur in clusters, this method will, in general, result in more hidden layer neurons than are necessary. The result would be long training times and slow operation during reference, due to the large amount of computation required.

A better approach finds the center of each cluster of input vectors, locating a hidden layer neuron at such a point. There are many clustering algorithms, some of which will be discussed in a later section.

Determining σ

The diameter of the receptive region, determined by the value of σ, can have a profound effect upon the accuracy of the system. The object is to cover the input space with receptive fields as uniformly as possible. If the spacing between centers is not uniform, it may be necessary for each hidden layer neuron to have its own value of σ. For hidden layer neurons whose centers are widely separated from others, σ must be large enough to cover the gap, whereas, those in the center of a cluster must have a small σ if the shape of the cluster is to be represented accurately.

While there are ways to provide an optimal value for σ, the following heuristic will often perform well in practice:

1. For each hidden layer neuron, find the RMS distance between its center $\mathbf{u}_i$, and the center of its N nearest neighbors.
2. Assign this value to σ_i.

Setting N to 1 (Saha and Keeler 1990) considers only the nearest neighbor, thereby simplifying the computation, while producing good results in many applications.

Training the Output Layer Weight Matrix W

Once the centers and σ's have been chosen, the output layer weight matrix $\mathbf{W}$ can be optimized by supervised training. A training set must be available, composed of pairs of vectors. Each pair of vectors consists of an input vector, designated $\mathbf{x}_i$, and a target vector $\mathbf{t}_i$. The target vector indicates the output desired from the network when its associated input vector is applied.

The training process consists of the following sequence:

1. Apply an input vector $\mathbf{x}$ from the training set.
2. Calculate the outputs of the hidden layer neurons, collectively referred to as vector $\mathbf{h}$.
3. Compute the network output vector, $\mathbf{y}$. Compare this to the target vector $\mathbf{t}$. Adjust each weight in $\mathbf{W}$ in a direction which reduces the difference. The following gradient descent algorithm is often used for this purpose

$$w_{ij}(n + 1) = w_{ij}(n) + \eta(t_j - y_j)x_i \tag{8-5}$$

where

w_{ij} = the weight between hidden layer neuron i and output layer neuron j

t_j = target or desired output for neuron j in the output layer

y_j = output of neuron j in the output layer

η = the learning rate coefficient (η is typically $\ll 1.0$)

4. Repeat 1–3 for each vector in the training set.
5. Repeat 1–4 until the error is acceptably small, training stops, or some other terminating condition occurs.

Because of the limited receptive field of each hidden layer neuron, most hidden layer outputs, h_i, will be nearly zero for a given input vector. As may be seen from the weight-update equation, the weight change is correspondingly small for all weights connected to such a neuron. Thus, these neurons may be ignored in the weight-update process, thereby greatly reducing the training time. Also, because there is only the linear output layer beyond the hidden layer, the network is guaranteed to converge to a global minimum. In practice, convergence often occurs 1000 times faster than a backpropagation network of comparable size.

It is possible to regard the problem of training the weight array $\mathbf{W}$ as one of solving a matrix equation. If for each input vector $\mathbf{x}_i$ in the training set, the outputs from the hidden layer are made a row in a matrix $\mathbf{H}$, target vectors $\mathbf{t}_i$ are placed in corresponding rows of target matrix $\mathbf{T}$, and each set of weights associated with an output neuron is made a column of the matrix $\mathbf{W}$. Training consists of solving the following matrix equation

$$\mathbf{T} = \mathbf{HW} \tag{8-6}$$

or,

$$\mathbf{W} = \mathbf{H}^{-1}\mathbf{T} \tag{8-7}$$

where $\mathbf{H}^{-1}$ indicates the matrix inverse of $\mathbf{H}$.

While appealing due to its noniterative nature, this method is not usable in every case. Matrix $\mathbf{H}$ is, in general, not square; it is not invertible, only its pseudoinverse can be found—if it exists. Finding the pseudoinverse involves inverting a matrix which is frequently ill-conditioned (singular or nearly so) and cannot be accurately inverted by simple methods. It is possible to approximate the inverse by singular value decomposition, but this may not be justified due to the resulting computational load, and the limited accuracy of the results. For these reasons, an iterative training technique is most frequently used.

GENERALIZED REGRESSION NEURAL NETWORK (GRNN)

This recently developed system (Specht 1991) subsumes the basis-function methods described above, as well as PNN (see Chapter 3). It has the desirable property of requiring no iterative training. It approximates any arbitrary function between input and output vectors, drawing the function estimate directly from the training data. Furthermore, it is consistent; that is, as the training set size becomes large, the estimation error approaches zero, with only mild restrictions on the function.

GRNN is based on nonlinear regression theory, a well-established statistical technique for function estimation. By definition, the regression of a dependent variable y on an independent variable $\mathbf{x}$ estimates the most probable value for y, given $\mathbf{x}$ and a training set. The training set consists of values for $\mathbf{x}$, each with a corresponding value for y ($\mathbf{x}$ and y are, in general, vectors). Note that y may be corrupted by additive noise. Despite this the regression method will produce the estimated value of y which minimizes the mean-squared error.

GRNN is based upon the following formula from statistics

$$E[\,y|\mathbf{x}] = \frac{\displaystyle\int_{-\infty}^{\infty} yf(\mathbf{x}, y)\, dy}{\displaystyle\int_{-\infty}^{\infty} f(\mathbf{x}, y)\, dy} \qquad (8\text{-}8)$$

where

$$y = \text{output of the estimator}$$
$$\mathbf{x} = \text{the estimator input vector}$$
$$E(\,y|\mathbf{x}) = \text{the expected value of out, given the input vector } \mathbf{x}$$
$$f(\mathbf{x}, y) = \text{the joint probability density function (pdf) of } \mathbf{x} \text{ and } y$$

GRNN is, in essence, a method for estimating $f(\mathbf{x}, y)$, given only a training set. Because the pdf is derived from the data with no preconceptions about its form, the system is perfectly general. There is no problem if the functions are composed of multiple disjoint non-Gaussian regions in any number of dimensions, as well as those of simpler distributions.

Specht shows that y_j, the function value, is estimated optimally as follows:

$$y_j = \sum_{i=1}^{n} h_i w_{ij} \bigg/ \sum_{i=1}^{n} h_i \qquad (8\text{-}9)$$

where

$$w_{ij} = \text{the target (desired) output corresponding to input training vector } x_i \text{ and output } j$$
$$h_i = \exp\,[-D_i^2/(2\sigma^2)], \text{ the output of a hidden layer neuron}$$
$$D_i^2 = (\mathbf{x} - \mathbf{u}_i)^T(\mathbf{x} - \mathbf{u}_i) \text{ (the squared distance between the input vector } \mathbf{x} \text{ and the training vector } \mathbf{u}\,)$$
$$\mathbf{x} = \text{the input vector (a column vector)}$$
$$\mathbf{u}_i = \text{training vector } i, \text{ the center of neuron } i \text{ (a column vector)}$$
$$\sigma = \text{a constant controlling the size of the receptive region.}$$

Note that Equation (8-9) is identical to Equation (8-4) of the radial basis-function (with normalization), except that the target values are used for the weights of the output network. Also, the resulting network topology is identical to Figure 8-4 for the normalized radial basis-function network. The major difference lies in the way that the weights w_{ij} are determined. In GRNN, instead of training the weights, one simply assigns to w_{ij} the target value directly from the training set associated with input training vector i and component j of its corresponding output vector.

Consider a single pair of vectors in the training set, one an input vector and the other a target vector. A hidden layer neuron is created to hold the input vector. For simplicity, assume that the target vector has only one component and the network has only one output neuron. The weight between the newly created hidden neuron and the output neuron is assigned the target value. If there is more than one output neuron, the weight from the hidden neuron to each is given the corresponding target value.

As a concrete example, suppose that the training set contains the following training pair

Input Vector: 1 2 5 3

Target Vector: 3 2

As shown in Figure 8-5(a), a hidden layer neuron is created to hold the input vector. Two weights go from this neuron to output neurons. These weights have values 3 and 2, respectively, corresponding to the target vector.

As another example, Figure 8-5(b) shows a network designed by this method which solves the celebrated exclusive–or problem. The values of σ are chosen to be small; for a given input one and only one hidden layer output is 1, the rest are nearly 0. Clearly, if the weights of the hidden layer neuron equal the input vector $\mathbf{x}$, the distance between them will be zero and Equation (8-9) will evaluate to 1. The small value of σ causes the rest to be arbitrarily close to 0, thereby solving the problem. Note that no normaliza-

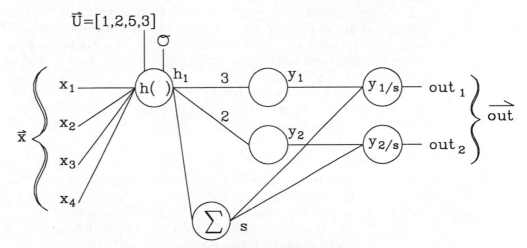

Figure 8-5(a). GRNN example.

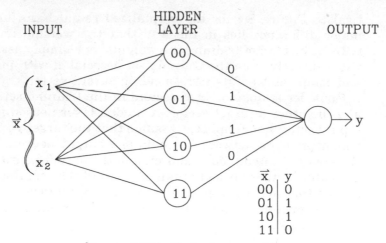

Figure 8-5(b). Exclusive–or problem.

tion is shown as it would have no effect. Only one hidden layer neuron output is 1 for each input; the rest are 0.

THE RELATIONSHIP BETWEEN PNN, AND GRNN

Since GRNN can approximate any continuous function, it can easily be made into a classifier. Doing so produces a normalized version of PNN where each output represents the probability of its associated class. This result may appear surprising considering the differing theoretical foundations of the two paradigms, PNN coming from Bayesian classification theory and GRNN from regression theory. It will be shown that, in fact, these two theories are closely related, therefore the transformation from GRNN to PNN is simple.

A classifier has binary target vectors, each of which has a single one indicating the target class. All other components are zero; the GRNN network used as a classifier will have its output layer weights set to ones and zeros. Classification then consists of applying an input vector and determining which output is greatest.

Each GRNN hidden neuron represents an input training vector, and each has that vector's classification as well as its weights. The following procedure (a specialization of the general method described above) is used to set the weights of a GRNN classifier.

For each hidden neuron:

1. Assign the weight going to the output neuron of the same class the value 1.
2. Assign weights going to all other output neurons the value 0. These will have no effect upon the output neurons, therefore, the weight can be removed from the network.

Performing these operations on the GRNN network produces the network of Figure 8-6. The removal of all zero-valued weights effectively partitions the hidden layer neurons by class. Adding the comparison function to the outputs to find the maximum exactly duplicates the PNN topology, when it is modified by normalization to produce the probabilities of each output class.

This result is suggested by observing that GRNN finds the regression $E(y|\mathbf{x})$. It has been shown (Geman, Bienenstock and Doursat 1992) that this is an optimal estimate in the mean-squared-error sense. Also, it has been shown (Richard and Lippman 1991) that any estimator that is optimal in a mean-squared-error sense will (with enough training data) approach a Bayesian classifier. Therefore, GRNN must approach a Bayesian classifier, as does PNN.

In the following, the mathematical relationship between PNN and GRNN is derived. For those not interested in the mathematical details this material may be skipped without loss of continuity.

The basis for PNN is Bayes theorem which states

$$P(y^i|\mathbf{x}) = P(\mathbf{x}|y^i)P(y^i)/P(\mathbf{x}) \tag{8-10}$$

where

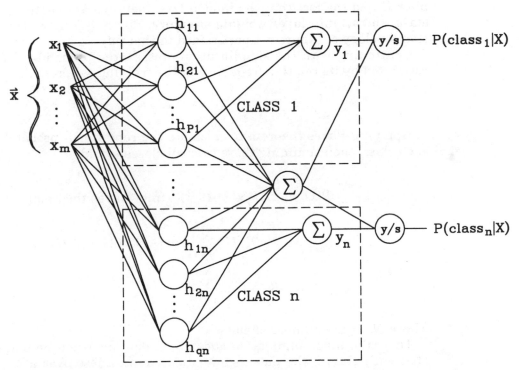

Figure 8-6. Normalization topology. (Note: All connections have weight of 1.0.)

$$P(y^i|\mathbf{x}) = \text{the probability that input vector } x \text{ is in class } y_i$$
$$P(y^i) = \text{the probability of class } i \text{ occurring}$$
$$P(\mathbf{x}) = \text{the probability of an input vector with value } \mathbf{x}$$

In PNN the pdf $P(\mathbf{x}|y^i)$ is approximated by Parzan windows, typically using the exponential function. By the previous definitions,

$$P(\mathbf{x}|y^i) = (K/N^i) \sum_{j=1}^{N^i} \exp\,[-D_j^{i2}/(2\sigma^2)] = (K/N^i) \sum_{j=1}^{N^i} h_j^i \qquad (8\text{-}11)$$

where

$K = 1/(2\,\pi^{d/2}\sigma^d)$, the scaling factor to produce a multidimensional unit Gaussian

$D_j^{i2} = (\mathbf{x} - \mathbf{u}_i)^t(\mathbf{x} - \mathbf{u}_i)$, the squared Euclidian distance between the current input $\mathbf{x}$ and training vector j in class i

$h_j^i = $ training vector (hidden layer neuron) output j in class i

$d = $ number of components in the input vector

$N^i = $ number of training vectors (hidden neurons) in class i

$N = $ total number of training vectors (hidden neurons)

This is very similar to the basis-function equations, except for the multiplier K and the fact that the hidden layer neurons are partitioned by their class, and all interlayer weights are unity. Figure 8-6 shows the basis-function topology of Figure 8-4 partitioned in this way.

Continuing with the simplification process, the probability of y_i may be estimated by its relative frequency in the training set as,

$$P(y^i) = N^i/N \qquad (8\text{-}12)$$

Applying Bayes theorem to calculate the conditional probability of $\mathbf{x}$ for each class, then summing these over all classes yields

$$P(\mathbf{x}) = \sum_{i=1}^{N^c} P(\mathbf{x}|y^i)P(y^i) \quad \text{(from Bayes theorem)}$$

$$= \sum_{i=1}^{N^c} (K/N^i) \sum_{j=1}^{N^i} \exp\,[-D_i^2/(2\sigma^2)(N^i/N)]$$

$$= (K/N) \sum_{i=1}^{N^i} \sum_{j=1}^{N^i} h_j^i$$

where $N^i = $ the number of classes.

Thus, the inner summation adds all hidden layer neuron outputs associated with class i; the outer summation counts these over all classes. The double summation may be eliminated by simply counting all hidden neuron outputs. Therefore,

$$P(\mathbf{x}) = (K/N) \sum_{i=1}^{N} h_i \tag{8-13}$$

substituting Equations (8-11), (8-12), and (8-13) into Equation (8-10), the constants cancel, producing,

$$P(y^i|\mathbf{x}) = \sum_{j=1}^{N^i} h_j^i \bigg/ \sum_{i=1}^{N} h_i \tag{8-14}$$

where N^i is the number of hidden layer neurons associated with class j.

This is identical to Equation (8-9) with the following exceptions:

1. Each output represents the conditional probability of a class, given the current input vector.
2. Hidden layer neurons are partitioned by class.
3. The numerator is summed only over those hidden layer neurons associated with a given class.

Since PNN is a classifier, the target t_i is either 0 or 1 for a given training vector. Therefore the summation in the numerator is taken only over those hidden layer neurons which are in class i.

NORMALIZATION OF TRAINING DATA

Since the weighting function of the simple basis function is radially symmetric, it is usually desirable to normalize the training and test sets so that each dimension has the same variance. The diameter of the receptive field (controlled by σ) should be selected so that the basis-functions cover the space between training vectors without excessive overlap. This is required for accurate interpolation. Figure 8-7 illustrates the problem: Here the data variance is much greater in y than in x. The diameter σ_1, that would be optimal for the variance in x, would result in poor overall coverage, and the diameter σ_2 that would cover y would overlap badly in x, producing poor smoothing.

This problem may be solved by the following normalization procedure. For each component of the input training vectors:

1. Find the standard deviation over the training set.
2. Divide the corresponding component of each training vector by this standard deviation, thereby producing a normalized training set.

The resulting set of standard deviations may be considered to constitute a variance vector S. It is important to save this vector and to divide all input vectors by it when the network is used in the reference mode.

This normalization method may fail if for a given dimension the data is

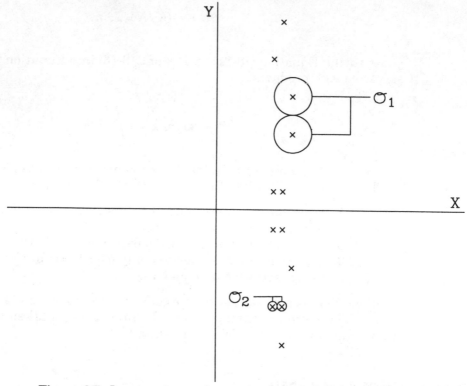

Figure 8-7. Input vectors and receptive fields before normalization.

not distributed fairly uniformly. If, for example, the distribution is multi-modal with large variance differences between modes, no single value of σ will give smooth interpolation. In these cases, separate values for σ may be required for each training vector. This problem is also faced in the RBF net-work; methods for dealing with the problem will be presented in a later section.

Characteristics of the Exponential Weighting Function

Parzen (1962) and Cacoullos (1966) have shown that any weighting function of the form of Equation (8-3) that satisfies the following conditions is consistent: It produces a pdf that converges to the underlying distribution (where it is continuous) as the number of training vectors approaches infinity:

$$\lim_{n \to \infty} \sigma(n) = 0$$

$$\lim_{n \to \infty} n\sigma^P(n) = \infty$$

where

$$n = \text{number of training vectors}$$
$$p = \text{number of components in a training vector}$$

This indicates that σ must decrease as the number of training vectors increases, but not too rapidly.

Alternative Distance Functions

The Euclidian distance function, otherwise referred to as the L^2 norm, is only one of a large number of functions that can be used. Specht (1991) reports that the L^1 or city block norm that also satisfies the Parzen consistency criterion can be used without significantly changing the results, but with a large reduction in the required computations. In this case the distance function is calculated as follows:

$$D_i^1 = \sum_k |x_k - \mu_k|$$

Advantages of Clustering

As with the RBF network, a very large training set may create an unnecessarily heavy computational load on the system. Again, some form of clustering is desirable to replace all training vectors in a cluster with a single vector. Once a cluster of input training vectors is identified, its central vector is found by averaging all vectors in the cluster. Its target (desired output) is likewise found by averaging the targets of the vectors in the cluster. This central vector is then substituted for the training vectors in the cluster. Since the central vector now represents a group of vectors, its "strength" must be increased proportionately. This is easily done by multiplying h_i in Equation (8-9) by m_i, the number of vectors in cluster i. This produces the following relationship

$$y_i = \sum_{i=1}^{n} m_i h_i w_{ij} \bigg/ \sum_{i=1}^{n} m_i h_i \tag{8-15}$$

CLUSTERING METHODS

All of the basis-function methods described in this chapter may benefit by clustering the training vectors when there is a large amount of training data.

For example, this is frequently the case in signal processing applications where the amount of training data is virtually unlimited. If the data forms a cluster, an entire cluster of training vectors can be replaced by a single representative vector, thereby reducing the number of vectors in the training set. This may substantially decrease the computation time in the reference mode. This is true because every training vector is involved in the calculation of the network output. Therefore, the computational load (and time) is directly proportional to the number of training vectors.

Specht (1991) proposes a simple and effective clustering method, wherein a radius r is first defined. The first training vector becomes the center of the first cluster. Each training vector is considered in turn. If its distance to the center of the nearest cluster is less than or equal to r, it is assigned to that cluster; if greater than r it becomes the first member of a new cluster. This procedure performs clustering in a noniterative fashion, requiring only one pass through the training set.

The following iterative method has also produced good results. Select the desired number of cluster centers, and place these in "good" starting positions.

1. Select an input vector $\mathbf{x_k}$ from the training set.
2. Find the cluster center $\mathbf{u_i}$ that is closest.
3. Adjust the position of this center as follows

$$\mathbf{u_i}(n + 1) = \mathbf{u_i}(n) + \eta * (\mathbf{x_k} - \mathbf{u_i})$$

4. Repeat steps 1–3 over all input vectors, gradually reducing η, until changes in $\mathbf{u_i}$ are negligible.

K-means clustering constitutes another well-established set of techniques that can be used to good effect in this application. These include K-means averaging (Tou and Gonzalez 1974), adaptive K-means (Moody and Darken 1989), and many others.

Burrascano (1991) reports an experiment in which learning vector quantization (Kohonen 1988) was used to reduce the training set for PNN. He found that there were only minor reductions in classification accuracy; it was reduced by only 1.6% when the training set size was reduced by a factor of 10. While not tested, it seems likely that this method would function well for the basis-function methods described in this chapter.

There is no guarantee that the locations found by these clustering algorithms (or any other) are optimal. Often the process must be repeated a number of times with different starting locations until an acceptable set of centers is found. Since the network training is so rapid, it is entirely feasible to rate each set of centers by the average error produced by a network trained with them. Cross validation is often used for this purpose. Here a subset of the training vectors are randomly selected and excluded from the training set, and the average error of the network taken over this subset is determined. This is repeated many times, with the mean overall repetitions indicating the error of the approximator. The cross-validation process is repeated with different sets of centers; the set producing minimum error is then used in the final network. If no set of centers produces an acceptably low error, a new set of centers is generated and the process repeated as many times as necessary.

K-means clustering requires a set of initial locations for the centers. These can be assigned at random, however, this is seldom optimal as centers will often start in a region where there are no input vectors. It is better to locate the centers only where there is data nearby. The previous reference shows a systematic way to accomplish this.

Some clustering algorithms may erroneously define a cluster center where no cluster exists. This can make it impossible to train the output weights associated with the associated hidden layer neuron. This is most probable in high-dimensional input-vector spaces, as the volume of the space rises exponentially with the dimensionality. If a cluster center is defined where no input vectors are nearby, the output of that hidden layer neuron will be essentially zero for all input vectors. Equation (8-5) shows that no training will occur in this case. Thus, clustering is most useful where there is an excess of training data forming dense clusters.

TRAINING THE CENTERS AND SHAPES OF THE BASIS FUNCTIONS

It is usually possible to improve accuracy by adjusting the location and/or shape of the basis functions (Lee and Kil 1991). This may be accomplished by generalizing the exponential function of Figure 8-1 to the following (that is within a constant multiplier of the multivariate normal density function (Duda and Hart 1973))

$$h_i = \exp\left[(-1/2)(\mathbf{x} - \mathbf{u}_i)^T \mathbf{K} (\mathbf{x} - \mathbf{u}_i)\right] \tag{8-13}$$

where

$\mathbf{K}$ = the inverse of the covariance matrix of the input vectors

$$\mathbf{K} = [E(\mathbf{x} - \mathbf{m})(\mathbf{x} - \mathbf{m})^T]^{-1} \tag{8-14}$$

$\mathbf{m}$ = the mean vector taken over all input training vectors

$\mathbf{u}_i$ = the vector which defines the center of basis function i. This will be referred to as the *mean vector* for a basis function. Note that if clustering is used, this may not be the same as any input vector in the training set.

The quantity $[(\mathbf{x} - \mathbf{u}_i)^T \mathbf{K} (\mathbf{x} - \mathbf{u}_i)]^{0.5}$ is called the *Mahalanobis distance* between $\mathbf{x}$ and $\mathbf{u}_i$. The contours of constant Mahalanobis distance in Equation (8-13) define hyperellipsoids in d-dimensional space. The shapes of the ellipsoids may be classified as follows:

1. If **K** is diagonal (all elements not on the major diagonal are zero) with equal diagonal elements, the resulting function is radially symmetric; Equation (8-13) reduces to Equation (8-1) (Figure 8-8(a)).
2. If **K** is diagonal with unequal elements, the function is not symmetrical, but the axes of the ellipsoids are aligned with the reference axis of the input vectors (Figure 8-8(b)).
3. If **K** is not diagonal, the shape and orientation of the hyperellipsoids is arbitrary (Figures 8-8(c) and (d)).

Any of these cases may be chosen. Case 1 provides the most rapid training; case 3 the highest accuracy.

Location Adjustment

It is often possible to improve network accuracy by adjusting the locations of the basis-function centers through some form of iterative supervised training. There is, however, a high price to pay. Training becomes nonlinear optimization with all of its attendant difficulties of local minima, long train-

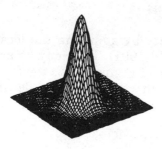
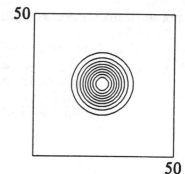

Figure 8-8(a). Radially symmetric basis function.

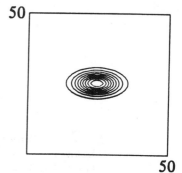

Figure 8-8(b). Diagonal inverse covariance matrix—equal components.

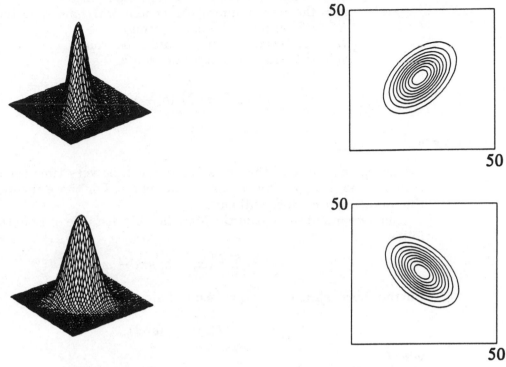

Figure 8-8(c) and (d). Nondiagonal inverse covariance matrices.

ing times, and various pathologies. Furthermore, it has been reported (Moody and Darken 1989) that basis functions may be moved entirely out of the region of training data. Nevertheless, if accuracy is a prime concern, this training may be worthwhile.

The location of each basis function may be adjusted by gradient descent, according to the following formula

$$\mathbf{u}_j^i(n + 1) = \mathbf{u}_j^i(n) + \sum_{l=1}^{d} k_{jl}^i(\mathbf{x}_l - \mathbf{u}_l^i)\theta_k^i \qquad (8\text{-}15)$$

where

i = the basis function (hidden neuron)
j = the component of the mean vector
l = the component of the current input vector $\mathbf{x}$
d = the number of components in the input vector
k = the output neuron
$\mathbf{u}_j^i(n)$ = the value of component j of the mean vector associated with basis-function i
k_{jl}^i = the value of component (j, l) of the inverse covariance matrix of basis-function i

$\mathbf{x}_l$ = component l of the current input vector
$\mathbf{u}_l^i$ = the corresponding component of the mean vector i
h_i = the output of hidden neuron i
t_k = the target vector for output neuron k
y_k = the output of output neuron k

$$\theta_k^i = h_i \sum_{k=1}^{N} (t_k - y_k) w_{ki}$$

Shape Adjustment

Adjusting the shape of the basis function can be very time consuming and troublesome in high-dimensional input spaces. For those inclined to do so, the following procedure will suffice.

It is convenient to expand the Mahalanobis distance of Equation (8-13) as follows

$$\sum_j \sum_k k_{jk}^i (x_j - m_j^i)(x_k - m_k^i) \tag{8-16}$$

Furthermore, k_{jk}^i may be expressed as follows

$$k_{jk}^i = c_{jk}^i / (\sigma_j^i \sigma_k^i) \tag{8-17}$$

where

c_{jk} = the correlation coefficient between components j and k
σ_j^i and σ_k^i = the marginal standard deviations for components j and k respectively

The correlation coefficient and marginal standard deviations are trained as follows:

$$c_{jk}^i(n + 1) = c_{jk}^i(n) - 1/2[(\mathbf{x}_j - \mathbf{u}_j^i)(\mathbf{x}_k - \mathbf{u}_k^i)/(\sigma_j^i \sigma_k^i)]\theta_k^i \tag{8-18}$$

$$\sigma_j^i(n + 1) = \sigma_j^i(n) + \sum_{l=1}^{d} k_{jl}^i (\mathbf{x}_j - \mathbf{u}_j^i)(\mathbf{x}_l - \mathbf{u}_l^i)/\sigma_j^i \theta_k^i \tag{8-19}$$

Note that an input vector with d components requires the training of d^2 correlation coefficients and $2d^2$ marginal standard deviations, a computational load which is often prohibitive in high-dimensional spaces. This load may be reduced to $O(d)$ if the covariance matrix is approximated by its main diagonal, an appropriate approximation if the off-diagonal elements are small.

DISCUSSION

Basis-function techniques are powerful methods with a definite range of applicability. They greatly accelerate the development and evaluation process, allowing experimentation and optimization that would not be practical with backpropagation. Also, their rapid training makes them suitable for situations where on-line incremental learning is necessary.

Unfortunately, the basis-function methods that train rapidly are slow in the reference mode; a feed-forward network trained by backpropagation is usually much faster. This results from the larger number of network coefficients typically required in the basis-function network. This means more arithmetic operations to process each input vector.

This inefficiency is due to the local nature of each basis function; its weights are effective over only a small portion of the input space. In contrast, the weights of backpropagation are used in a more global fashion, thereby encoding the characteristics of the training set into a more compact form. While clustering and training will help, training time goes up rapidly, usually destroying the paradigm's principal advantage over backpropagation. Furthermore, the nonlinear optimization techniques required reintroduce backpropagation's training pathologies.

There have been many efforts to solve this problem, most of which have not been tested on a wide enough range of applications to allow their evaluation. Some of the more promising will be presented here as a guide to the reader who wishes to pursue these methods.

1. Hartman and Keeler (1991) describe a method which uses semi-local "Gaussian bars" as basis functions. These are intended to provide the advantages of the highly nonlocal sigmoids and the speed advantages of radial basis functions.
2. Sanger (1990) describes a variable-sized tree-structured network which uses only those dimensions of the input vector that are necessary to the approximation accuracy desired. Since the computation increases with the dimensionality of the input space, this method can make significant speed improvements with certain types of data.
3. Chen, Cowan, and Grant (1991) describe a method for selecting and optimally locating a minimal number of hidden neurons using an orthogonal least squares method.

In applying basis-function methods, questions arise regarding the number of training examples required and the best value for σ. The answers are not very satisfying. About all that can be said is that the number of training vectors must be adequate to cover the input space with a density sufficient to provide the needed accuracy. In other words, if the network does not generalize well enough, increase the size of the training set. Relative to the value of σ, it must be large enough to produce adequate generalization without excessively smoothing the function estimate. Since the underlying function is usually unknown, one is again reduced to experimentation. Figures 8-9(a), (b), and (c) show the results of a GRNN approximation of a sine function with ten equally spaced neurons (training vectors) and σ at 0.01, 0.05, and 0.1, respectively. As may be seen, there is an optimal value for σ that produces minimum error. Figures 8-10(a), (b), and (c) show the same function

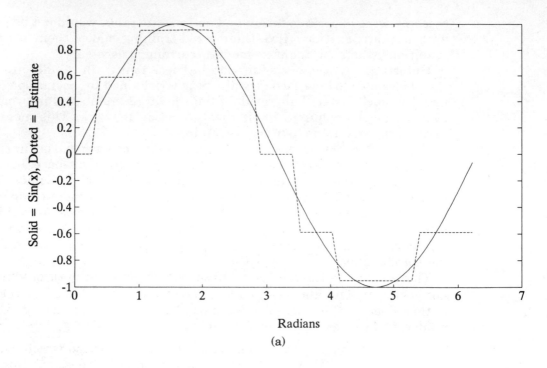

(a)

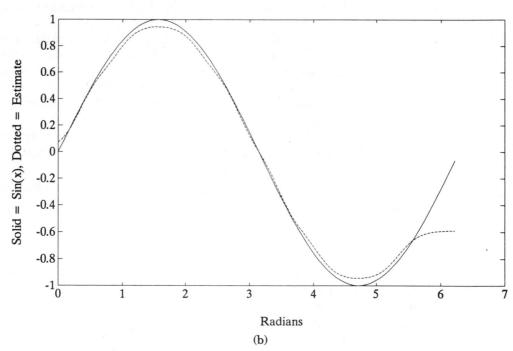

(b)

Figure 8-9. GRNN estimate of sine function. (a) 10 neurons, $\sigma = 0.01$. (b) 10 neurons, $\sigma = 0.05$. (c) 10 neurons, $\sigma = 0.1$.

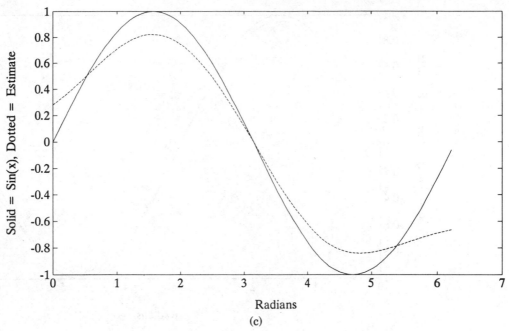

(c)

Figure 8-9. (*Continued*)

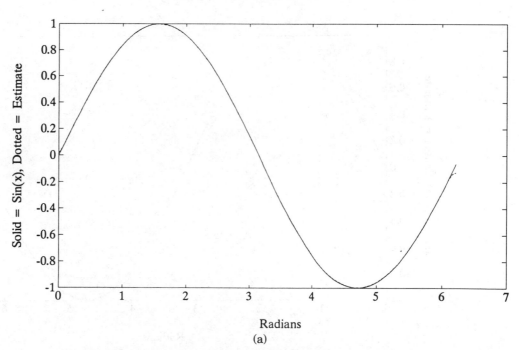

(a)

Figure 8-10. GRNN estimate of sine function. (a) 50 neurons, $\sigma = 0.01$.
(b) 50 neurons, $\sigma = 0.05$. (c) 50 neurons, $\sigma = 0.1$.

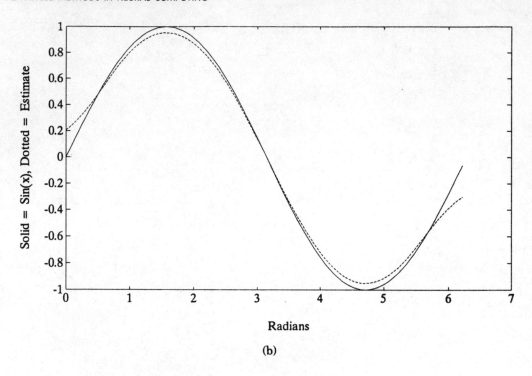

(b)

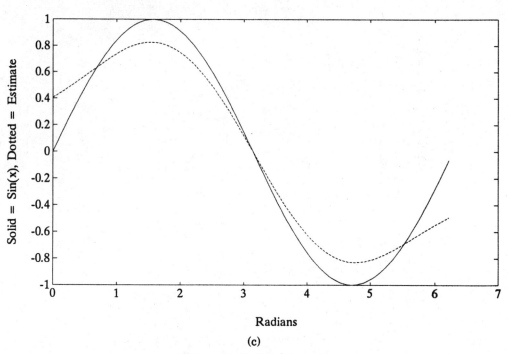

(c)

Figure 8-10. (*Continued*)

being approximated by a 50-neuron GRNN with the same values for σ. Note that the optimal value for σ is lower in this case. In general, as the density of the training examples increases, a smaller value for σ should be used. This makes sense in the limiting case where an infinite number of training examples are used with infinitesimally small σ. Clearly, this is a perfect approximation, as every possible point in x is paired with the desired output value, and σ is so small that there is no interaction.

The high level of interest and research in the basis-function area is at least in part an indicator of the frustration produced by training feed-forward networks using backpropagation. Unfortunately, the rapid, reliable training of basis-function networks comes at the price of slow operation in the reference mode due to the large number of variables involved. It may be that research will lead to methods which overcome this disadvantage, perhaps through the use of basis functions with greater extent. The Ni1000 VLSI integrated circuit, recently delivered to DARPA by Intel Corp., should greatly alleviate the speed problem. With 1024 neurons it processes 40,000 input vectors per second, implementing the PNN algorithm.

REFERENCES

Aizerman, M. A., E. M. Braverman, and L. I. Rozonoer. 1964. Theoretical foundations of the potential function method in pattern recognition learning. *Automation and Remote Control*, vol. 25, pp. 821–837.

Baldi, Pierre. 1991. Computing with arrays of bell-shaped and sigmoid functions. In: *Advances in Neural Information Processing Systems 3*, eds. R. P. Lippmann, J. E. Moody, and D. S. Touretzky, pp. 735–742. San Mateo, CA: Morgan Kaufmann.

Bashkirov, O. A., E. M. Braverman, and I. B. Muchnik. 1964. Potential function algorithms for pattern recognition learning machines. *Automation and Remote Control*, vol. 25, pp. 629–631.

Bishop, Chris. 1991. Improving the generalization properties of radial basis function neural networks. *Neural Computation* 3(4):579–588.

Botros, Sherif M. and Christopher G. Atkeson. 1991. Generalization properties of radial basis functions. In: *Advances in Neural Information Processing Systems 3*, eds. R. P. Lippmann, J. E. Moody, and D. S. Touretzky, pp. 707–713. San Mateo, CA: Morgan Kaufmann.

Broomhead, D. S. and D. Lowe. 1988. Multi-variable functional interpolation and adaptive networks. *Complex Systems*, vol. 2, pp. 321–355.

Burrascano, Pietro. 1991. Learning vector quantization for the probabilistic neural network. *IEEE Transactions on Neural Networks* 2(4):458–461.

Cacoullos, T. 1962. Estimation of a multivariate density. *Ann. Inst. Statist. Math.* (Tokyo) 18:1065–1076.

Chen, S., C. F. N. Cowan, and P. M. Grant. 1991. Orthogonal least squares learning algorithm for radial basis function networks. *IEEE Transactions on Neural Networks* 2(2):302–309.

Duda R. O. and P. E. Hart. (1973) *Pattern Classification and Scene Analysis.* New York: Wiley.

Friedman, Jerome H. 1991. Adaptive spline networks. In: *Advances in Neural Information Processing Systems 3*, eds. R. P. Lippmann, J. E. Moody, and D. S. Touretzky, pp. 675–683. San Mateo, CA: Morgan Kaufmann.

Gagarine, N., I. Flood, and P. Albrecht. 1992. Weighing trucks in motion using Gaussian-based neural networks. Proceedings International Joint Conference on Neural Networks, June 7–11. Baltimore, MD.

Geman S., E. Bienenstock, and R. Doursat. 1992. Neural networks and the bias/variance dilemma. *Neural Computation* (4)1–58.

Girosi, F., T. Poggio, and B. Caprile. 1991. Extensions of a theory of networks for approximations and learning: outliers and negative examples. In: *Advances in Neural Information Processing Systems 3*, eds. R. P. Lippmann, J. E. Moody, and D. S. Touretzky, pp. 750–756. San Mateo, CA: Morgan Kaufmann.

Hartman, E. J., J. D. Keeler, and J. M. Kowalski. 1990. Layered neural networks with Gaussian hidden units as universal approximations. *Neural Computation* 2(2):210–215.

Hartman, E., and J. D. Keeler. 1991. Predicting the future: Advantages of semilocal units. *Neural Computation* 3(4):566–578.

Jokinen, P. A. 1992. On the relations between radial basis function networks and fuzzy systems. Proceedings International Joint Conference on Neural Networks, June 7–11. Baltimore, MD.

Kadirkamanathan, V., M. Niranjan, and F. Fallside. 1991. Sequential adaptation of radial basis function neural networks and its application to time-series prediction. In: *Advances in Neural Information Processing Systems 3*, eds. R. P. Lippmann, J. E. Moody, and D. S. Touretzky, pp. 721–727. San Mateo, CA: Morgan Kaufmann.

Kavuri, Surya N. and V. Venkatasubramanian. 1992. Solving the hidden node problem in networks with ellipsoidal units and related issues. Proceedings International Joint Conference on Neural Networks, June 7–11. Baltimore, MD.

Kelly, P. M., D. R. Hush, and J. M. White. 1992. An adaptive algorithm for modifying hyperellipsoidal decision surfaces. Paper read at International Joint Conference on Neural Networks, June 7–11. Baltimore, MD.

Kohonen, T. 1988. *Self-Organization and Associative Memory*, 2nd ed. Berlin: Springer-Verlag.

Lane, S. H. 1991. Multi-layer perceptrons with B-spline receptive field functions. In: *Advances in Neural Information Processing Systems 3*, eds. R. P. Lippmann, J. E. Moody, and D. S. Touretzky, pp. 684–692. San Mateo, CA: Morgan Kaufmann.

Lee, S., and R. M. Kil. 1991. A Gaussian potential function network with hierarchically self-organizing learning. *Neural Networks* 4(2):207–224.

Lee, Y. 1991. Handwritten digit recognition using K nearest-neighbor, radial-basis function, and backpropagation neural networks. *Neural Computation* 3(3):440–449.

Leonard, J. A., M. A. Kramer, and L. H. Ungar. 1992. Using radial basis functions to approximate a function and its error bounds. *IEEE Transactions on Neural Networks* 3(4):624–627.

Mel, B. W. and S. M. Omohundro. 1991. How receptive field parameters affect neural learning. In: *Advances in Neural Information Processing Systems 3*, eds. R. P. Lippmann, J. E. Moody, and D. S. Touretzky, pp. 757–763. San Mateo, CA: Morgan Kaufmann.

Moody, J., and C. Darken. 1988. Learning with localized receptive fields. In: *Proceedings of the 1988 Connectionist Models Summer School*, eds. D. Touretzky, G. Hinton, and T. Sejnowski, pp. 133–143. San Mateo, CA: Morgan Kaufmann.

Moody, J., and C. J. Darken. 1989. Fast learning networks of locally-tuned processing units. *Neural Computation* 1(2):281–294.

Musavi, M. T., K. Kalantri, and W. Ahmed. 1992. Improving the performance of probabilistic neural networks. Proceedings, International Joint Conference on Neural Networks, June 7–11. Baltimore, MD.

Omohundro, S. M. 1991. Bumptrees for efficient function, constraint, and classification learning. In: *Advances in Neural Information Processing Systems 3*, eds. R. P. Lippmann, J. E. Moody, and D. S. Touretzky, pp. 693–699. San Mateo, CA: Morgan Kaufmann.

Park, J. and I. W. Sandberg. 1991. Universal approximation using radial-basis-function networks. *Neural Computation* 3(2):246–257.

Parzan, E. 1962. On estimation of a probability density function and mode. *Ann. Math. Statistics* 33:1065–1076.

Pati, Y. C. and P. S. Krishnaprasad. 1991. Discrete affine wavelet transforms for analysis and synthesis of feedforward neural networks. In: *Advances in Neural Information Processing Systems 3*, eds. R. P. Lippmann, J. E. Moody, and D. S. Touretzky, pp. 743–749. San Mateo, CA: Morgan Kaufmann.

Platt, J. 1991. A resource-allocating network for function interpolation. *Neural Computation* 3(2):213–225.

Platt, J. C. 1991b. Learning by combining memorization and gradient descent. In: *Advances in Neural Information Processing Systems 3*, eds. R. P. Lippmann, J. E. Moody, and D. S. Touretzky, pp. 714–720. San Mateo, CA: Morgan Kaufmann.

Richard, M. D. and R. P. Lippmann. 1991. Neural network classifiers estimate Bayesian *a posteriori* probabilities. *Neural Computation* 4(3):461–483.

Saha, A. and J. D. Keeler. 1990. Algorithms for better representation and faster learning in radial basis function networks. In: *Advances in Neural Information Processing Systems 2*, ed. D. S. Touretzky, pp. 482–489. San Mateo, CA: Morgan Kaufmann.

Saha, A., J. Christian, and D. S. Tang. 1991. Oriented nonradial basis functions for image coding and analysis. In: *Advances in Neural Information Processing Systems 3*, eds. R. P. Lippmann, J. E. Moody, and D. S. Touretzky, pp. 728–734. San Mateo, CA: Morgan Kaufmann.

Sanger, T. D. 1990. Basis-function trees for approximation in high-dimensional spaces. *Proceedings of the 1990 Connectionist Models Summer School*, eds. D. S. Touretzky, J. L. Elman, T. J. Sejnowski, and G. E. Hinton, pp. 145–151. San Mateo, CA: Morgan Kaufmann.

Sanger, T. D. 1991. Basis-function trees as a generalization of local variable selection methods for function approximation. In: *Advances in Neural Information Processing Systems 3*, eds. R. P. Lippmann, J. E. Moody, and D. S. Touretzky, pp. 700–706. San Mateo, CA: Morgan Kaufmann.

Sarajedini, A., and R. Hecht-Nielsen. 1992. The best of both worlds: Casasent networks integrate multilayer perceptrons and radial basis functions. Paper read at International Joint Conference on Neural Networks, June 7–11. Baltimore, MD.

Specht, D. F. 1968. A practical technique for estimating general regression surfaces. Lockheed Missiles & Space Company Inc. Palo Alto, CA, LMSC-6-79-68-6. Also available as Defense Technical Information Center AD-672505 or NASA N68-29513.

Specht, D. F. 1991. A general regression neural network. *IEEE Transactions on Neural Networks* 2(6):568–576.

Specht, D. F. 1992. Enhancements to probabilistic neural networks. Proceedings International Joint Conference on Neural Networks, June 7–11. Baltimore, MD.

Stinchcombe M. and H. White. 1989. Universal approximation using feedforward networks with non-sigmoid hidden layer activation functions. In: *Proceedings of the International Joint Conference on Neural Networks* (June). Washington, DC. June. IEEE Neural Network Committee, vol. 1, pp. 607–611.

Tau, J. T. and R. C. Gonzalez. 1974. *Pattern Recognition Principles*. Reading, MA: Addison Wesley.

Traven, Hans G. C. 1991. A neural network approach to statistical pattern classification by "semiparametric" estimation of probability density functions. *IEEE Transactions on Neural Networks* NN-2, pp. 366–377.

Watkins, S. S. and P. M. Chau. 1992. A radial basis function neurocomputer implemented with analog VLSI circuits. Paper read at International Joint Conference on Neural Networks, June 7–11. Baltimore, MD.

Weymaere, N. and J.-P. Martens. 1991. A fast and robust learning algorithm for feedforward neural networks. *Neural Networks* 4(3):361–369.

Xu, L., A. Krzyzak, and A. Yuille. 1992. Kernel regression and radial basis function net: some theoretical studies. Paper read at International Joint Conference on Neural Networks, June 7–11. Baltimore, MD.

9

Chaos in Artificial Neural Networks

INTRODUCTION TO CHAOS

Chaotic systems are all around us—in electronic circuits, mechanical systems, fluid flow, biology—even in population dynamics. Despite its ubiquity, chaos was long ignored by the scientific community. With the phenomenon frequently dismissed as noise, techniques were developed to avoid it rather than understand it.

Chaos is unpredictable. This characteristic is anathema to scientists and engineers alike, who seek to extract order from apparent disorder. After all, who would care to publish a paper saying that their results were random? Only recently has chaos been recognized as a fruitful area for scientific study. The results, while far from complete, have produced important insights with hints of major breakthroughs in the offing.

What is chaos? Watch the flow of water in a rocky stream; the irregular swirls and eddies are a beautiful and fascinating chaotic system. With careful observation, patterns emerge. Water may swirl behind a rock in an endless number of ways, but there is always a swirl. It may be larger or smaller, but it will never disappear or exceed some indefinite upper size. Order in disorder—patterns in randomness—this apparent paradox is at the heart of chaotic systems.

Nature and mathematics provide many examples of aesthetically satisfying chaotic systems, however, a great deal of engineering effort has centered on less benign manifestations of chaos. The sudden onset of flutter in an airplane wing, violent wind-driven motions of a suspension bridge, instabilities in space shuttle control systems—these all represent potentially dangerous and destructive chaotic modes. Now that the possibility of such conditions has been recognized, engineers want to know how to prevent them. The answers are incomplete and less than satisfying. Chaos is subtle and extraordinarily complex to describe rigorously. Mathematicians are grappling with the problem but it is easy to pose questions for which there are no answers—so far.

Randomness and Determinism

Generally speaking, chaos is random behavior in a deterministic nonlinear system. Eighteenth-century thinkers would have considered this statement a contradiction in terms; to them randomness could never mix with determinism. For example, in 1776, Pierre Simon de Laplace wrote in his *Philosophical Essays on Probabilities:*

> "An intellect which at any given moment knew all the forces that animate Nature and the mutual positions of the beings that comprise it, if this intellect were vast enough to submit its data to analysis, could condense into a single formula the movement of the greatest bodies of the universe and that of the lightest atom: For such an intellect nothing could be uncertain, and the future just like the past would be present before its eyes."

In other words, given the equations describing all of nature along with the position and velocity of every particle in the universe, Laplace thought that he could predict the future (and the past) for all time.

Heisenberg's uncertainty principle proved this ideal to be unrealizable. He showed it to be impossible in principle to know both the position and velocity of a particle to arbitrary accuracy. Chaos is another counterexample to this deterministic point of view.

Determinism has been highly fruitful; most of modern engineering is based upon faith in cause and effect. Pointing out exceptions to a well-understood and highly successful philosophy does not engender joy in its adherents. Thus, it is not surprising that research into chaos has been rejected or ignored by so many for so long.

Another obstacle has been the nonlinear nature of the problem. Engineers are trained to deal with linear systems (those where response is directly proportional to excitation). When a nonlinear system is encountered, engineers are taught to approximate it by a linear system. Despite the pervasive appearance of nonlinearities in physical systems, the linear approximation approach is not mere prejudice. The behavior of a linear system is fully predictable from its eigenvectors and eigenvalues; a nonlinear system is not. The time behavior of a linear system is described by a set of differential equations that have closed-form solutions; few nonlinear systems have such solutions. For linear systems there is a transient solution that describes system behavior while it is "settling down" after some disturbance, and a steady state solution which specifies the condition approached by the system after a long period has elapsed. A system is said to be "attracted" to its steady-state solution. Since a linear system can stabilize in only three fully predictable modes, there are only three types of attractors: a constant value (a fixed point attractor), a continuous periodic oscillatory state (a periodic attractor), or a quasi-periodic state (a quasi-periodic attractor), the latter being a sum of periodic functions.

Steady state responses of nonlinear systems are far more diverse and complicated. In addition to the steady states of linear systems, a nonlinear system is capable of chaotic modes (a chaotic attractor), where the long term behavior of the system is, in practice, impossible to determine from its current condition. This refutes Laplace, renders linear-system theory useless in such cases, and creates engineering problems which have no known solution.

Paths of Chaos

Mackey-Glass Equations

Like linear systems, chaotic systems can be described by differential equations. The Mackey–Glass equation which follows is a typical example

$$dx[t]/dt = -bx[t] + ax[t - \tau]/(1 + x[t - \tau])^{10} \tag{9-1}$$

By selecting suitable values for the coefficients a, b, and τ, a wide range of attractors can be produced, including fixed points, periodic attractors, and chaotic attractors. In Figures 9-1 through 9-4, $x[t]$ is plotted against $dx[t]/dt$, producing a so-called phase plane plot. In Figure 1, $a = 0.2$, $b = 0.01$ and $\tau = 17$. This produces a system that moves from the starting point on the left, spiraling into the central fixed point attractor. Figure 9-2 shows the result of setting $a = 0.2$, $b = 0.05$, and $\tau = 17$. In this case the system quickly converges to a periodic attractor, endlessly repeating the same orbit.

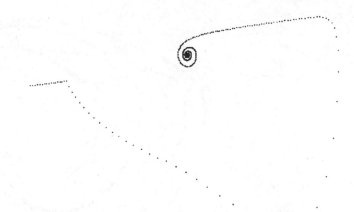

Figure 9-1. Fixed point attractor. Mackey–Glass equation, $a = 0.2$, $b = 0.01$.

Figure 9-3 shows the nonperiodic attractor that results from setting $a =$ 0.2, $b = 0.1$, and $\tau = 17$. Note that the orbits are bounded but never repeat exactly. With $a = 0.23$, $b = 0.12$, and $\tau = 17$ the chaotic attractor of Figure 9-4 is produced.

Mandlebrot Set

From 1950–1970 Benoit Mandelbrot, then at IBM, developed a new mathematics to describe the irregular patterns which he encountered in nature

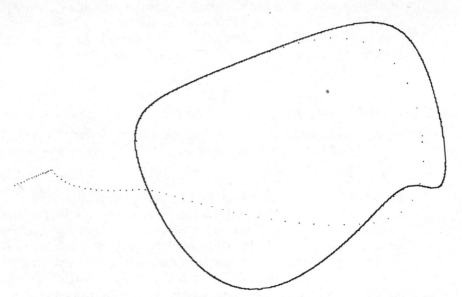

Figure 9-2. Periodic attractor. Mackey–Glass equation, $a = 0.2$, $b = 0.05$.

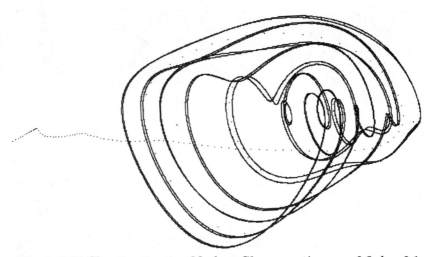

Figure 9-3. Chaotic attractor. Mackey–Glass equation, $a = 0.2$, $b = 0.1$.

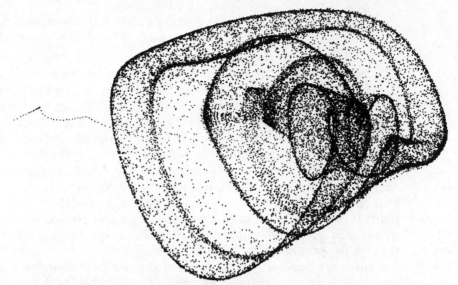

Figure 9-4. Chaotic attractor. Mackey–Glass equation, $a = 0.23$, $b = 0.12$.

and mathematics (Mandlebrot 1983). He coined the name *fractal* for the shapes he saw in clouds, mountains, and coastlines. A key feature of such shapes is their self-similarity; regardless of the scale, they look much the same. For example, if one takes a map of a section of coastline and expands it by a factor of 100 (or any other multiple), it still looks like a coastline. Mandlebrot's fractals exhibit this property of self-similarity despite any degree of expansion or contraction.

At first, there was no clear connection between fractals and chaos. Today, they are recognized as two different aspects of the same phenomenon. They may be used to describe the behavior of a chaotic system, or they may be considered as a geometric tool for describing irregular and self-similar shapes.

The Mandlebrot set (named for its inventor) is a fractal shape with the highest complexity of any known mathematical object. All of this complexity results from the iteration of the following simple equation

$$x(n + 1) = x(n)^2 - y(n)^2 + a$$
$$y(n + 1) = 2x(n)y(n) + b \tag{9-2}$$

where

$$n = 0, 1, 2 \cdots$$
$$x(0), y(0) = 0.0.$$

$[x(n), y(n)]$ = the x, y coordinates of a point at step n.
(a, b) = the starting coordinates in the x, y plane.

To plot the Mandlebrot set, pick a starting point (a, b) and iterate Equation (9-2). Figure 9-5, plotted for 307,000 regularly spaced starting points, shows the overall shape of the set. If the point goes off to infinity after a few iterations, it is outside the set. Plot it in black. Some points never go to infinity; these comprise the interior of the set. Plot them in white. At the periphery of the set are points that go off at various rates; these are assigned a shade proportional to the rate with which they go to infinity. These peripheral points are the interesting region of the set. They contain an unimaginable wealth of intricate and beautiful patterns.

It has been shown that a starting point (values for a and b) that lead to a point $[x(n), y(n)]$ more than two units from the origin, is headed for infinity in the x, y plane. The general rule is to assign to each point (a, b) a shade that is determined by the number of iterations required for $[x(n), y(n)]$ to exceed a distance of two units from the origin. Of course it is necessary to set some maximum number of trial iterations before deciding the point is in the interior of the set; 50–100 produces good results.

In addition to starting values for a and b, it is necessary to define a stepsize and maximum value for each. This determines the scale of the display, and the region of the set being displayed. Note that each point (a, b) must be mapped to a corresponding pixel in the display.

Figure 9-5. Full Mandlebrot set. $\tau = -2$, $i = -2$, side = 3.5.

Figures 9-6, 9-7, and 9-8 show a region of the Mandlebrot set of Figure 9-5 expanded by 35, 7000, and 35,000, respectively. This demonstrates the self-similarity of the set. Differences are clearly apparent between the magnifications, yet the overall patterns are similar. This property holds on all scales. Pick an arbitrarily small section on the periphery of the set, expand it, and you will find a new landscape that still has the characteristic shapes of the set.

The set never repeats its patterns exactly; this is a characteristic of fractals and chaotic attractors. Despite an arbitrary degree of magnification, no exact repetition will ever be found. Thus, limited only by time and the precision of your computer, you can explore the set without limit, forever discovering new and fascinating landscapes, most of which have never been viewed before.

Defining Chaos

Considering the ubiquity of chaotic phenomena, it is surprising that there is no generally agreed upon definition of chaos. In general, it is the trajectory of some nonlinear system. It is usually further defined by what it is not; it is not a fixed point, periodic attractor, or quasi-periodic attractor. Other characteristics of chaos are its boundedness (it never goes to infinity), its continuous and broadband frequency spectrum, and its consequent narrow

Figure 9-6. Mandlebrot set ×35.

Figure 9-7. Mandlebrot set ×7000.

Figure 9-8. Mandlebrot set ×35,000.

autocorrelation function. In fact, the spectrum of a chaotic system's trajectory looks much like $1/f$ noise.

Sensitivity to Initial Conditions

In 1903 the French mathematician Henri Poincaré wrote the following:

> "A very small cause which escapes our notice determines a considerable effect that we cannot fail to see, and then we say that the effect is due to chance. If we knew exactly the laws of nature and the situation of the universe at the initial moment, we could predict exactly the situation of that same universe at a succeeding moment. But even if it were the case that the natural laws had no longer any secret for us, we could still only know the initial situation *approximately*. If that enabled us to predict the succeeding situation with *the same approximation*, that is all we require, and we should say that the phenomenon had been predicted, that it is governed by laws. But it is not always so; it may happen that small differences in the initial conditions produce very great ones in the final phenomena. A small error in the former will produce an enormous error in the latter. Prediction becomes impossible, and we have the fortuitous phenomenon."

Poincaré wrote about the extreme sensitivity to initial conditions that he had observed in chaotic systems. As an example, imagine two identical chaotic systems with arbitrarily similar, but not identical, initial conditions. Set into chaotic motion, the two system responses will, after a time, diverge until they appear to be unrelated. The more nearly identical the initial conditions, the longer the system responses remain similar. Eventually, their chaotic nature will cause the two system responses to diverge. Since the initial conditions can only be known to a finite precision, it is impossible to predict the long term behavior of such a system.

Similar experiences led Edward Lorenz of MIT to propose his well-known "butterfly effect." While studying weather prediction, he found weather to be a chaotic system, and hypothesized that a single butterfly flapping its wings could produce major changes in global weather at some time in the future, perhaps producing a hurricane in the Bahamas, or preventing a drought in the Sahara.

A billiards game on a frictionless table has been proposed as another example of sensitivity to initial conditions (Crutchfield *et al.* 1986). Here, a single shot causes an endless series of collisions. Suppose that one wished to predict the position of one of the balls after a period of time following the shot. To do so would require the calculation of every force acting on all of the balls. Neglecting the gravitational attraction of a single electron at the edge of the universe would produce a significant prediction error after only one minute.

Why Study Chaos?

One may reasonably ask why we should embark an unpromising study of such an unpredictable, analytically intractable subject as chaos. Many have contemplated the problem and decided to work on something easier. In the words of Sir Edmund Hillary, we must study it because "it's there," or more accurately, because its everywhere. Chaos can no longer be ignored. Its effects are so pervasive and its practical consequences so significant that its problems must be attacked on a broad scale, regardless of the difficulties involved. Such an effort is now underway. The progress is slow, but the results are exciting. Research is gradually revealing a wealth of beauty and complexity which promises a major expansion in our understanding of natural phenomena.

Fractal Dimension: Measuring Chaos

When studying an entity it is often useful to define a measure of its complexity. In the case of chaotic systems, fractal dimension is such a measure. Dimension generally refers to the number of coordinates needed to define a point in space. For example, a point in three-dimensional space requires three numbers to specify its location. Similarly, a dynamic system has a dimension which refers to the number of variables required to define the state of the system. The spaces we are most familiar with have an integral number of dimensions. A chaotic system, however, traces a pattern in its state space that has a nonintegral number of dimensions; i.e., it may have a fractal dimension such as 2.7, a concept that may be new and nonintuitive. In one sense, fractal dimension is a measure of the roughness, complexity, or convolutedness of a pattern. For example, the pattern of human arteries has a dimension of about 2.7, a coastline is typically between 1.15 and 1.25, and a snowflake is approximately 1.26.

To see how this applies to attractors, think of the time course of a dynamic system as though it were a point moving in space. For simplicity, suppose there are only two variables $x(t)$ and $y(t)$. This allows us to plot the system behavior as a trace on a piece of graph paper with x–y axes. Further, suppose that this paper is marked off in squares of side length E. Now, count the number of squares, N, through which the curve passes. By one definition (Parker and Chua 1989)

$$N = k/E^D \tag{9-3}$$

where D approaches the fractal dimension of the system as E approaches zero.

This may be written

$$\ln N = D \ln (1/E) + \ln k \tag{9-4}$$

From this it may be seen that D is the slope of a log–log plot of N verses $1/E$. Thus, $\ln k$ can be disregarded as it does not affect the asymptotic slope. This yields the following equation

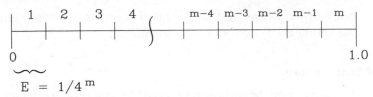

$$E = 1/4^m$$

Figure 9-9. A line subdivided to calculate fractal dimension.

$$D = \lim_{E \to 0} (\ln N)/\ln (1/E) \tag{9-5}$$

We can test this formula by calculating the dimension of a straight line of length 1.0. Suppose we subdivide the line into sublines of length $E = 1/(4^m)$, where m is an arbitrary integer (Figure 9-9). It then requires 4^m sublines to cover the unit line. Calculating the fractal dimension, we find it to be: $D = \ln (4^m)/\ln (4^m) = 1$. This result is consistent with our knowledge that a line is a one-dimensional figure.

As with many other aspects of chaos, there is no final agreement about how the dimension should be calculated. The following five definitions are commonly used: Fractal dimension (capacity), as defined in Equation (9-4), information dimension, correlation dimension, kth nearest-neighbor dimension, and Lyapunov dimension. Furthermore, calculating dimension for high dimensional spaces can be computationally expensive; numerous algorithms have been developed to ease this task. Anyone with serious intentions about performing calculations on chaotic systems should refer to a book such as Parker and Chua's (1990) as a guide. In this area an inefficient algorithm can consume prohibitive amounts of computer time.

Much has been written about chaos. For a semitechnical treatment read Gleick (1987) or Stewart (1989). Also, there is an excellent article (Parker and Chua 1987) that, along with other articles in the same special issue, presents chaos from an engineering standpoint.

CHAOS IN THE MAMMALIAN BRAIN

There has been significant progress in understanding certain functions of the brain and the peripheral nervous system. The complicated electrochemical activities of individual neurons are becoming well understood, major neural pathways have been traced, and the functions of many regions of the brain have been identified.

We know how externally applied sensory stimuli are converted to neuronal pulses, how these are directly or indirectly transmitted to the area of the cerebral cortex (the outer layer of the brain) appropriate to the sense of taste, touch, sight, hearing, and smell, and something about the processing of these signals. What is less clear is how these sensory stimuli are represented within the various layers of the cortex. There is, however, a growing body of evidence that patterns of stimuli are represented as chaotic attractors in certain areas of the cortex.

Chaos in the Olfactory System

Consider how odors are processed by the olfactory system. A "sniff" conveys an odor to a set of sensors in the nose. Their response is relayed to the olfactory bulb in the brain. After processing, the sensory signal is transmitted to the olfactory region of the sensory cortex. There are a number of puzzling aspects of this process of olfaction, e.g., the mechanism of generalization. Every sniff of a specific odor must produce the same response, despite the fact that differing air currents may cause the odor molecules to fall on entirely different sets of sensors. How can widely separated sets of sensors produce the same response? Also, the cortical response to the sniff is remarkably fast and widespread. About 0.1 sec after the application of the stimulus a coherent response is detected over a significant region. This finding is inconsistent with the longer delay predictions made using the known firing rates of the individual neurons and their axonal propagation times.

Recent work has identified some remarkable characteristics of this process; it appears that each odor is represented in the brain by a chaotic attractor (Freeman 1975; Freeman 1987a,b; Yao and Freeman 1989; Yao and Freeman 1990; Freeman 1991). This is consistent with anatomical studies which reveal that the mammalian olfactory system (like many other parts of the brain) can be modeled as a distributed, nonlinear feedback system with multiple loops. Clearly, such a system is capable of exhibiting chaotic behavior; it may even be inevitable.

Chaotic attractors in the brain were detected by an elegant experiment (Freeman 1987a, 1991). An array of 64 electrodes was placed on the exterior surface of the olfactory bulb of a rabbit trained to respond to specific odors. The olfactory bulb is a small part of the brain that processes odor sensory responses from receptors in the animal's nose. As each odor was sniffed, the 64 electrical signals from the electrodes were recorded simultaneously. In the absence of an odor the olfactory bulb showed a low, but substantial degree of activity, with neurons firing in a seemingly random pattern. When the rabbit sniffed a known odor, a highly irregular but essentially similar pattern appeared on all electrodes. The amplitudes of the signals varied among electrodes; also, there were different time delays. Nevertheless, there was a great similarity between the signals; the same patterns of dips and peaks occurred over the entire array. Furthermore, these signals were found to be characteristic of a low dimension attractor, with each distinct odor producing a characteristic pattern.

From this, Freeman concluded that the olfactory system represents each odor as a distinct chaotic attractor, perhaps involving all neurons on the olfactory bulb. When there is no odor present, a state of low excitation is entered which "primes" the system so that it can switch rapidly into the appropriate chaotic state.

A Chaotic Model of the Olfactory System

Based on anatomical evidence and computer simulation, Freeman and his co-workers (Yao and Freeman 1990) have developed the model of the olfactory system shown in Figure 9-10. Here receptors in the nose are stimulated by an odor, sending signals to the olfactory bulb (OB) via the primary olfactory nerve (PON). These signals activate periglomerular neurons (P), these being heavily interconnected by excitatory synapses. This causes the spread of excitation over a broad region of the bulb. Mitral cells (M) have excitatory connections from the periglomerular neurons as well as the primary olfactory nerve. These, likewise, are heavily interconnected by excitatory synapses. Granule cells (G) receive excitatory inputs from the mitral cells, but return inhibitory signals. Also, granule cells are densely interconnected and mutually inhibitory. Thus, mitral cells excite granule cells, that in turn inhibit mitral cells. This feedback results in these cell groups forming low frequency oscillators.

The mitral cells transmit their output by way of the lateral olfactory tract (LOT) to the anterior olfactory nucleus (AON) and the prepyriform cortex

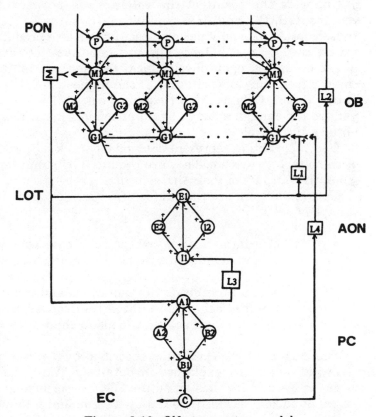

Figure 9-10. Olfactory system model.

(PC). Note that cell groups of E and I neurons in the AON, like the A and B neuron groups in the PC, form oscillators like the M- and G-cell groups in the OB.

Despite the complexity of the model, it is actually highly simplified relative to the microscopic complexity of the olfactory system; it has been found that millions of neurons and billions of synapses participate in the process of olfaction. Freeman proposes, however, that the surface activity he has recorded reflects the local mean fields of microscopic activity, measured at a macroscopic level. He suggests that the similarity of single neuronal activity, to the massed activity he sees in brain waves may be an example of the scale invariance which is characteristic of chaotic systems. He believes that the microscopic sensory input to the cortex determines the transitions of the activity of large populations from one chaotic attractor to the next. This may be an example of the sensitivity to initial conditions of chaotic systems, similar to the "butterfly" that starts the hurricane. If so, then a major advantage of chaotic dynamics may prove to be the selective amplification that the sensory cortex provides for exceedingly minute but important sensory inputs, such as the flash of a headlight, a faint whiff of smoke, or the cracking of a distant twig.

Chaos is the result of the interactions between the three oscillatory regions, OB, PC, and AON, conducted by paths L_1, L_2, L_3, and L_4. Without these connections only periodic oscillations are produced. For a chaotic system, OB-, PC-, and AON-cell groups must oscillate at incommensurate frequencies. Based upon physiological measurements, it has been found that the OB frequency of oscillation is the highest, AON is next highest, and PC is the lowest. OB and AON frequencies are all within a factor of two of PC, yet are far enough apart to avoid phase locking which would cause them to enter a limit cycle.

L_1, L_2, L_3, and L_4 represent delayed feedback paths between separate areas of the olfactory system. They are produced by summing and averaging, over time, the outputs of their source units.

Note that there are four kinds of feedbacks operating between cells and groups of cells:

1. Mutual excitation, where cells pass excitatory signals between them, causing the effect of a stimulus to be expressed over a wide area.
2. Mutual inhibition that sharpens and localizes responses.
3. Delayed negative feedback that causes oscillations.
4. Delayed feedback that leads to chaos.

The system of Figure 9-10 is described by a set of nonlinear coupled differential equations, explained in detail by Yao and Freeman (1989). Each circle in Figure 9-10 has an output Xmn described by a second-order differential equation; each is followed by a sigmoidal nonlinearity $Q(.)$, defined as follows

$$Q(v) = Qm[1 - e^{-k/Qm}] \qquad \text{if } v > -u_0$$

$$Q(v) = -1 \qquad\qquad\qquad \text{if } v \le -u_0 \qquad (9\text{-}7)$$

where

$$k = e^v - 1$$
$$u_0 = -\ln[1 - Q_m \ln(1 + 1/Q_m)]$$
$$a, b = \text{loop rate constants}$$

Every connection between circles has a weight. Most weights are fixed. However, certain weights are adaptive, being set during learning.

Inputs to the system are operated by a sigmoidal function that is time invariant through sequences of bursts, but is subject to increased steepness with increasing motivation and arousal. Also, the steepness of the sigmoid is greater in several parts of the olfactory cortex than in the bulb (Eeckman and Freeman 1991). The basal activity is maintained by the periglomerular (P) cells, which are stabilized by the sigmoid without the necessity for inhibitory feedback control (Freeman 1974). This maintains a basal level of excitation in the system in the absence of external input, thereby ensuring a rapid change to the desired attractor.

Learning

Trainable weights exist as excitatory connections between M_1 units. These weights are modified during training using a Hebbian correlation method. Initially, all weights are set to K_{low}. A binary-input vector V is applied. If components i and j of V are both 1, then the corresponding weight is set to K_{high}; otherwise it is unchanged. Thus, weights are binary and learn in a single pass.

Parameters

The system that has been described involves a large number of parameters determined by physiological measurements as well as computer simulations. These are defined by Yao and Freeman (1989).

The computational load for the system simulation was substantial. For 8 inputs, Runge–Kutta integration was used to solve 9 second-order and 10 eighth-order differential equations with a parallel algorithm, using a time step of 0.5 ms.

Pattern Classification

An eight-input version of the system was tested on a simple pattern classification task in software (Yao and Freeman 1989) and in hardware (Eisenberg, Freeman, and Burke 1989). The network was trained on patterns $A = (1\ 0\ 0\ 1\ 0\ 0\ 1\ 0)$ and $B = (0\ 1\ 0\ 0\ 1\ 0\ 0\ 1)$. The outputs of the G cells were observed. In the absence of an input excitation, the cells showed a low-level, aperiodic, chaotic, noise-like activity. When pattern A or B was applied, the array of G cells showed higher d.c. offsets for cells with a 1 applied, than for cells with an input of 0. Also, applying a pattern moves the system out of its basal level of activity into a mode which is closer to a limit cycle.

One hypothesis is that training forms a chaotic attractor for each pattern. With no pattern applied the system remains in a basal chaotic state which primes it for rapid change to one or the other attractor when an input pattern is applied.

The system has been shown to generalize. Applying the pattern $A^* = (0\ 0\ 0\ 1\ 0\ 0\ 1\ 0)$ (which has the first bit changed relative to pattern A), produced the same qualitative pattern of responses as did pattern A; the same G cells have high or low d.c. levels. Similarly, pattern $B^* = (0\ 0\ 0\ 0\ 1\ 0\ 0\ 0)$ produces the same response as pattern B. Also, the system discriminates among input patterns, producing different d.c. levels on the G cells for input patterns $(0\ 0\ 1\ 0\ 0\ 1\ 0\ 0)$ and $(0\ 0\ 1\ 0\ 0\ 0\ 0\ 0)$.

Comparisons to the Biological System

The system was designed to simulate the olfactory system, and it does so in the following significant respects:

1. The overall response to input stimulation has been shown to be a global increase in chaotic activity, indicating a chaotic attractor involving the entire system.
2. With proper system parameters, the stimulated activity pattern is qualitatively independent of the number of inputs. This scaling invariance is required of any biologically plausible model of the olfactory system, as function must continue despite the loss of neurons with age.
3. The response is independent of initial conditions. Unlike other artificial neural systems with attractors, there is no need to return to a state of low excitation before accepting a new input. Seldom, if ever, does an animal in a real-world environment experience a gap in excitation between stimuli.
4. Spatial coherence is observed. Like its biological counterpart the pattern of activity (its peaks and dips) is consistent throughout the system, even though there are amplitude and time-delay differences.
5. After training, applying one of the training vectors causes the system to consistently produce the same spatial pattern of excitation; no such pattern is produced for input vectors unlike the training vectors.

Despite these similarities, the simulation differs from the biological system in two major respects. It produces a pattern of d.c. levels, whereas, the olfactory bulb represents patterns in the amplitudes of its oscillations. Freeman reports that with a new (and still unpublished) parameter set, his model now classifies correctly on the basis of amplitudes of oscillation, rather than d.c. shifts.

Also, the simulation is slow to switch between chaotic attractors, requiring roughly 50 ms versus around 6 ms for the olfactory system.

An Industrial Application

The chaotic olfactory system model described above has been applied to the detection of defects in small mechanical components (machine screws, ball studs, and Phillips tips) (Yao et al. 1991). The system uses ultrasonic energy to measure characteristics of parts as they move down a chute (Buckley 1975). Classification results compare favorably to those produced by a binary associator, standard statistical approaches, and a three-layer backpropagation network.

A feature vector having 64 components was presented to the olfactory model simulated on a Cray X-MP/14 computer. Despite the size of the system, scaling invariance ensures that the qualitative performance characteristics of smaller systems are duplicated.

The system's task was to separate good parts from those known to be defective. The task was known to be difficult; parts can come down the chute reversed, and at any angular rotation. Nevertheless, 100% of the unacceptable objects were correctly classified, as were 80% of the acceptable objects. A backpropagation network with the same problem correctly classified 50–100% of the unacceptable objects, and 12.5–100% of acceptable objects, depending upon the type of object being classified.

DISCUSSION

Freeman and his co-workers have compiled an impressive body of theoretical and experimental evidence that the olfactory system represents patterns as chaotic attractors. Furthermore, he has shown that an artificial neural system that models what is known of the biological system has accuracy advantages over conventional artificial neural network techniques, as well as standard statistical methods in at least one practical application.

The artificial system has prodigious computational requirements to solve the large number of simultaneous differential equations. With the cost of computation being reduced by 50% every two to three years, this alone should not affect the ultimate utility of the method. Also, the implementation in analog hardware yields a more economical system.

Despite the many parallels between the artificial and biological systems, one may reasonably ask if the brain really works this way, particularly the other sensory systems that operate through the neocortex rather than the simpler paleocortex.

Freeman's work is controversial; while respected, his results are not universally accepted among knowledgeable researchers, a situation faced by most innovators. Time, further study, and application experience will tell if this is an accurate model of the olfactory system, and if it has performance advantages which justify its use in a broad range of real-world applications.

REFERENCES

Buckley, S. 1975. Phase monitored inspection. *Proceedings of the 3rd North American Metalwork Res. Conference*, pp. 701–712.

Crutchfield, J. P., J. D. Farmer et al. 1986. *Scientific American* (December), pp. 46–57.

Eisenberg, J., W. J. Freeman, and B. Burke. 1989. Hardware architecture of a neural network model simulating pattern recognition by the olfactory bulb. *Neural Networks* 2(4):315–325.

Freeman, W. J. 1975. *Mass Action in the Nervous System.* New York: Academic Press.

Freeman, W. J. 1979. Nonlinear gain mediating cortical stimulus-response relations. *Biological Cybernetics* 33:237–247.

Freeman, W. J. 1987a. Methods of Analysis of Brain, Electrical, and Magnetic Signals, *EEG Handbook* (revised series, vol. 1, Chapter 18), eds. A. S. Gevins and A. Remond. New York: Elsevier.

Freeman, W. J. 1987b. Simulation of chaotic EEG patterns with a dynamic model of the olfactory system. *Biological Cybernetics* 56:139–150.

Freeman, W. J. 1989. Perceptual coding in olfaction and vision. Accepted for publication in *Scientific American*.

Freeman, W. J. and Y. Yao. 1990. Chaos in the biodynamics of pattern recognition by neural networks. *Proceedings of the International Joint Conference on Neural Networks* 1:243–249.

Gleick, J. 1987. *Chaos: Making a New Science.* New York: Viking Penguin.

Mandlebrot, B. 1983. *The Fractal Geometry of Nature.* New York: Freeman.

Stewart, I. 1990. *Does God Play Dice: The Mathematics of Chaos.* Cambridge: Blackwell.

Parker, T. S and L. O. Chua. 1987. Chaos: A tutorial for engineers. *Proceedings of the IEEE* 75(8):982–1007.

Parker, T. S. and L. O. Chua. 1989. *Practical Numeric Algorithms for Chaotic Systems.* New York: Springer-Verlag.

Yao, Y. and W. J. Freeman. 1989. Pattern recognition in olfactory systems: Modeling and simulation. *Proceedings of the International Joint Conference on Neural Networks* 1:699–704.

Yao, Y. and W. J. Freeman. 1989. Model of biological pattern recognition with spatially chaotic dynamics. *Neural Networks* 3:153–170.

10

Fuzzy Logic

WHY FUZZY LOGIC?

In Japan, fuzzy logic technology is a well-developed, broadly applied computational method. The Japanese have installed fuzzy logic systems in hundreds of consumer and industrial applications, such as trains, elevators, air conditioners, VCR cameras, and even golf swing analyzers. For example, in 1985, Hitachi installed a fuzzy logic controlled subway system in Sendai, Japan, an application which has demonstrated the superiority of fuzzy over conventional controllers. The trains accelerate more quickly and smoothly, while providing energy savings of more than 10% when compared to their conventional counterparts.

Quick to sense technology which can lead to commercial advantage, Japanese government and industrial firms have funded a 70 million dollar, five-year program to develop fuzzy methods. Directors of this program include top executives from many of the leading Japanese electronics firms.

In dramatic contrast, fuzzy logic has found a cold reception in the West, with responses ranging from indifference to outright hostility. Engineers have ignored its proven advantages, researchers have generally found it uninteresting, and statisticians have said that fuzzy logic is not distinct from statistics, devoid of content, even "silly." The reasons for this response are unclear, perhaps representing a Western cultural bias rather than reality. Since the time of Aristotle, Western logic has been two valued; that is, a statement cannot be simultaneously partially true and partially false. This law of noncontradiction, along with the law of the excluded middle (that A and not A cover all possibilities), are at the basis of Western mathematics and statistics. Fuzzy logic violates these assumptions.

Eastern philosophy and religion make different assumptions. The idea of contradiction, that something can and must coexist with its opposite, is essential to their world view. This concept of reality makes fuzzy logic seem natural, even inevitable.

In the West, Aristotelian logic deals with the truth value of statements, classifying them as true or false. Unfortunately, much of human experience is not black or white; infinite shades of gray best describe the world. Is a car fast or slow, a house large or small, a man wise or foolish? A yes/no answer to these questions is usually a misleading oversimplification. Converting continuous variables into binary 1's and 0's discards most of the significant information, yet this is what is required to apply the rules of Aristotelian logic.

The Western answer to this dilemma has been statistics; we can express the probability that a car is fast or slow as a real number from 0–1. Fuzzy logic produces the same result, mapping cars by speed into numbers between 0 and 1. This has produced a great deal of confusion, leading some to declare that statistics and fuzzy logic are identical. As we shall see, the differences are fundamental; the basic axioms of the two systems are different and incompatible.

FUZZY CONTROLLERS

Fuzzy systems have been used in control applications more often than any other area. These controllers are easy to design, often requiring only a few hours to develop a sophisticated system. Despite their simplicity, typical performance has been high, usually exceeding that produced by conventional control theory methods. Furthermore, fuzzy controllers capture the "common sense" knowledge of the engineer which is often lost in formal synthesis procedures.

Designing a fuzzy system requires no knowledge of fuzzy logic or the underlying theory. To show how this is done, a simple fuzzy controller will be described for a hypothetical application: an elevator controller. Master this example and you will be able to design your own fuzzy control systems; read the theory which follows and you will know why it works.

The first step in designing a fuzzy system is to decide on a set of fuzzy rules. The following are two of those required for the elevator controller (many more would be needed for a complete system).

1. If the elevator is slowly moving upward and its position is far below the desired position, then make the motor move it rapidly upward.
2. If the elevator is moving upward at a medium speed, and it is a

little below the desired level, then make the motor move it slowly upward.

These rules can be more expressed in conventional IF–AND–THEN format, using appropriate abbreviations:

1. IF velocity is SP (small positive), AND position is LN (large negative), THEN motor voltage is LP (large positive).
2. IF velocity is MP (medium positive), AND position is SN (small negative), THEN motor voltage is SP (small positive).

The task of a fuzzy controller is to process these two rules (and possibly others) when specific values of position and velocity have been determined.

Figure 10-1(a) shows a fuzzy control system. Suppose that the "velocity input," the current rate at which the elevator is moving, has been measured to be 0.1 ft/sec. Similarly, the elevator's current position, the "position input," is −10 ft from the desired level. The controller first determines to what degree each of the fuzzy rules is applicable to the currently measured situation. It then combines all the relevant rules to produce a single output that sets motor voltage to a level that causes the elevator to rise at the desired rate.

A rule is made up of two parts: The *antecedent* and the *consequent*. The antecedent comes after the "if" and before the "then" part; the consequent comes after the "then." For example, the antecedent of rule #1 is, "If velocity is SP and position is LN," then the consequent is, "then motor voltage is LP." Note that the antecedent can contain many *clauses* linked by the logical operators "and," "or," and "not." For example, the clauses in the antecedent of rule #1 are "velocity is SP" and "position is LN." Clauses can be further decomposed into *variables* and *adjectives*. The variables in rule 1 are "velocity" and "position"; the adjectives are "SP," "LN," and "LP."

The degree to which a rule is relevant to a measured situation is the same as the degree to which the rule's antecedent is true, in a fuzzy sense. The *fuzzy truth* value of an antecedent depends upon the fuzzy truth value of each of its clauses, and upon the logical operators linking them.

In fuzzy logic each *adjective* such as SP is assigned a *membership function*. Given a value for the variable, the membership function is used to calculate the truth value of that variable. Note that the variable name SP may be assigned a different membership function for each rule. The dashed line in Figure 10-2 shows a membership function plotting the extent to which a person of a given height can be truthfully described as a "tall man." A man much shorter than 5'11" cannot be truthfully described as "tall," so the fuzzy membership function is 0 at this point. On the other hand, a man much larger than 5'11" can be truthfully described as "tall," and so the fuzzy membership function is 1 in this region. In between, there is a region where the fuzzy membership function takes on a range of values from 0–1, indicating the fuzzy truth value of the variable "tall" in this region.

Using the fuzzy membership functions, each clause in an antecedent can be assigned a fuzzy truth value. The next step is to assign a truth value to the entire antecedent. For example, consider how the velocity and position information are processed by rule #1. Figure 10-1(a) shows how a fuzzy controller would process the two rules when specific values of position and velocity have been determined. Following the dashed line up from the velocity input of 0.1 to the SP membership function of rule #1, the truth of describing the velocity as "SP" is found to equal 0.6. Similarly, the truth of describing the position as "LN" is 0.8. Since the two clauses are separated by an "and," fuzzy logic rules combine the two truth values by taking their minimum. (The reason for this rule of combination will be explained in a later section.) Thus, the truth value of the entire antecedent of rule #1, equals 0.6. Similarly, Figure 10-1(a) shows the truth value of the antecedent of rule #2 to be 0.2.

The final step is to combine the output values of each of the two rules in a manner that reflects the truth value of each rule. This process is called *defuzzification*. At this point there is no clear consensus among theoreticians or practitioners on exactly how to defuzzify. Figure 10-1(a) shows one method, called the min-max defuzzification. Here the output motor voltage of the controller is given a collection of adjectives such as LP and SP, each with its respective membership function. It is important to note that these membership functions are not necessarily the same as those defined for the antecedents of the rules. The consequent of rule #1 is "motor voltage is LP"; therefore, rule #1 uses the LP function for motor voltage. The truth value of rule #1 is used to "clip" (truncate) the consequent membership function; only the region shaded with diagonal lines will be used to determine the combined defuzzified output value. Rule #2 and all other rules are processed in a similar way. In a fuzzy system all rules process their inputs simultaneously, and all contribute to the final output to varying degrees. As shown in Figure 10-1(a), the final motor voltage is calculated to be the center of gravity of all the motor output membership functions.

Figure 10-1(b) shows an alternative method of defuzzification, called the product-max technique. Here, the peak of the output membership functions is scaled down rather than being clipped. This method reduces the computational load; since it has no clear disadvantages it is very commonly used.

To summarize, the example illustrates the following important points:

1. A membership function determines the degree to which an adjective truthfully describes the value of a variable.
2. The truth value of a fuzzy variable can be any real number from 0–1. In conventional logic, truth has only two values—1 or 0; either something is true or it is false. Thus, fuzzy logic is a natural generalization of conventional logic allowing variables to have degrees of truth.
3. The form of the membership function is up to the designer; however, triangular and trapezoidal functions are often used.
4. The logical "and" function is implemented by taking the mini-

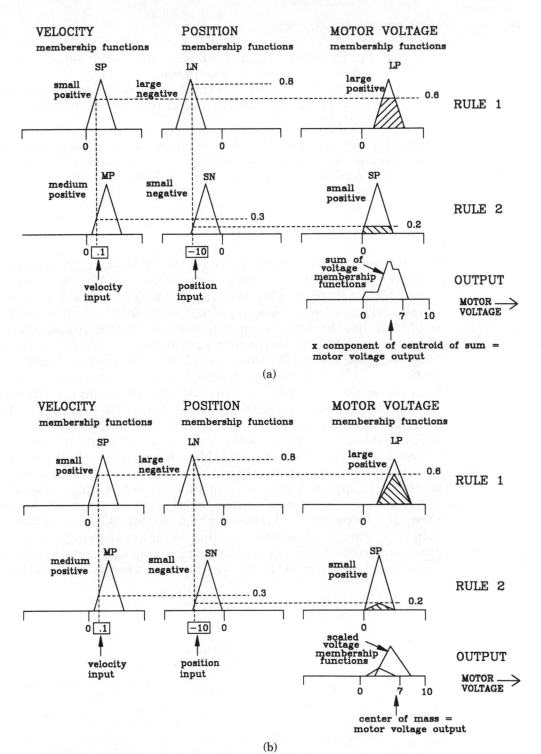

Figure 10-1. Fuzzy logic system. (a) Min-max method. (b) Product-max method.

mum of the values of the variables. Later we shall see that the logical "or" uses the maximum.

5. Fuzzy rule outputs are combined, producing a "defuzzified" output, by finding the center of gravity of the summed, limited rule outputs.

These points will be justified in detail in later sections. For now, please take them on faith. You know enough to design workable fuzzy controllers even if you do not know exactly why they work.

FUZZY LOGIC, CONVENTIONAL LOGIC, AND SET THEORY

Like conventional set theory, fuzzy set theory is concerned with the concept of set membership. For example, conventional set theory allows the statement "John is a tall man" to have only one of two truth values (true or false), usually written 1 or 0. Now suppose John is 6'10". By most judgments he would fall into the set of tall men, so the statement would be true. Likewise, if John were 4'10", he would not be in the set of tall men, so the statement would be false. But what if John were 5'10"? Conventional set theory would require us to "round him up or down," either including, or excluding him from the set. Fuzzy set theory does not force this unnatural decision. John can belong partially to a fuzzy set. We can say, for example, that he has a membership of 0.5 in the set of large men. Since this implies a membership of 0.5 in the set of "not tall men," John belongs to both the set and its complement, a situation which is forbidden in conventional set theory.

This shows fuzzy set membership to be a generalization of conventional set theory. Suppose that we wish to know if x is a member of set A. Conventional logic defines a membership function which maps x to either 0 or 1. Formally, $f(x): x \rightarrow \{0, 1\}$. Here nonmembership is indicated by 0, membership by 1. Fuzzy logic generalizes this mapping, allowing x to be mapped to any value from 0–1. Hence, a fuzzy membership function would be expressed formally as $g(x): x \rightarrow [0, 1]$. Figure 10-2 shows these two membership func-

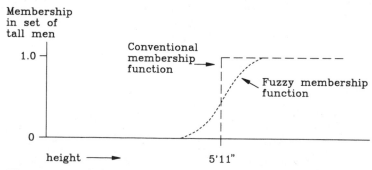

Figure 10-2. Conventional vs. fuzzy logic membership function.

tions, plotting set membership against height. Viewing a set as a function capable of defining partial membership is the cornerstone of fuzzy set theory.

Dealing with set membership values other than 1 and 0 require a new mathematics. Zedah (1965, 1983, 1984) has produced a body of work which establishes the mathematical foundations required. Kosko (1986, 1987) has added new concepts and methods. Today, fuzzy logic rests on a sound theoretical and mathematical foundation, sounder some say than traditional statistics.

Conventional and Fuzzy Logic

Conventional logic uses "and," "or," and "not"; any relationship can be described by combinations of these operators. Assuming that there are two variables, X and Y, Table 10-1 shows the possible truth values.

For example, $X = 1$ and $Y = 1$ corresponds to the statement "both X and Y are true." This has the truth value, true = 1, only in the row where both $X = 1$ and $Y = 1$.

Fuzzy logic functions have been developed that extend conventional logic to a fuzzy logic system. These functions must operate on truth values that can be decimal fractions, while continuing to produce the same results as conventional logic for values of 0 and 1. An infinite number of functions exist that satisfy these requirements. The ones chosen are intuitively satisfying, avoid contradictions, and above all, are useful.

The fuzzy logical "and" function can be implemented by using the minimum of the values of X and Y. Thus, the truth value of $X = 1$ and $Y = 0$ is 0, allowing us to say the following

$$\text{and } (X, Y) = \min (X, Y) \tag{10-1}$$

This function holds true for both conventional and fuzzy logic. Try it on the entries of Table 10-1; it produces the same answers as the conventional "and" function.

Similarly, the "or" function can be extended by using the maximum of the variables

$$\text{or } (X, Y) = \max (X, Y) \tag{10-2}$$

TABLE 10-1 CONVENTIONAL LOGIC
TRUTH TABLE

Variables		Truth Values		
X	Y	X and Y	X or Y	not X
0	0	0	0	1
0	1	0	1	1
1	0	0	1	0
1	1	1	1	0

To have a complete, minimal set of logical functions, we need the complement function. This can be implemented as follows

$$\text{not } (X) = 1 - X \qquad (10\text{-}3)$$

From these definitions, all of the other logical relationships involving an arbitrary number of variables can be derived, both for conventional and fuzzy logic.

Conventional and Fuzzy Set Theory

The extensions needed for fuzzy set theory follow naturally from the logical functions defined above. Figure 10-3 shows two sets, A and B, along with the crosshatched regions defined by their "and," "or," and "not" functions. These correspond to the set relationships intersection, union, and complement, respectively. A is the set of all points in the circle labeled A, B is defined similarly, and box U is assumed to contain all possible points, "the universe of discourse."

Define $m_A(x)$ as the value of the membership function for point x in set A. Similarly, $m_B(x)$ is the value of the membership function for point x in set B. We can define the value of the membership function of point x in both A and B, or mathematically in $A \cap B$ as follows

$$m_{(A \cap B)}(x) = \min\,[m_A(x),\, m_B(x)] \qquad (10\text{-}4)$$

This is compatible with the definition of the "and" function. It also satisfies the intuitive requirement that something should belong to the intersection of two sets no more than it belongs to either set. This is the relationship used in our controller example above.

As with the fuzzy logic "or" function, fuzzy membership in either set A or set B (or mathematically in the union of the sets) is defined similarly as follows

$$m_{(A \cup B)}(x) = \max\,[m_A(x),\, m_B(x)] \qquad (10\text{-}5)$$

The value of the membership function for a point x in the complement, A^c

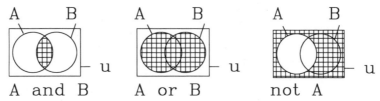

Figure 10-3. Venn diagram: Logical combinations of sets.

of set A, can be defined as follows

$$m[A^c(x)] = 1 - m_A(x) \qquad (10\text{-}6)$$

Kosko's Cube

Kosko (1986a,b,c, 1987, 1988) has developed an alternate formulation for fuzzy systems with many interesting and useful insights. A videotape course called FuzzyTapes (Schwartz 1990) provides a good introduction to this topic, as well as more conventional fuzzy logic. Only the essential set of Kosko's ideas will be presented here; the interested reader will find a complete treatment with derivations in the references.

As we have seen, Zedah defines a fuzzy set by a fuzzy membership function, whereas, in Kosko's view, a fuzzy set is a point in a unit hypercube. Figure 10-4 shows a square with a side length of 1.0 (a two-dimensional unit hypercube), with the two-element set $A = (.7, .3)$ located at these coordinates. If, for example, the axis were labeled "tall" and "friendly," the point A would represent a person who is rather tall (.7) but not very friendly (.3). This square contains all fuzzy sets having two elements. Similarly, any fuzzy set with three elements would be represented as a point in a three-dimensional unit cube. Adding elements to the set increases the dimensionality of the unit hypercube, but the concept remains the same.

Each element of a fuzzy set has a value between 0 and 1, representing its degree of membership in the set indicated by the name on its axis. The four corners of the square then represent the fuzzy sets (0 0), (0 1), (1 0), and (1 1). These are all the sets possible using conventional set theory, where an

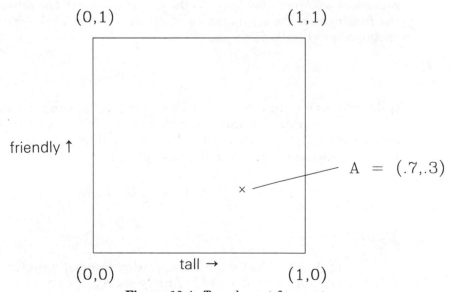

Figure 10-4. Two-element fuzzy set.

element must definitely be in the set (1), or out (0). Using our previous example, the point (0, 0) would mean definitely not tall and definitely not friendly, whereas (1, 1) would indicate definitely tall and definitely friendly.

Combining fuzzy sets in this formulation is accomplished with the fuzzy set operations previously described: Intersection is pairwise minimum, union is pairwise maximum, and complementation is accomplished by subtracting each element from 1.0. For example:

$$A = (.5 \quad .3 \quad .6 \quad .2)$$

$$B = (.4 \quad .5 \quad .8 \quad .3)$$

$$A \cap B = (.4 \quad .3 \quad .6 \quad .2) \quad \{\text{minimum}\}$$

$$A \cup B = (.5 \quad .5 \quad .8 \quad .3) \quad \{\text{maximum}\}$$

$$A^c = (.5 \quad .7 \quad .4 \quad .8) \quad \{1 - A\}$$

$$A \cap A^c = (.5 \quad .3 \quad .4 \quad .2)$$

$$A \cup A^c = (.5 \quad .7 \quad .6 \quad .8)$$

Unlike conventional logic, the intersection of A and A^c is not always a set of zeros, and the union is not always ones; this condition exists only for sets at the vertices. Furthermore, the position of the point indicates the degree to which the set is fuzzy. Figure 10-5 shows a two-component set $A = (.6 \quad .4)$, with $A^c = (.4 \quad .6)$, $A \cup A^c = (.6 \quad .6)$ and $A \cap A^c = (.4 \quad .4)$. The symmetry of these points will be found in all fuzzy sets. Their positions indicate the degree of fuzziness. If they were at the corners the set would not be fuzzy, it would represent a conventional set. As the points approach the center of the square, the fuzziness of the set increases, until they merge at the center $(.5 \quad .5)$ indicating a maximally fuzzy set.

Fuzzy Distance

Calculations on fuzzy sets require a scalar representing the distance between two sets. The Fuzzy–Hamming distance provides a useful measure in this case. It is easily computed as the sum of the differences between corresponding components of the set. This may be expressed as,

$$D(A, B) = \sum_i |A_i - B_i| \tag{10-7}$$

where

$D(A, B)$ = the fuzzy Hamming distance between fuzzy sets A and B.
A_i = component i of fuzzy set A.
B_i = component i of fuzzy set B.

This leads to a simple definition of size $S(A)$ of fuzzy set A as the sum of its components, or equivalently, as the fuzzy Hamming distance from the set to the origin. This may be expressed as follows

$$S(A) = \sum_i A_i \qquad (10\text{-}8)$$

Fuzzy Entropy

As we have seen, the position of the set in the unit hypercube determines its fuzziness. It is frequently useful to have a scalar measure of the degree to which a set is fuzzy. Since entropy is a measure of uncertainty, the term *fuzzy entropy* is defined to quantify fuzziness. Entropy varies from 0–1, with 0 representing total certainty, 1 total uncertainty. For sets at the vertices of the fuzzy cube there is no uncertainty, hence the entropy (and fuzziness) must be 0. For a set at the center of the cube, fuzziness is maximal as is uncertainty. Its entropy must be 1. To be consistent with these notions, fuzzy entropy $E(A)$ is defined as,

$$E(A) = S(A \cap A^c)/S(A \cup A^c) \qquad (10\text{-}9)$$

As shown in Figure 10-5, fuzzy entropy has a geometric interpretation. It is the ratio of the distance from a point (a fuzzy set) to the nearest vertex and the distance to the furthest vertex. For example, in Figure 10-5, the distance from A to the nearest vertex (labeled 1, 0) is ($|.6 - 1| + |.4 - 0|$) = .8. Similarly, the furthest vertex is (0, 1), hence $D[A, (0, 1)] = 1.2$. Therefore, the fuzzy entropy is .8/1.2 = .666.

Fuzzy Sets and Logical Paradoxes

Using conventional logic, propositions having truth values at the center of the fuzzy hypercube represent paradoxes. For example, Bertrand Russell

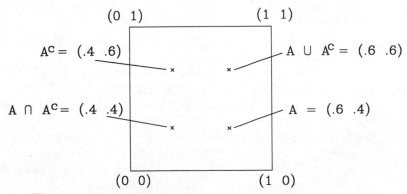

Figure 10-5. Logical functions of a two-component fuzzy set.

posed the famous barber's paradox which may be paraphrased as follows: In town there was a barber who shaved everyone who did not shave himself. The question is, did the barber shave himself? If we assume that he shaved himself, then he did not, and vice versa; therefore, the logical contradiction indicating the paradox. If the proposition P = "shaved himself" has a truth value truth(P), then truth(P) = truth(not P). Using the fuzzy complement, truth(not P) = 1 − truth(P). Thus truth(P) = 1 − truth(P). Solving for truth(P), we get truth(P) = .5, the center of the fuzzy cube (the unit line in this case).

Russell's paradox has confounded set theorists for decades. This impasse arose from their insistence on two valued logic. With fuzzy logic, propositions are allowed to have intermediate truth values anywhere within the fuzzy cube, and the paradox does not exist. Conventional logicians accuse fuzzy theorists of devising fictitious constructs. Clearly, removing all restrictions on the imagination can produce explanations for virtually anything. For example, consider the superstitions of primitive peoples that explained natural phenomena in terms of supernatural entities. Ultimately, mathematical theories are judged by their consistency, beauty, and utility. Fuzzy theory passes examination on all counts, in addition to resolving these logical paradoxes.

Expert Systems, Fuzzy Systems, and Artificial Neural Networks: A Comparison

The goal of artificial intelligence is to produce intelligent machines. That is, computers that duplicate certain aspects of human intelligence. Expert systems, fuzzy systems, and artificial neural networks all attempt (and to some extent succeed) in meeting this objective. Despite having similar objectives, the three techniques are profoundly different in both structure and performance. Failure to understand the advantages and limitations of these methods has led to expensive application failures. In the following sections these three methods will be explored, with special emphasis on the way that knowledge is represented in the system, and how it is obtained.

Expert Systems

Expert systems represent knowledge in sets of if–then–else rules. A typical rule might be:

IF A man is over six ft tall AND he weighs more than 200 lbs THEN he is a large man ELSE he is not a large man.

Propositions are proven by discovering a chain of rules. This may be done through either forward or backward chaining. In forward chaining, a rule such as A implies D is proven by finding a chain of rules such as A implies B, B implies C, and C implies D. Backward chaining proves the same—rule A implies D by finding a chain of rules—C implies D, B implies C, and A implies B. In either case, discovery of a rule chain implies that statement A implies D is true.

Expert systems have had a measure of success on certain well-defined problems. There have, however, been many failures. Most of the problems have arisen from the difficulty of obtaining a consistent, complete set of rules. The rule acquisition process requires the interaction of two specialists: A knowledge engineer and a domain expert. As a result of a set of meetings with the domain expert, the knowledge engineer creates a preliminary set of rules. These rules are evaluated on trial data, and errors are noted. Further meetings are held to resolve erroneous performance, and a modified data base of rules (a rule base) is constructed. The process is repeated in the hope that all errors and limitations of the rules will be eliminated. Often this hope is not realized.

There are several problems with this process. First, the domain expert may not be fully cooperative. After all, he is being asked to participate in the development of a system that will replace him with a computer. More often, the domain expert only appears to be uncooperative; he simply cannot create a set of rules that explain how he does certain things. Think how difficult it would be to create a set of rules for riding a bicycle, painting a picture, or simply walking across the room. From one point of view, only trivial things can be reduced to a set of rules; all important aspects of human intelligence are beyond a simple rule set.

A great deal of confusion has arisen from the "confidence factors" that some expert systems apply to the clauses of the antecedent as well as to the entire rule. Despite the superficial similarity, these are not equivalent to fuzzy set membership or to probabilities. A confidence factor is simply a single number applied to a specific clause or rule, representing the degree of confidence that the domain expert places on its correctness. In contrast, fuzzy set membership is a continuous function of the value of a variable used in a fuzzy rule, taking on any value from 0–1 depending upon the value of that variable. Furthermore, confidence factors are not probabilities; assigning a confidence factor of 0.75 to a rule does not indicate that it will be true three times out of four. Finally, there is no consensus (or conclusive theory) regarding the way that confidence factors are to be combined over the logical operators "and," "or," and "not"; different expert system shells perform this combination in various ways with significantly different results.

Fuzzy Systems

Like expert systems, fuzzy systems rely on a set of rules. These rules, while superficially similar, allow the input to be fuzzy, more like the natural way that humans express knowledge. Thus, someone might refer to a man as "somewhat tall," "a little overweight," or "a bit nearsighted." This linguistic input can be expressed directly by a fuzzy system. Therefore, the natural format greatly eases the interface between the knowledge engineer and the domain expert. Furthermore, infinite gradations of truth are allowed, a characteristic that accurately mirrors the real world, where decisions are seldom "crisp."

The exact meaning of each fuzzy term such as "somewhat tall" is defined by the membership function. Here human judgment plays a critical role. Membership function shapes must be matched to the subjective meaning of the terms they represent, as membership functions determine the performance of the system. In control systems (a major applications of fuzzy systems), the membership functions control speed of response, smoothness, and even system stability. In other systems the significance and effects of the membership functions may be entirely different.

Artificial Neural Networks

Artificial neural networks and fuzzy systems are similar in many ways. First, they both store knowledge and use it to make decisions on new inputs. Also, they are continuous vector mappers; they produce an output vector that is a function of the input vector. Both can generalize; both produce correct responses despite minor variations in the input vector. There are, however, fundamental differences between the techniques, some of which weigh heavily in the favor of fuzzy systems in certain applications.

Artificial neural networks acquire knowledge through training. That is, they are presented with a training set composed of numerical values, each of which represents some aspect of the outside world. Application of this training set modifies the network so that it produces the desired output for each input in the training set, as well as similar inputs that are not included in that set. This has a major advantage: Often the training set can be composed of actual observations of the physical world, rather than being formed of the human opinions used for fuzzy (or expert) systems. In other words, the neural network "lets the data speak for itself." This can be a major disadvantage: The training set must be adequate to fully represent the domain of interest, otherwise, the network can be called upon to make decisions in areas where it has no experience. In both humans and machines this can lead to serious errors.

Collecting an adequate training set can be a serious problem; its acquisition may be costly and time consuming. For example, a system to diagnose automobile engines would require a training set that covers all conceivable malfunctions, along with their combinations. This may make the collection of this type of data set impractical due to time and cost.

Adaptive fuzzy systems (Anderson and Nielsen 1985) have been developed that allow the system to learn from experience, thereby improving its decisions. Therefore, the line between neural networks and fuzzy systems is becoming increasingly difficult to define. Perhaps this represents a trend toward the eventual fusion of these apparently disparate methods into a single science of artificial intelligence.

Why Are Fuzzy Systems So Successful?

Expert systems have been extensively studied and applied. While there are many successful applications, there have been many failures. In general, expert systems have not lived up to the expectations of their advocates. Artificial neural networks have long been the subject of intensive research; yet, for reasons that are not completely clear, the total number of deployed applications is small. In contrast, the Japanese have used fuzzy systems successfully in hundreds of high-volume commercial applications. There are many reasons for this difference, not the least of which is the production orientation of the Japanese. Still, one must look more deeply to discover the major reasons for this discrepancy.

Like expert systems, fuzzy systems acquire knowledge from human domain experts rather than objective observation. Fuzzy and expert systems differ in one critical respect: Fuzzy systems allow the representation of imprecise human knowledge in a natural, logical way, rather than forcing the use of precise statements, then softening them with confidence values as in expert systems. Fuzzy systems allow the approximate terms that are nearly always employed by humans to express their judgments, thereby permitting more accurate knowledge representations.

Artificial neural networks suffer from a lack of perceived reliability. They can provide useful answers in the vast majority of cases, and then without warning produce a totally incorrect result. This can usually be traced to an inadequate training set. Still, there is often no way to determine when the output will be incorrect. Therefore, expensive or dangerous consequences can occur. Understandably, this leaves many users feeling insecure, despite assurances that the statistical error rate is low.

Even worse, it is usually impossible to determine how an artificial neural network made an incorrect decision so that the problem can be corrected. This situation arises from the fundamental structure of the network: Knowledge is distributed over the entire pattern of weights, a large percentage of which may be involved in each decision. Furthermore, network operation is obscured by nonlinearities. For these reasons the weight patterns leading to decisions are seldom discernible in problems of practical size.

Since it is usually impossible to determine what an artificial neural network knows (and does not know), the only way to fully characterize the response of a network to a novel input is to apply every possible input and see what happens. In all but trivial cases this is impractical; a full set of inputs cannot be assembled and if they could, the time required to test them would be prohibitive.

With artificial neural networks one must be satisfied with a probabilistic statement of reliability. This is achieved by separating the training set into two parts through random selection. The network is trained on one set; the error rate is called its training accuracy. Its performance is then tested on the second set, with the resulting error rate called its test accuracy. Test accuracy is a measure of the anticipated performance of the network provided that the test set is an adequate statistical representation of the input domain. Examples outside the domain of the test and training sets can produce high error rates. Since it is usually impossible to define these domains precisely, accuracy remains a matter of conjecture.

Training sets for artificial neural networks are either objective or subjective; they are either generated from measurements of a system or they are a set of opinions from a human expert. Obtaining a sufficiently large amount of objective data will often require prohibitively expensive testing. With subjective training data, artificial neural network systems have the same problem as expert systems. How can you find a true expert, and how can you extract answers that are accurate and complete?

Fuzzy rules are compact representations of human knowledge. For example, a rule such as, "When approaching an intersection, slow the automobile," incorporates a huge amount of information regarding cars, pedestrians, and the law. The fuzzy concepts "approaching" and "slow" encode the continuous nature of these concepts in a natural, efficient fashion. Representing these concepts in an artificial neural network could require thousands of training vectors.

THE INVERTED PENDULUM: A FUZZY CONTROL APPLICATION

Togai (1990) has developed a software system that facilitates the development of fuzzy systems. It has produced software that simulates a fuzzy controller maintaining an inverted pendulum in the vertical position, despite external disturbances. This is like balancing a broom on the palm of your hand. Available from Togai on a floppy disk (for a nominal charge), it demonstrates the dynamics of this system on an IBM PC or compatible computer. Figures taken from the screen of this demonstration are included here as an example of the most common application of fuzzy technology: Automatic control.

There are two inputs to this system: Theta, the angle between the pendulum and the vertical axis, and DTheta, the rate of change of that angle. Membership functions for Theta and DTheta and Motor Current are given the following names:

Z   Zero
NS   Negative Small
NM   Negative Medium
PS   Positive Small
PM   Positive Medium

Note that membership functions for Theta, DTheta, and Motor Current are the same, although in general they may differ both in name and form.

The box on the right in Figure 10-6 shows the names of the input membership functions associated with Theta and DTheta along the horizontal and vertical axes, respectively. In the interior squares of the box the functions of Motor Current are placed to indicate the output membership functions. In this case a rule is activated by the fuzzy "and" of the two inputs.

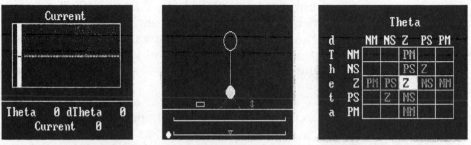

Figure 10-6. Fuzzy logic controller in equilibrium.

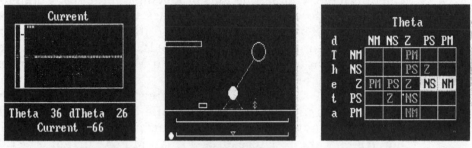

Figure 10-7. Fuzzy logic controller after impulse to right.

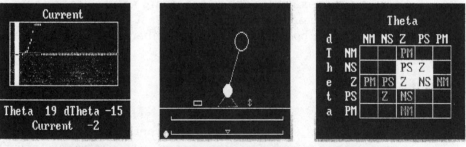

Figure 10-8. Fuzzy logic controller recovering from impulse.

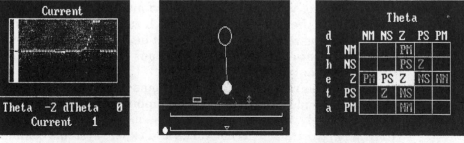

Figure 10-9. Fuzzy logic controller after slight overshoot.

For example, Figure 10-6 shows the pendulum (center box) to be stationary in its upright (desired) position. Both Theta and DTheta are zero, activating the Z-input membership function for each variable. The light square labeled Z indicates that the zero Motor Current output membership function is active. This produces no Motor Current as shown by the Current value of 0.0 in the left-hand box. This is the correct response for the current state of the pendulum.

Figure 10-7 shows the system after an impulse has been applied to the pendulum, forcing it to the right. The pendulum is shown toward the right (Theta = 36), and still continuing in that direction; hence, its velocity DTheta is 26. Since the pendulum is displaced to the right, both PS and PM membership functions are activated for Theta, activating both NS and NM Motor Current membership functions producing a large restoring Motor Current of −66 to flow, forcing the pendulum back toward its central position.

Figure 10-8 shows the pendulum on its way back. Now, three Motor Current membership functions are active: PS, NS, and Z. This causes a restoring Motor Current of −2 to flow. Note that Motor Current membership function Z is activated by two different rules.

Figure 10-9 shows the pendulum after it has passed its center position and has overshot slightly to the left. While this is not desirable behavior, it is typical of many control systems. At this point two rules are firing, activating both the PS and Z. This causes a small Motor Current of +1.0 to flow, tending to restore the pendulum to its central position.

Triangular membership functions combined with simple "and" rules are used in this example. The membership values become zero for input values far from the center of their range; thus it is possible to speak of rules "firing" if and only if both of their input membership functions are nonzero.

DISCUSSION

Fuzzy systems are simple to design, yet they present both theoretical and practical challenges. For example, there is no comprehensive theory that predicts the dynamic performance of fuzzy control systems. They constitute a complicated nonlinear system that is capable of producing fixed points, periodic oscillations, limit cycles, and even chaotic attractors. Furthermore, the crafting of the membership functions is largely intuitive; it is this skill that defines the true meaning of each fuzzy set. Determining the membership functions remains an art; a great deal of trial and error may be required to devise a set of membership functions that lead to stable systems having desirable dynamic performance.

Despite their problems, fuzzy systems have proven to be an effective technology in a wide variety of practical applications. In terms of sheer numbers, it seems likely that there will soon be more fuzzy systems in day-to-day use than all artificial neural networks and expert systems combined. While there is a growing interest in the U.S., most activity is confined to Japanese firms.

Unless this situation changes quickly, fuzzy systems will become another technology invented in the U.S. but economically exploited almost entirely by others.

REFERENCES

Anderson, T. R. and S. B. Nielsen. 1985. An efficient single output fuzzy control algorithm for adaptive applications. *Automatica* 21(5):539–545.

Kosko, B. 1986a. Counting with fuzzy sets. *IEEE Transactions on Pattern Analysis and Machine Intelligence* 8:556–557.

Kosko, B. 1986b. Fuzzy knowledge combination. *International Journal of Intelligent Systems* 1:293–320.

Kosko, B. 1986c. Fuzzy entropy and conditioning. *Information Sciences* 40:165–174.

Kosko, B. 1987. Foundations of fuzzy estimation theory, Ph.D. dissertation, Department of Electrical Engineering, University of California, Irvine.

Kosko, B. 1988. Hidden patterns in combined and adaptive knowledge networks. *International Journal of Approximate Reasoning* 2(4):377–393.

Schwartz, T. 1989. *Fuzzy Tapes*. Tom Schwartz Associates, Mountain View, CA.

Togai Infralogic, Inc. 1990. Fuzzy-C Pendulum Demonstration, Version 3.1. Irvine, CA.

Zadeh, L. A. 1965. Fuzzy sets. *Information and Control* 8:338–353.

Zadeh, L. A. 1983. A computational approach to fuzzy quantifiers in natural language. *Computers and Mathematics* 9(1):149–184.

Zadeh, L. A. 1984. Making computers think like people. *IEEE Spectrum*, pp. 26–32. New York: IEEE Press.

11

Neural Engineering

INTRODUCTION

Artificial neural networks have emerged from the laboratory and are finding their way into a large number of practical applications. As this happens, engineers are learning to use them as problem-solving tools, rather than as subjects for research. Since most of the literature is directed toward the researcher, it is difficult to determine which methods have the greatest probability of success, which have subtle problems that only become evident after much wasted effort, and which have never been applied to any but theoretical problems.

This chapter is written as a guide for the perplexed neural engineer. It is largely based on practical experience with a wide variety of paradigms used in diverse applications. Where the theory will help to illuminate an issue, it is used, however, this is a fledgling technology and many important questions have no definitive answers. It discusses these issues from a purely pragmatic viewpoint. There is an abundance of theory in the literature, the other chapters of this book as well as the companion volume, *Neural Computing, Theory and Practice*. The sole aim here is to aid the development of successful applications by pointing out potential problems and useful techniques.

The information that follows has been drawn from many sources, but mostly from the author's personal experience with real-world applications. As such it has certain limitations:

1. It is incomplete.
2. Often it is anecdotal, conjectural, and heuristic, rather than rigorously scientific.

3. It will become dated as more is learned about this technology.

4. Much of it is controversial.

Despite these caveats, the techniques have been proven useful. Applying them has solved many problems, producing good performance in a wide range of applications.

The wide range of neural network applications makes it difficult to formulate general rules; engineering judgment and ingenuity are nearly always required. Nevertheless, considering the points described in this chapter should illuminate some of the pitfalls and suggest paths leading to successful engineering solutions.

SELECTING THE RIGHT PROBLEM

A good solution requires a good problem. Despite the exciting capabilities of artificial neural networks, they are not a panacea; restraint and judgment must control enthusiasm if a successful application is to result.

Using an artificial neural network where it is inappropriate will often lead to an inferior solution, if not outright failure. For example, if an existing mathematical technique or algorithm is known to provide good results, in most cases it should be used rather than an artificial neural network. The literature has many examples where artificial neural networks have been applied to problems that have well-known closed-form solutions. While these examples are useful to show the capabilities of networks, they should not be considered appropriate applications to engineering problems. Neural networks typically require more computation and produce less accurate results than function evaluation. In a competitive world, a practical solution must not only work—it must be superior to all other alternatives.

All neural networks perform the same fundamental function, despite the many descriptive names applied to the various paradigms. Generally speaking, all artificial neural networks map one vector space to another. An *input vector* is applied to the network; in response, the network produces an *output vector*. Each vector consists of one or more *components*, each of which represents the value of some variable. Mappings may be static, in which case a feed-forward neural network will suffice. Or, they may be dynamic, involving previous network states; in this case a network with feedback is required.

Artificial neural networks are best applied when the complexity or inaccessibility of the system makes the mapping relationship unknown and perhaps unknowable. For example, optimizing cattle feed composition might be a suitable problem for an artificial neural network. Each component of an input vector might represent the amount of a dietary constituent; the output vector might consist of weight gain, meat grade, and other significant characteristics. Since our understanding of biological systems is fragmentary, no set of equations can be written to describe the complicated, nonlinear relationships between input and output vectors. Based on sufficient observations, however, a set of input- and output-vector pairs, called a *training set*, could be produced that would allow a network to be trained to extract this relationship. In this way the effects of dietary changes could be determined and perhaps optimized, resulting in significant economic benefits.

Inverting a matrix is an example of a problem not well suited to an artificial neural network. While it might be possible, such a solution would require an extensive training set, more computation, and would produce results that are less accurate than the deterministic methods in common use.

OVERCOMING OBJECTIONS

The experienced engineer knows the necessity of selling ideas to management, particularly if the technology is new and relatively unproven. This section addresses the problem, providing reasonable, realistic responses for some of the common questions and objections applying to artificial neural networks.

"They're Too New"

As with all new technology, artificial neural networks have been greeted with a combination of enthusiasm and scepticism. To paraphrase William James:

> When something is new, people say,
>   "It's not true."
> Later, when its truth becomes obvious, they say,
>   "It's not important."
> Finally, when its importance cannot be denied, they say:
>   "Anyway, it's not new."

In fact, artificial neural networks have a long history, going back at least to the late 1940's. Recent developments have overcome the limitations of earlier networks, raising tremendous current interest with many successful, practical applications in industry and the military.

While being the first to use a new technology is hazardous, being among the last may be disastrous. Technical leadership is essential to maintaining a firm's competitive position in our rapidly evolving global economy. Artificial neural networks are at the stage where judicious application can produce major benefits; failure to consider them may result in inferior, noncompetitive products.

"Neural Nets Have Never Been Successfully Applied"

There are many published application successes. An excellent source of these is the series of books *Intelligent Engineering Systems Through Artificial*

Neural Networks. Each volume contains over 1000 pages of engineering-oriented applications. Other sources include the applications oriented portions of the International Joint Conferences on Neural Networks (IJCNN) published annually by IEEE Press. Collecting several papers that show similar examples is often an effective way to demonstrate the utility of this technology.

Many of the most successful practical applications are either classified by the military or are trade secrets of the corporations who developed them. Furthermore, neural networks are often implemented as an embedded component in a larger system and never identified as such. Despite these difficulties, examples of application successes can usually be found through careful study of the literature.

"Neural Networks are Unreliable and Inaccurate"

It is true that artificial neural networks rarely produce correct answers 100% of the time, however, neither will the human they are often intended to replace. The accuracy of both must be expressed in statistical form. This objection often comes from the expectation that "computers do not make mistakes," an assumption that is inappropriate for this new technology. In many cases 100% accuracy is not required; an optimal solution must only satisfy the accuracy requirements of the application while reducing cost, improving performance, or making functions possible that could not have been implemented by conventional computational techniques.

"Minsky Disproved Neural Networks in 1969"

Minsky and Papert (1969) rigorously proved that single-layer artificial neural networks could not solve some simple problems (such as emulating an exclusive–or gate). Times have changed. A variety of new network techniques (including backpropagation) have been developed which employ multilayer networks, thereby overcoming these limitations. Nevertheless, one still encounters this objection from those who have not kept up with the field.

"Expert Systems are a Better Alternative"

A conventional expert system is, in essence, a complicated, automated rule book that has been developed by asking a "domain expert" what he or she would do under each circumstance. With the virtual eclipse of artificial neural networks, during the 70's and early 80's, it was thought that expert systems would solve all problems of artificial intelligence. This proved to be overoptimistic. Major development efforts, both military and industrial, failed to produce expert system performance that met expectations. While there were a few outstanding successes, there were numerous failures.

As it turned out, determining an expert's behavior under all circumstances is an extraordinarily difficult problem. For all but trivial tasks, an expert may not be able to explain in logical terms why a given course of action was chosen, yet an answer must be produced. The result can be a contradictory set of rules producing absurd consequences.

It is now obvious that human intelligence cannot be captured in a rule book. A human brain trained through experience is a far more powerful mechanism for making such judgments. Artificial neural networks attempt to emulate certain aspects of this mechanism, producing results that are more similar to those of human intelligence.

In recognizing the limitations of conventional expert systems, there has been an effort to incorporate some of the characteristics of neural networks into their structure, either by making their rules adaptive, or by creating hybrid neural network/expert systems. This appears to be a promising technique for emulating more accurately the human decision process which combines pattern recognition of neural networks with the logical reasoning of expert systems.

SOFTWARE AND HARDWARE TOOLS

Artificial Neural Network Software

Due to the limited availability of specialized neural network hardware, most artificial neural network development is performed on general purpose computers. The first thought of many engineers entering the field of artificial neural networks is to buy one of the "shrink-wrapped" software packages. This approach has many precedents; much of the software used by engineers for computer-aided design can be purchased off the shelf, and performs very well.

A number of sophisticated software packages are available that provide the beginner with a useful introduction to one or more paradigms. Reliable sources include the following:

> HNC Inc., San Diego, CA
> SAIC Inc., San Diego, CA
> NeuralWare Inc., Sewickley, PA
> Nestor Inc., Providence, RI
> Olmsted & Watkins, Escondido, CA
> The Math Works, South Natick, MA

While useful for beginners who wish to gain a fundamental understanding of neural network methods, standard software often proves to be an inadequate solution for a real-world application. Since the source code is seldom available, the network architectures and training algorithms can only be modified to a limited degree. Therefore, one has no recourse if the performance is not acceptable.

This inadequacy stems from the immaturity of the neural network science; theory and methods are not developed to the point where a fixed set of algorithms will solve all problems. Instead, the user has several basic paradigms available, each having a large number of variations. All of these variations may be useful in combinations under specific circumstances. Frequently, no combination of known methods will suffice. The engineer is then obliged to use ingenuity to invent new variations that can solve the problem at hand. This is impossible unless the source code is available, and the engineer is able to understand it in enough detail to perform modifications.

Thus, experienced neural network engineers will often write their own programs. In this way they gain a detailed understanding of how the algorithm functions, along with the capability to modify it if it does not perform as needed. Artificial neural network programs are often short but intricate, representing a large amount of theory and experience in a few lines of code. Since this information is difficult to convey to a programmer, it is often the case that today's neural network engineer is also the author of the programs he or she uses.

Artificial Neural Network Hardware

Artificial neural networks often require substantial computational resources. For those without access to a super computer, training a large network with a paradigm such as backpropagation can be an unacceptably lengthy process, perhaps requiring days or weeks to train a single network. There are two major ways to solve this problem: a hardware accelerator board or specialized integrated circuits.

Neural-network hardware systems are in a state of rapid change, therefore, the following information will quickly become of historical interest only. Nevertheless, it is included to give the reader a "snapshot" of currently available systems. HNC, NeuralWare, SAIC (and several others) sell artificial neural accelerator boards that plug into an IBM PC or compatible, and implement various paradigms. These can reduce training times by a factor of 10–100 if well programmed. Again, the software provided with these boards may not be optimal for the task at hand, and it may not be possible to modify it as needed. The boards are relatively expensive. If, however, the value of time is a consideration, they can often provide a rapid payback.

Alternatively, it is now possible to develop a dedicated artificial neural network hardware system using integrated circuits specifically developed for the purpose. Examples include the following:

1. Intel Corp. introduced an integrated circuit at the International Joint Conference on Neural Networks in 1989 (Holler 1989). Named the Electronically Trainable Artificial Neural Network (ETANN) or the 80170, it contains 64 processing elements and 10,240 programmable weights that are accurate to approximately five bits. It is capable of implementing a network trained by the backpropagation algorithm, as well as the Madeline III algorithm, but requires that training be performed on a separate computer and weight values loaded onto the chip. Since the com-

putation is done in parallel analog form, a direct comparison with digital techniques is difficult. Nevertheless, an equivalent computational rate of 2 billion connections per second is achievable. Questions remain regarding the effect of the limited accuracy of the weights on the overall performance. Intel is now selling an evaluation board along with software for training and programming the ETANN.

2. Micro Devices has developed a bit-slice digital device, the MD1220, that contains eight processing elements with up to 256 inputs per processing element (more with some sacrifice in speed). Weights are stored in external memory as 16-bit integers. It is rated at 10 million interconnects per second for each integrated circuit. A number of circuits may be combined to increase network size and computation rate. These devices take advantage of the inherently parallel nature of artificial neural network computation through the use of VLSI circuits. Thus, effective computational rates approach or exceed those achieved with super computers. This approach requires considerable electrical engineering skill and a substantial investment in design to achieve a workable system.

3. Neural Semiconductor has announced a digital integrated circuit, the SU3232, with 32 processing elements and 1024 weights. This circuit is not available as of this writing.

4. Bell Laboratories is expected to make an integrated circuit available that combines analog and digital processing in a configurable architecture. It has 32,000 one-bit weights, or it can be arranged for more bits per weight and fewer weights. It runs at 300 billion connections per second in the one-bit mode, substantially slower with more bits per weight.

5. Adaptive Solutions provides a system designed around their CNAPS integrated circuit. This circuit contains 64 processors in an architecture capable of emulating all known neural network paradigms. Its throughput in the feed-forward configuration is 1.6 billion connections per second, and does 250 million connection updates per second in the backpropagation mode. The development system operates as a server on an Ethernet, and is compatible with several workstations. The system can be supplied with up to 512 processors (four chips) that yield a peak performance of 7.68 billion multiply-accumulate operations per second.

SELECTING A PARADIGM

There is justifiable confusion regarding the numerous paradigms available to the artificial neural-network engineer. The literature abounds with algorithms having colorful names. There are thousands of papers emphasizing the virtues of each, often omitting their limitations.

Despite this apparent diversity, we have seen that all neural networks perform the same task: mapping input vectors to output vectors. They differ only in the way they perform this task. A formal taxonomy of artificial network paradigms is beyond the scope of this volume, however, only certain major distinctions are required in many cases. Therefore, three of the most important characteristics will be considered.

A somewhat artificial distinction may be drawn between paradigms that map their input vectors to continuous valued outputs, and those that perform classification. In the latter case, only a single output vector component is "true," all others being "false." Obviously, the latter is a subset of the former; a classifier cannot perform continuous mappings.

Another important distinction may be made between paradigms that require supervised training, and those that are unsupervised (sometimes called self-organizing systems). Supervised training requires a training set consisting of input-output vector pairs. The network is trained by applying each input vector and adjusting the network weights in a direction that minimizes the error between the network output and the desired output vector. Unsupervised training uses only input vectors in its training set. Based upon some distance measure, input vectors are grouped so that similar vectors produce the same output.

A third critical characteristic separates recursive from nonrecursive algorithms. Nonrecursive (feed-forward) networks offer the advantages of simplicity of implementation and analysis. For static mappings, a nonrecursive network with a single hidden layer of nonlinear neurons is completely general. Given enough hidden layer neurons, it can approximate any static continuous mapping on a compact set (Hornik, Stinchcombe, and White 1989).

Despite the generality of nonrecursive networks for static mappings, adding feedback expands the networks range of behavior; its output now depends upon both the current (and perhaps previous) input and network states. Despite their greatly enhanced capabilities, recursive networks have found limited practical application, primarily because training is more complicated and lengthy. Nevertheless, recursive networks can provide a compact model for systems that have dynamic behavior. Since virtually all physical systems have some dynamic characteristics, the recursive network is a natural choice for their emulation.

Most practical applications use one of a small number of paradigms, or their variations. It should be remembered that the choice of a paradigm is most often based upon its success in previous applications; thus, applications of the better established paradigms tend to proliferate, perhaps more than their characteristics warrant. The following short list of paradigms are used in approximately 80–90% of the applications. While these probably represent fewer than 1% of the total number of published methods, an engineer seeking reliable results with minimum effort is well advised to select from these, at least as a first attempt. Many paradigms that are highly touted in the literature have subtle flaws and limitations that become obvious only after substantial investments have been made.

Backpropagation

Despite the proliferation of published algorithms, more practical applications use Backpropagation (Rumelhart, Hinton, and Williams 1986) than any other. Its primary use is to perform supervised training on multilayer, non-recursive networks; however, training algorithms for recursive networks have also been developed (Williams and Zipser 1989, Narendra and Parthasarathy 1991). With suitable training it may be used for either continuous mappings or classification.

Backpropagation suffers from a variety of ills. Perhaps the worst of these is its very long training times. This has given rise to a small industry devoted to devising heuristics intended to increase its training speed (see Chapter 6). While these methods can yield substantial reductions in training time, their performance is highly problem dependent.

Another problem with backpropagation results from its fundamental training mode—gradient descent. Because of this a training session can result in a network trapped in a local minimum, a nonoptimal solution that may not be acceptable. Various methods have been suggested to overcome this problem, including the marriage of backpropagation and the Cauchy machine (Wasserman 1989). While they have been found useful, these methods have not been validated on a large enough range of problems to prove their general effectiveness.

Finally, backpropagation training is subject to a pathology called paralysis. If this occurs, training virtually ceases and there is little that can be done other than to repeat the training process with different initial conditions, and perhaps a smaller weight adjustment step size. For a more complete treatment of backpropagation see Wasserman (1989).

Statistical Methods

In a seminal paper by Geman and Geman (1984), a method was described for optimization by analogy to the gradual cooling of an initially molten metal. As the metal cools, it converges to a minimum energy state. This may be thought of as an optimization process, where system variables are randomly adjusted with changes whose size decreases over time.

The Boltzmann machine and a recent modification, the Cauchy machine, are artificial neural networks that mimic the thermodynamic phenomenon. The network starts at a high artificial temperature where large random changes in network weights are made. Weight changes that are beneficial according to some criteria are kept. Deleterious changes are usually reversed, except that a randomly determined number of such changes are kept. This ensures that the system will not become trapped in a local minimum.

It has been shown that such a system does not suffer from the local minima problem of backpropagation. However, the random nature of the training process results in training times that may be orders of magnitude longer than those required for backpropagation. For a more complete treatment of this algorithm see Wasserman (1989).

Probabilistic Neural Networks (PNN)

PNN (see Chapter 3) is a classifier that overcomes many of the problems of backpropagation. It uses supervised training, is nonrecursive, and trains virtually instantaneously. It is capable of learning arbitrarily complicated classification tasks with an accuracy approaching that of a Bayesian classifier (the standard of optimality). Relatively little known, it is a powerful method with many advantages where a Bayesian classifier is desired. A practical difficulty lies in its use of the entire training set for each classification; this increases storage requirements and lengthens classification times. Various clustering techniques have been developed that reduce the size of the training set. However, with memory prices dropping rapidly, this is not the problem that it once was. Nevertheless, classification times can become much longer than for feed-forward networks if the training set is large.

Counter-Propagation Networks

This network performs continuous mappings by first feeding data into a Kohonen network using nonsupervised training and then feeding the output to a Grossberg Outstar with supervised training (Wasserman 1989). This paradigm has advantages in speed and certainty of training, but lacks the generality of backpropagation.

Adaptive Resonance Theory (ART)

This paradigm, in its many variations, has found increasing application in situations where its characteristics of rapid training and incremental learning are important. It allows the incorporation of new information without affecting that which was previously learned. For an explanation of this important paradigm see Wasserman (1989).

Radial Basis Functions

The past few years have seen a great deal of interest in radial basis-function neural networks as an alternative to backpropagation (see Chapter 8). They train rapidly (GRNN, a closely related method does not require training at all), and do not suffer from the local minima and other training pathologies of backpropagation. Unfortunately, they require all, or a substantial portion, of the training set to be involved in their operation; therefore they can be slow in the final application.

THE TRAINING SET

The performance of a network depends heavily upon the vectors used to train it; the network learns from nothing else. The training set must provide a full and accurate representation of the problem domain; otherwise the network will not meet expectations. While the theory is far from complete, there are certain useful guidelines to help decide the set's size and content. In the absence of a complete and rigorous theory, the neural network engineer must rely on experience, common sense, and creativity. The following topics will cover a mixture of theory and rules-of-thumb that have been proven useful.

Training Set Statistics

The training set should be a statistically representative sample of the problem domain. Considering a training vector to be a point in N-dimensional space, where N is the number of vector components, the probability of randomly selecting a vector within a given volume from the training set should be the same as the probability of selecting one from the underlying population. For example, suppose we had a one-dimensional input vector (one component) representing height, and a one-dimensional target vector (assuming supervised training) representing weight. Suppose that we select 1000 men at random from the population of the U.S. and make a histogram of their heights, shown in Figure 11-1(a). By normalizing the area under the curve to unity, a probability density function is produced. Suppose that we were now to repeat the process for all 100,000 men in the population (Figure 11-1(b)). If the two distributions were enough alike, we would say the sample of 1000 was statistically representative of the population.

The necessity for a statistically representative set can be illustrated by a simple example. Suppose that we wished to train a network to input height and output weight. Consider the case where the sample was taken in an area where only short men lived. A network trained to input height and output weight would probably produce incorrect responses when tall men were input, as there were no similar examples in its training set. The same argument holds if tall men were not entirely excluded, but merely under represented. Here, the output would tend to produce outputs skewed toward the weights of short men; therefore, the output would be less accurate for tall men.

Objective and Subjective Training Sets

Training sets may be characterized as objective and subjective. For example, consider two training sets to be used for a medical prognosis system. Both have symptoms of the patient as components of their input vectors. In the first set, the output vector represents the judgment of a particular physician regarding the probability of each outcome; this is a subjective set as it is based on human judgment and experience. In the second set, the output vec-

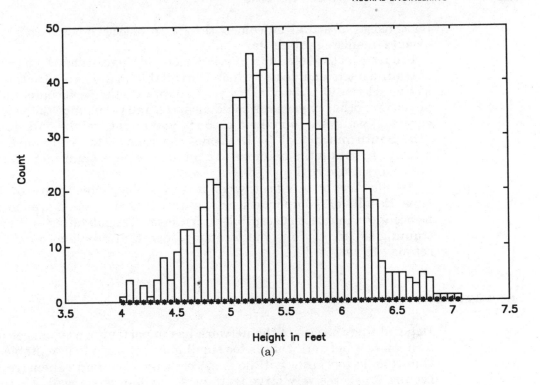

Height in Feet

(a)

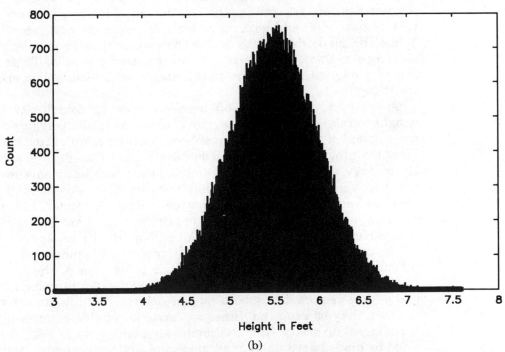

Height in Feet

(b)

Figure 11-1. Height distribution. (a) 1000 samples. (b) 100,000 samples.

tor consists of actual outcomes; this is an objective set if there can be no disagreement regarding the results.

From a practical standpoint it is vital to distinguish between the two types of training sets and decide which is available in a given situation. The subjective set would, at best, allow you to duplicate the performance of a specific physician; other physicians could disagree and pronounce the machine inaccurate. If you were to make a product, you might well be obliged to make a "Dr. Smith machine," "a Dr. Jones machine," etc. You could, of course, attempt to obtain the opinions of a number of physicians and average them, but others could still disagree.

An objective training set, when it is available, solves many of these problems. Results based upon observation rather than opinion are more likely to be accurate, and less susceptible to criticism. The advantages of an objective training set are obvious, but for many important problems obtaining such a set may be impossible.

NETWORK SIZING

Determining the size of the network has important consequences for its performance. A network that is too small may not train to acceptable accuracy. One that is too large will be unnecessarily slow and expensive, and may require an excessively large training set to generalize well. There has been a great deal of research on the relationship between network complexity, training set size, and generalization (Mehrotra, Mohan, and Ranka 1991). While the methods used to derive the results involve mathematics beyond the scope of this book, the results are relatively simple. These will be presented along with references to the literature for those who are mathematically inclined.

One aspect of the trade-off between network complexity (neuron and weight counts) and training set size can be seen intuitively by observing that more complex networks are capable of learning more patterns. Therefore, a large training set is required to define all that a complex network can learn. By analogy, an organism with a simple brain, such as an earthworm, is capable of only a limited range of behaviors; therefore, only a small set of examples are required to teach it all it can learn. A human brain, by way of contrast, is orders of magnitude more complex, so many books and a lifetime of experience can be learned without exhausting its capacity.

The optimal network size is highly problem dependent in ways that are difficult to determine at this time. It is a function of the diversity of the training set as well as the complexity of the desired function between input and output vectors. Since both may be arbitrarily high, an arbitrarily large network may be required. Since we have no reliable relationships between training set diversity, function complexity, and network size, these decisions must be made based upon experience and some experimentation.

A pragmatic approach to network sizing uses the smallest network that will produce adequate accuracy on both the training and test vector sets. This requires the training and evaluation of several networks, a time-consuming task if backpropagation is used. If speed and cost are important to the application, it may be worthwhile as small networks train faster, compute more rapidly, and cost less to implement in hardware.

Generalization and Network Complexity

Neural networks are useful primarily because they generalize; that is, similar inputs produce similar outputs. Generalization allows the network to approximate the correct output for an input not in the training set. A network that did not generalize (one that could produce a correct output only when its training vectors were input) would be of little value; it could be replaced by a look-up table.

Generalization in neural networks is closely related to classical interpolation; both are concerned with estimating values that are "between" those in a given data set. Since polynomial interpolation is widely used and well understood, it will be used to illustrate general characteristics of the interpolation problem. Figure 11-2 shows a case where three different polynomials are used to interpolate between five data points. Since all curves pass through the "training points," which is "best"? In fact, without additional information, optimal generalization in neural networks, like interpolation,

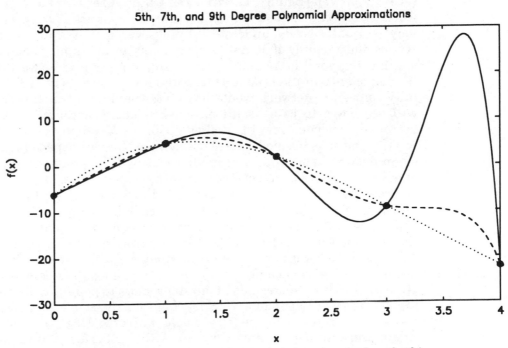

Figure 11-2. Polynomial approximations to samples of cubic.

is an ill-posed problem. There is no single answer that is better than an infinite number of others.

Still, humans do generalize with great success; therefore, applying a suitable bias is done largely subconsciously like so many other functions of human intelligence. Implicit in this process problem is the belief that the data points (training set) are samples of some *underlying function* that is being estimated. Thus, selecting among the three curves of Figure 11-2 requires a preconceived notion regarding the shape of the curve. For example, one might reject the 9th-degree polynomial approximation (solid line) as unacceptable due to its large excursions. This shows a *bias* toward smooth functions; it may be based upon knowledge of the system that generated the data, personal experience, or general observations about nature. Thus, it may seem that the user is predetermining the result; rather than "letting the data speak for itself," however, *without this bias, it is impossible to perform optimal interpolation; many different answers are equally valid.* Hence, the usefulness of the results will depend heavily upon the correctness of the bias. A decision that the underlying function is best fit by a 5th-degree polynomial (dotted line), may be grossly in error if the 9th-degree approximation is correct. Therefore, predetermining the correct bias is critical to a successful application.

Bias in neural networks is most often controlled by the network complexity, e.g., the number of weights and neurons if a feed-forward network, as well as by the nature of its nonlinearities. It has been long observed and recently proven (Baum 1989) that the training set size must grow with network complexity if good generalization performance is to be achieved. This may be qualitatively understood by observing that a network produces a correct output only if it has been trained on an input that is sufficiently similar. Suppose, for example, that a single layer feed-forward network has N components in its input vector. If the layer consists of M neurons, then a fully connected network would have NM weights in this layer; this product will be shown to be a useful measure of network complexity. Each input vector may be considered to define a point in N-dimensional space. Suppose $N = 1$, and it is deemed necessary to have K evenly spaced training vector examples to ensure that any input vector will have a training vector close enough to produce a correct network output. Considering the general N-dimensional case, suppose that each dimension is partitioned into K subdivisions. Then the "volume" of this space is K^N, measured in hypercubes of equal size. If it is desired to have a training example in each hypercube, then the training set size is also K^N, a number that grows with alarming rapidity as the number of components in the input vector increases. For example, a vector with 256 components in a space where each dimension is divided into 10 sectors would require 10^{256} training vectors to populate it uniformly, placing one in each hypercube. Considering that there are only about 10^{79} electrons and protons in the observable universe (ten vigintsextillion, the Eddington number estimated by Sir Arthur Stanley Eddington, the astrophysicist), the severity of the problem becomes apparent. Fortunately, this view of the problem is excessively pessimistic. Rarely is this space uniformly populated; regions with no real-world examples do not require training vectors. Later in this chapter research results will be shown that give a more realistic estimate of the required training set size. Nevertheless, training set size grows rapidly with network complexity, perhaps exceeding the bounds of available data sets; excessive network complexity must be avoided, for this and other reasons to follow.

These intuitive concepts may be made more rigorous by considering a neural network as a learning system. This allows the application of a measure known as the Vapnik–Chervonenkis or VC dimension (Blumer *et al.* 1989). In a sense the VC dimension is a measure of the learning capacity of a system as determined by its complexity. The generality of the VC concept is surprising; it may be applied to virtually any learning system, however, calculating it may be very difficult. For example, the VC dimension of a single-layer feed-forward neural network is simply the number of its weights. In multilayer nonlinear networks there is, as yet, no explicit formula for calculating the VC dimension, although upper and lower bounds have been defined (Baum and Haussler 1989). The lower bound is the number of weights in the network, so this number is often used as an estimate of the VC dimension. This may be pessimistic, demanding a much larger training set than is actually required.

For example, consider a linear network with L inputs, M neurons in the first layer, and N neurons in the second layer. The total number of weights (if the network is fully connected between layers) is $LM + MN$. However, it is easy to show by the associativity of matrices that the total number of free variables is only LN, as the two-cascaded weight matrices are exactly equivalent to a single matrix equal to their product. Something similar occurs in nonlinear networks as well, but it has not been quantified.

A theorem derived from VC-dimensional theory (Vapnik 1982) shows that a system having VC dimension d that has been successfully trained on a set of m examples will, with a high confidence level, have a worst case generalization error that is less than e, where $e \leq O(d/m \ln (m/d))$, and $O(.) =$ "on the order of."

Furthermore, it has been shown (Ehrenfeucht *et al.* 1988) that there are classes for which $e \geq O(d/m)$, thereby bounding the worst case on the lower side to within $\ln (m/d)$. Using this somewhat optimistic lower bound can still produce a discouraging result. For example, a network with M inputs, N-hidden-layer neurons, and P-output neurons would have an estimated VC dimension of $MN + NP$. If $M = 256$, $N = 32$, $P = 16$, and $e = 0.01$, then $d = 8704$; a training set of 870,400 vectors would be required.

Neural network practitioners have objected to these results on the basis of experience; many networks of this complexity have been successfully trained with far fewer training vectors (LeCun *et al.* 1990). This bound was stated as a worst case, therefore it may be pessimistic in many applications. The objection regards its practical significance. As a partial answer Cohn and Tesaro (1992) have shown perfectly reasonable problems for which this bound is "tight"; fewer training vectors will not produce adequate generalization. While the significance of the VC bound is problem dependent, it must be kept in mind when sizing a network, otherwise, the number of training vectors may exceed the available data, and/or the capacity of the computational facilities may become inadequate to train the network in a reasonable amount of time.

Neural Networks and Statistics

The development of neural network theory has made clear the strong relationships between neural networks and statistical approximation methods. Viewing neural networks in this way allows the application of a huge body of knowledge that illuminates many aspects of neural network theory and applications.

The field of nonparametric statistical inference is a highly developed science that deals with model-free estimation, that is, estimating an arbitrary function based upon samples of the input and output data, with no *a priori* knowledge regarding the underlying statistics of the generating process. This can take the form of general function estimation, or its subset, classification. This is precisely the goal of neural network learning and recall.

Estimators may take many forms with a wide range of characteristics. One way to evaluate an estimator is to determine if it is *consistent*. Given an infinite training set, does it converge to the desired function? This is a property shared by many nonparametric estimators including Parzen windows and nearest neighbor methods (Duda and Hart 1973), regularization methods (Wahba 1982), as well as those techniques normally associated with neural networks, including Boltzmann machines and feed-forward architectures with nonlinear hidden layers. Note that convergence may require an estimator of arbitrary complexity. As we have seen, a feed-forward neural network with at least one nonlinear hidden layer of unlimited size, is a universal approximator, capable of approximating to an arbitrary degree of accuracy any continuous function on a compact set. This also is a property of many other estimators, including those constructed using trigonometric or algebraic polynomials. Thus, neural networks share their useful properties with other, more conventional techniques, and may be studied in the same context.

One outcome of nonparametric statistical inference theory is a clear understanding of the limitations of the method, concisely defined as the "bias/variance dilemma" (Gemen, Bienenstock, and Doursat 1991). Total estimation error may be expressed as the sum of *bias* and *variance* terms. Both relate to the accuracy of an estimator of finite complexity trained on a finite data set, measures that are more useful in real-world applications than is consistency.

To estimate bias and variance, suppose that a large training set is available, each element of which consists of an input vector and an associated target vector. These vector pairs, taken together, define an underlying function. Further suppose that a large number of estimators of finite complexity are trained, each on a different data set of finite size, drawn at random from the training set with the same sampling rule. All estimators have the same structure (such as neural nets with the same number of layers and weights). Then suppose that all estimators are evaluated by inputting a large number of test vectors drawn at random from the training set, again with the same sampling rule. Because the estimators are trained on different data, they will differ in the accuracy with which they estimate the underlying function. Variance is a measure of the variation among these classifiers; bias measures the amount by which the average classifier differs from the underlying function. In equation form

$$MSE = \{E[f(\mathbf{x})] - y(\mathbf{x})\}^2 + \quad \{bias\}$$
$$E\{[f(\mathbf{x}) - E(f(\mathbf{x}))]^2\} \quad \{variance\}$$

where

$\mathbf{x}$ = an input vector
MSE = mean-squared estimation error
$E(.)$ = estimated value (arithmetic mean)
$y(x)$ = value of the underlying function at point x

Note that both bias and variance are functions. By averaging their value over the range of the input vector, more useful numbers, *cumulative variance* and *cumulative bias* are produced.

In neural networks, network complexity can be adjusted to a trade-off between bias and variance. A network with insufficient complexity (e.g., having too few neurons in the hidden layers) will not train accurately to a complicated function, regardless of the size of the training set, therefore it will exhibit high bias.

Conversely, a network that is excessively complex (e.g., too many hidden-layer neurons) will train precisely to each specific training vector, thereby producing high variance among classifiers trained on different subsets of the training vector population. This is sometimes called as "training to the noise."

These results support the common wisdom that an optimal number of weights exists for a neural network in a given application. Either too many or too few will increase generalization error.

As we have seen, polynomial interpolation is closely related to neural network approximation methods. Experience with polynomial interpolators shows that an excessive number of free variables (such as a polynomial of excessively high degree or a neural network with too many weights) produces results that "overfit" the data, training to fit insignificant fluctuations rather than approximating the underlying relationship.

In Figure 11-3 an "underlying" cubic function is shown as the dotted line and samples for a training set are generated by adding random noise; these

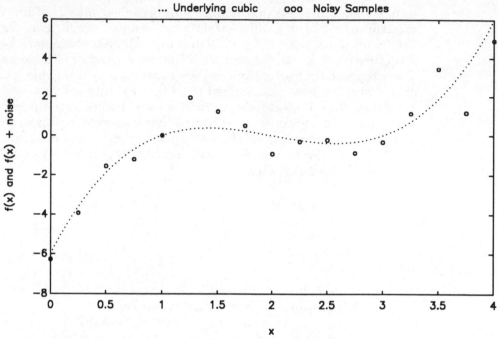

Figure 11-3. Cubic and noisy samples.

points are marked as "∘." Figure 11-4 shows the result of a least squared error fit by a quadratic. Obviously, the two coefficients, analogous to neural network weights, are inadequate to fit either the samples or the underlying cubic. Figure 11-5 shows a cubic approximation; this fits the underlying cubic quite well, but is a poor fit to the data points. In Figure 11-6, a 10th-degree polynomial was used; this fits the noisy data points quite well, but deviates considerably from the underlying curve. In the practical case, the underlying curve is unknown; only the noisy data points are available. Analogously, a network with too many weights may fit the training set well, but may produce large errors at intermediate points. In other words, the network will memorize the training set rather than generalizing around it. Conversely, a network with too few weights will fit both data points and the underlying function poorly.

Network complexity influences the degree of bias introduced into the approximation. A network with a small number of free variables (related to the number of weights) can approximate only a small number of functions, hence, it is biased toward these. Unless one of them is a good fit to the underlying function, generalization will be poor. On the other hand, a very large network can approximate a large number of different functions. Therefore, it imposes little bias, but will produce errors dominated by its variance. An arbitrarily large network can fit any continuous function on a compact set with arbitrary precision, so bias goes to zero in this case, but the network

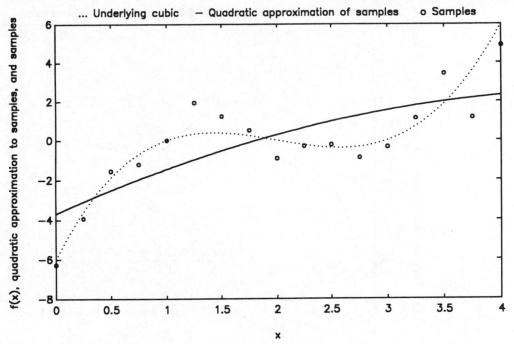

Figure 11-4. Cubic, noisy samples, and quadratic approximation.

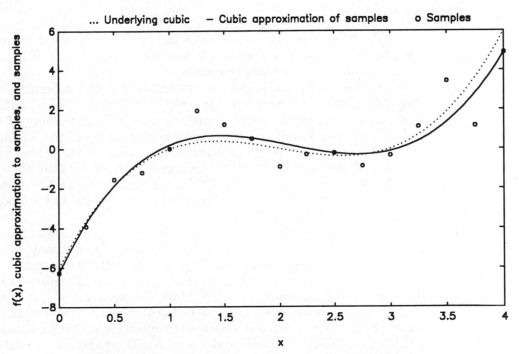

Figure 11-5. Cubic, noisy samples, and cubic approximation.

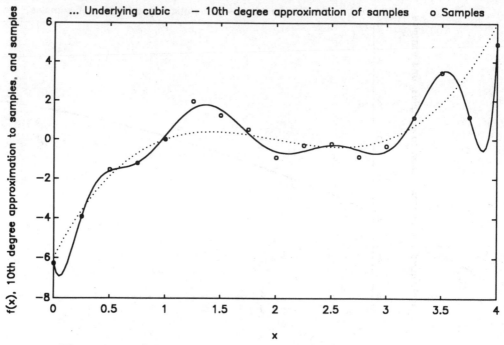

Figure 11-6. Cubic, noisy samples, and 10th-degree approximation.

will train to the statistical peculiarities of the training set rather than to the underlying function. Note that bias can be imposed in many ways, including the shape of the neuron's nonlinearity and the topology of the network; its effect is, however, the same.

Thus, there is an optimal network complexity that minimizes total error; calculating bias and variance over a range of complexities will allow an optimal value to be found at the cost of training a large number of estimators. Using backpropagation, such an undertaking can require a formidable computational capability; however, the computational power offered by the newer specialized architectures will make these methods feasible at a reasonable cost. In other cases such as the PNN classifier or the GRNN regression estimator, training is virtually instantaneous; the method is already practical on small computing platforms.

These estimates require a large training set population to ensure that different estimators are not trained on the same data; it may not be possible in a practical sense to assemble such a data set. Furthermore, estimating bias by the straight-forward method described above requires knowledge of the underlying function. This is seldom if ever available; if it were, there would be no need for a neural network to estimate it. Statisticians have faced these problems and have devised techniques for making estimates of bias and variance that make efficient use of whatever data is available, thereby circumventing the need to know the underlying function. For example, the

Jackknife, and Bootstrap (Efron 1982), are methods widely used among statisticians that may be adapted to neural network use.

Numbers of Neurons and Hidden Layers

As can be seen from the preceding section, there is no simple answer to the frequently asked question, "How many neurons should I use in the hidden layer of a feed-forward network?" Deciding on the number of hidden layers is even more difficult; there is very little theoretical guidance. It has been shown that the set of functions that may be implemented with a single hidden layer network of finite complexity is a subset of those possible with two hidden-layers. Many successful applications have incorporated two or more hidden layers, attempting to allow the network's output layer to construct complex relationships from more elementary ones in the layers near the input. Still, we have seen that a single hidden layer (of some undetermined size) can implement any function; therefore, it is often the configuration of choice due to its relatively rapid training when using backpropagation and other gradient descent algorithms.

NORMALIZATION

Neural network performance can often be improved if the data set is modified by removing insignificant characteristics. For example, the important aspects of the data are often independent of the value of offsets and standard deviations; these may merely obscure the issue and complicate the network's task. Recognizing an object in a television image should not be affected by the settings of brightness and contrast; these correspond to mean and standard deviation of the data respectively and should be removed by normalization prior to attempting identification.

Normalization is a complicated topic. It can take many forms and has many hazards; it is all too easy to inadvertently remove the precise information required for accurate operation. On the other hand, correct normalization can transform a poorly performing network into one that is nearly error free. Therefore, careful selection of normalization techniques may pay large dividends in the success of a project.

Removing the Mean

In many cases significant information is contained in small variations added to a large offset. The offset should be removed if it is known to be irrelevant to the problem, as it may inhibit training. For example, a large offset in the input vectors may saturate nonlinear neurons, thereby inhibiting the network's training. Offset in output target vectors may place the levels beyond the range of the sigmoidal output neurons. If the offset is unrelated to the characteristics of interest, and if it is constant over all components of all vectors, it can be removed simply by subtracting from each vector component the arithmetic mean over all vectors and all components. This will be called *total normalization*. The following pseudocode algorithm does the job, assuming that each vector occupies a row in the array named "data[m][n]" where m and n represent the vector and component, respectively

```
sum = 0;
for each vector v from 1 to m
    for each vector component c from 1 to n
        sum = sum + data[v][c];
    end
end

average = sum/(m * n)
for each vector v from 1 to m
    for each vector component c from 1 to n
        data[v][c] = data[v][c]/average;
    end
end
```

Correctly determining the significance of the offset is critical. In some cases the average value of a vector contains significant information and removing it will damage network performance. An even more subtle hazard exists that can destroy the meaning of the data. Suppose that the components of a vector represent different types of data with different offsets. For example, component 1 might be the consumer price index, while component 2 might be the price of gold. Furthermore, assume that consecutive vectors represent the values on consecutive days. If the price of gold changes dramatically from one day to the next, but the consumer price index is constant, normalization as shown above will make the consumer price index appear to vary.

In this case one should average the same component over all vectors, and subtract the average from only that component. This will be referred to as *vertical offset normalization*, and may be computed as follows:

```
for each vector component c from 1 to n
    sum[c] = 0;
    for each vector v
        sum[c] = sum[c] + data[v][c];
    end
    average[c] = sum[c]/n;
end

for each vector component c from 1 to n
    for each vector v
        data[v][c] = data[v][c]/average[c];
    end
end
```

Neither total nor vertical normalization is appropriate if the adjacent components of a vector represent consecutive samples of a continuous process such as speech or music. Suppose that each vector represents a different human utterance, and that components of a given vector represent consecutive samples in time. Vertical normalization would divide a given vector component by the average corresponding time samples of all utterances. This would, again, mix unrelated data and create serious errors. The correct approach in this case is to average over all components of a given vector, and divide its components by that average. This will be called *horizontal offset normalization*.

```
for each vector v from 1 to m   sum[v] = 0;
    for each vector component c from 1 to n
        sum[v] = sum[v] + data[v][c];
    end
    average[v] = sum[v]/n;
end

for each vector v from 1 to m
    for each vector component c from 1 to n
        data[v][c] = data[v][c]/average[v];
    end
end
```

Normalizing Vector Magnitudes

Large variations in the magnitude of the components of a vector may not convey meaningful information, but can confuse the network. Suppose the task is to recognize human speech, and we are given a set of vectors, each of which represents sequential samples of the same utterance at different loudness levels. The loudness is not useful in identifying the utterance and should be removed. This can be done by dividing each component of a given vector by the standard deviation over its components. This is *horizontal deviation normalization*. Similar arguments can be made for *vertical variation normalization* in cases where a vector has unrelated components.

Multimodal Distributions

The data distribution is often multimodal with the modes having different (and possibly insignificant) standard deviations and/or offsets. Consider, for example, the case where a vector component represents the rotational rate of a motor that may be either running at one of two rates; slowly or at high speed. If it is running slowly, both the average value and the standard deviation of its rotational rate signal will be low. When it is running at high speed, both will be higher. Obviously there is no normalization that will be appropriate for both cases. The solution may be some form of local normalization, with a standard deviation and offset calculated for each operating mode.

Detrending Data

In some cases data will show a linear increase or decrease over the vector components. For example, electrocardiogram data will often show a gradual increase or decrease with time that is totally insignificant. This may be removed from the data (along with any offset) by fitting a degree 1 polynomial (a straight line) to the data, evaluating it for each component, and subtracting the result. Fitting higher degree polynomials is also possible but seldom necessary. This method may be applied either horizontally or vertically.

Nonlinear Normalization

In many cases the raw data may range over several orders of magnitude, where the significant information is contained in the percent deviation. If the largest values are scaled to avoid exceeding the network's range, percentage variations in small values may be lost in the round-off error. In this case, taking the logarithm of the data will adjust its range so that large values are "squashed" more than small values, thereby allocating a constant range to a given percentage deviation, independent of the data's value.

Other nonlinear normalizations may be appropriate. If the distribution of component values is monotonically increasing or decreasing, one of the following normalizations from Tukey's transformational ladder (Tukey 1977) may be appropriate. Distributions that are rising would use a transformation in the top half of the list; those decreasing would use one in the bottom half.

$$\exp\left[\exp\left(y\right)\right]$$

$$\exp\left(y\right)$$

$$y^4$$

$$y^2$$

$$y$$

$$y^{0.5}$$

$$y^{0.25}$$

$$\log\left(y\right)$$

$$\log\left[\log\left(y\right)\right]$$

Summary

From these examples it is clear that a detailed knowledge of the nature of the data is required before normalization can be successful. Correct normalization will pay large dividends in performance; done incorrectly, normalization can render a data set meaningless.

REPRESENTATION

Most experienced neural network researchers agree that a "good" representation of the input data is critical to a successful application of artificial neural networks. The desire for generalization leads to a serious conflict in how this representation is to be accomplished. On one hand, one would like to give the network training vectors with all available information, so that it can train to the optimal set of weights. After all, one of the major advantages of an artificial neural network is its ability to extract complicated nonlinear relationships from the input data, thereby discovering useful and previously unknown features. Unfortunately, doing so may produce long input vectors and networks so large that the training set size (and training time) become impractical. For example, an image recognition problem might have an input vector with one element per pixel. With a 1000×1000 pixel image, a one-million element input vector would result. Many millions of training vectors would be required if the network is to generalize well, and training time would be prohibitively long. Much smaller problems on a backpropagation network have required weeks of training time.

As we have seen, an attempt to use a small training set on a large network can produce poor generalization; the network will train to recognize insignificant irregularities in the training set ("training to the noise") rather than fitting the underlying function.

Alternatively, one may compress the input data through preprocessing, extracting a small set of features that are known to correlate with the desired outputs. In speech recognition, one may know that the energy in certain frequency bands at certain times correlates with specific utterances. The input data could then be preprocessed, extracting values for each frequency-time region and constructing the input vectors from these values.

This is intuitively appealing. Why should one ignore known relationships? Should not the network be given the advantage of all available information associated with the problem? In many cases such an approach does improve network performance. However, there is a risk; our knowledge may be inadequate. We may inadvertently delete important information that a network might use to extract significant features if it had access to all of the data. Experiments with artificial neural networks have shown them to be capable of solving problems in ways that their developers never imagined, sometimes extracting features from the data that are as important as they are unanticipated.

The most desirable solution would reduce the number of components in the input vector (the dimensionality of the problem) without losing significant information. Various transformations are available that attempt to approximate this ideal. For example, if the input vectors are known to consist of 1000 samples of three sinusoids, applying the discrete Fourier transform (DFT) (Oppenheim and Schafer 1975) will accurately represent each vector with six coefficients (real and imaginary parts of each), yielding a proportional reduction in network complexity and training set size. The DFT applied to an inappropriate problem can, however, drastically complicate the problem. In the situation that is the inverse of the above, three delayed impulses in the time domain would transform into the frequency domain as 1000 samples representing the sum of three sinusoidal components, thereby greatly complicating their separation.

In general, the DFT is most appropriate where it transforms extended representations in the time domain into compressed representations in the frequency domain, a property that is characteristic of the data as well as the transform.

Thus, selection of a "good" representation depends upon the characteristics of the training set; applying a given transformation may simplify one problem while complicating another.

At this point we can list some characteristics of a "good" representation, noting that these are not independent:

1. Compactness: Input vectors should have a small number of components.
2. Information Preservation: The representation should contain all of the significant information in the training set; information is preserved if an invertible transformation is selected.
3. Decorrelation: Transformed vectors should be as dissimilar as possible to minimize overlap.
4. Separability: The transformation should be such as to group like training examples, separating them from those which are significantly different.

Karhunen–Loeve Transformation

The Karhunen–Loeve transformation (KLT) (Papoulis 1965) provides a solution that achieves the first three objectives optimally (in a specific sense). Briefly, it requires the following steps:

1. Find the real symmetric covariance matrix R:

$$R = (1/N) \sum_i [\mathbf{x}(\mathbf{i}) - \mathbf{u}][\mathbf{x}(\mathbf{i}) - \mathbf{u}]^T$$

where

N = number of training vectors
$\mathbf{x}(\mathbf{i})$ = training vector i
$\mathbf{u}$ = a vector equal to the mean of each component taken over all training vectors

$(.)^T$ = the vector transpose
(column vectors are assumed)

2. Find the eigenvectors and eigenvalues of R.

3. Sort the eigenvectors by eigenvalue. The eigenvalues indicate the mean-squared error introduced in the representation if the corresponding eigenvector is deleted. Next, find the fractional error contribution of each as the ratio of an eigenvalue to the sum of all eigenvalues. Often it will be found that only a small subset of the eigenvectors (those with the largest eigenvalues) will represent the input training vectors to the desired degree of accuracy; just sum the eigenvalues until the desired accuracy level is reached, and use the associated set of eigenvectors $\mathbf{v}(\mathbf{i})$ each as a row of the matrix $\mathbf{V}$

4. Find the coefficient vector of the transformation as follows:

$$\mathbf{c}(\mathbf{i}) = [\mathbf{Vx}\ (\mathbf{i})^t]$$

Since the number of elements in each vector $\mathbf{c}(\mathbf{i})$ is, in general, smaller than the number of elements in $\mathbf{x}_i$, a more compact representation is produced. This will reduce network size and consequently the required training set size.

While the KLT produces a statistical representation of the training set, usually the original training vectors cannot be recovered precisely from the reduced set of eigenvectors and eigenvalues. Thus, information is usually lost in the transformation.

Orthogonal Transformations

Any orthonormal basis set that spans the training vector space may be used to produce an arbitrarily accurate representation of a training vector. This representation may, in certain cases, be made more compact than the original vector set. For example, the Fourier transform discussed above uses sine and cosine functions as the basis vectors. Often a vector representing a time series will have a spectrum that has a magnitude significant for only a subset of the Fourier coefficients. Disregarding coefficients outside that subset will produce a more compact approximate representation. Similarly, a series representation, using algebraic polynomials, can often be truncated to a small number of coefficients without significantly affecting accuracy.

The wavelet transforms (Daubechies 1988) provide another important set of orthonormal functions. Unlike the Fourier transform whose sine and cosine basis functions are of infinite extent, the wavelets have local support; they are zero outside of a specified range. The wavelet basis functions are produced by successive dilations (expansions) and shifts of a "mother wavelet." First, the smallest wavelet is shifted across the signal, in steps, and its correlation with the signal is found at each position. Each such correlation produces a coefficient in the transformation. Next, the wavelet is expanded (typically by a factor of 2) and the process is repeated.

Thus, each wavelet coefficient represents the local value of a sequence of data points. This is particularly useful in those applications involving sound, vibration, images and other continuous functions. By rough analogy, the notes on a musical score indicate the frequency (tone) to be produced at a given time. Similarly, the wavelet coefficient indicates the amount of that frequency that exists at a given position.

Unfortunately there are problems with these transformations. First, even though they can represent the training vectors to an arbitrary degree of accuracy, there is no guarantee that they make it easy to separate classes. That is, two different classes may be so represented in the transform space as to require a complicated decision surface to separate them. Also, transformations of this sort perform averaging of the input data. If an important feature is represented by a small characteristic of the input vectors, its contribution to the average may be so low that it may be discarded. Thus, like most preprocessing, transformations must be used with intelligence and restraint.

Nonorthogonal Transformations

There are a large number of nonorthogonal transformations that may be applied to the data, each of which can be useful under specific circumstances. For example, the Gabor functions (Gabor 1946) like wavelets, have the property that they minimize the region of support in both time and frequency domains, thereby allowing simultaneous localization of a signal's frequency and time of occurrence. Furthermore, there are indications that these functions are similar to the responsive fields of neurons in the human visual cortex. With Gabor functions, the original signal may not be reconstructed as a simple linear combination of the basis functions. However, in neural networks, reconstruction is usually less important than representation. Certain other non-orthogonal wavelet transformations do allow exact inversion (Daubechies 1992), thereby proving that the representation is unique.

DISCUSSION

Neural engineering is in its infancy. Unlike other engineering disciplines, there is no complete, rigorous body of science to support design decisions. Nevertheless, by a combination of heuristics, experience, and whatever science is available, workable neural systems are being produced and applied with good effect. The current acceleration in research efforts is rapidly broadening the scientific foundation. Therefore, an ongoing study of the literature is required if the engineer is to maximize performance.

REFERENCES

Baum, E. B. 1989. What size net gives valid generalization? In *Neural Information Processing Systems 1*, ed. D. S. Touretzky, pp. 81–89. San Mateo, CA: Morgan Kaufmann.

Blumer, A., A. Ehrenfeucht, D. Haussler, and M. Warmuth. 1989. Learnability and the Vapnik-Chervonenkis dimension. *Proceedings of the 1988 Workshop on Computational Learning Theory*. San Mateo, CA: Morgan Kaufmann.

Daubechies, I. 1988. Orthonormal bases of compactly supported wavelets. *Communications of Pure and Applied Mathematics* 41:909–996.

Daubechies, I. 1992. Ten Lectures on Wavelets. Philadelphia: Society for Industrial and Applied Mathematics.

Duda, R. O. and P. E. Hart. 1973. *Pattern Classification and Scene Analysis*. New York: Wiley.

Efron, B. 1982. *The Jackknife, the Bootstrap and Other Resampling Plans*. Philadelphia: Society for Industrial and Applied Mathematics.

Ehrenfeucht, A., D. Haussler, M. Kearns, and L. Valiant. 1988. A general lower bound on the number of examples needed for learning. *Proceedings of the 1988 Workshop on Computational Learning Theory*. San Mateo, CA: Morgan Kaufmann.

Gabor, D. 1946. Theory of Communications. *Journal of the IEE*, vol. 93 (III), pp. 429–457.

Geman, S. and D. Geman, 1984. Stochastic relaxation, Gibbs distributions and Bayesian restoration of images. *IEEE Transactions on Pattern Analysis and Machine Intelligence*, vol. 6, pp. 721–741.

Gemen, S., E. Bienenstock, and R. Doursat. 1992. Neural networks and the bias/variance dilemma. *Neural Computation* 4:1–58.

Holler, M., S. Tam, H. Castro, R. Benson. 1989. An electrically trainable artificial neural network (ETANN) with 10240 "floating gate" synapses. *Proceedings of the International Joint Conference on Artificial Neural Networks*, Washington, DC, New Jersey: IEEE TAB Neural Network Committee.

Hornik, K. M., M. Stinchcombe, and H. White. 1989. Multilayer feedforward networks are universal approximators. *Neural Networks* 2:359–366.

LeCun, Y., B. Boser, J. S. Denker, D. Henderson, R. E. Howard, W. Hubbard, and L. D. Jackel. 1990. Handwritten digit recognition with a back-propagation network. In *Advances in Neural Information Processing Systems 2*, ed. D. S. Touretzky. San Mateo: Morgan Kaufmann.

Mehrotra, K. G., C. K. Mohan, and S. Ranka. 1991. Bounds on the number of samples needed for neural learning. *IEEE Transactions on Neural Networks* vol. 2, no. 6. New York: IEEE.

Metropolis, N., A. W. Rosenbluth, M. N. Rosenbluth, A. H. Teller, and E. Teller. 1953. Equations of state calculations by fast computing machines. *Journal of Chemistry and Physics* 21:1087–91.

Minsky, M. L. and S. A. Papert. 1969. *Perceptrons*. Cambridge: MIT Press.

Narendra, K. S. and K. Parthasarathy. 1991. Gradient methods for the optimization of dynamical systems containing neural networks. *IEEE Transactions on Neural Networks*, vol. 2, no. 2. New York: IEEE.

Oppenheim, A. V. and R. W. Schafer. 1975. *Digital Signal Processing*. London: Prentice-Hall International.

Papoulis, A. A. 1965. *Probability, Random Variables, and Stochastic Processes*. New York: McGraw-Hill.

Rumelhart, D. E., G. E. Hinton, and R. J. Williams. 1986. Learning internal representation by error propagation. In *Parallel distributed processing*, vol. 1, pp. 318–362. Cambridge, MA: MIT Press.

Tukey, J. W. 1977. *Exploratory Data Analysis*. Reading: Addison-Wesley.

Vapnik, V. N. 1982. *Estimation of Dependencies Based on Empirical Data*. New York: Springer–Verlag.

Wahba, G. 1982. Constrained regularization for ill posed linear operator equations, with applications in meteorology and medicine. *Statistical Decision Theory and Related Topics III*, vol. 2, ed. S. S. Gupta and J. O. Berger, pp. 383–418. New York: Academic Press.

Wasserman, P. D. 1989. *Neural Computing, Theory and Practice*. New York: Van Nostrand Reinhold.

Williams, R. J. and D. Zipser. 1989. A learning algorithm for continually running fully recurrent neural networks. *Neural Computation* 1(2):270–280.

Index

Index

D